Blackstone Outdoor Gas Griddle
Cookbook

Elevate Your Grilling Skills with 200 Simple, Delicious Recipes, Pro Tips, and Innovative Techniques All Year Round. Impress Your Guests with Delectable Meals

Ray Hampton

Disclaimer

The information provided in this cookbook is for general informational purposes only. All recipes and cooking techniques are offered "as is" without any guarantees or warranties of any kind, either express or implied. The author makes no representations or warranties regarding the accuracy, reliability, or completeness of the content.
The use of the information in this cookbook is at the reader's own risk. The author assumes no responsibility or liability for any errors or omissions in the content, nor for any losses, injuries, or damages resulting from the use or misuse of the information provided.

Don't Miss Out on Exclusive Bonuses!

As a token of our appreciation for choosing the "Blackstone Gas Griddle Cookbook," we've prepared some exciting **BONUSES** just for you! These exclusive extras are designed to take your griddle cooking to the next level. To access them, simply scan the QR code provided. It's our way of saying thank you for joining us on this culinary adventure. Enjoy these special resources and continue making the most of your Blackstone Gas Griddle. Happy cooking!

- Ray

Table of Contents

Introduction

Why Griddle Cooking?

The Blackstone Outdoor Gas Griddle is a game-changer in the world of outdoor cooking. Launched by Blackstone Products in 2005, this versatile cooking appliance has rapidly gained popularity among home cooks and professional chefs alike. Known for its large, flat cooking surface and efficient heat distribution, the Blackstone griddle is designed to bring the convenience and quality of indoor cooking to the great outdoors. This guide will delve into the history, technical aspects, features, troubleshooting tips, and maintenance of the Blackstone griddle, providing you with all the information you need to maximize your culinary adventures.

The Blackstone Outdoor Gas Griddle's primary function is to provide a reliable and spacious cooking surface that heats evenly. This allows users to prepare a wide array of dishes, from breakfast staples like pancakes and eggs to dinner favorites such as steaks, stir-fried vegetables, and seafood. The griddle's versatility makes it an indispensable tool for outdoor kitchens, camping trips, and backyard gatherings.

The Blackstone Outdoor Gas Griddle is a versatile and reliable tool that enhances outdoor cooking experiences. By understanding its technical aspects, utilizing its features effectively, and maintaining it properly, users can enjoy a wide range of culinary creations with ease and confidence. Whether you are a seasoned chef or a home cook, the Blackstone griddle can elevate your cooking techniques and help you create delicious meals for family and friends. With proper care and maintenance, this appliance will remain a valuable asset in your outdoor kitchen for years to come.

Key Benefits of Using the Blackstone Outdoor Gas Griddle

Time Efficiency

One of the most significant advantages of the Blackstone griddle is its ability to reduce cooking time compared to traditional methods. The large cooking surface allows you to prepare multiple items simultaneously, cutting down the time spent in the kitchen. For example, you can cook pancakes, bacon, and eggs all at once for a quick and hearty breakfast. This is particularly beneficial during large gatherings or busy mornings when time is of the essence.

Energy Efficiency

The Blackstone griddle is designed to be more energy-efficient than conventional cooking methods. Its efficient burners and excellent heat retention minimize energy consumption. Traditional ovens and stovetops often lose heat to the surrounding environment, but the griddle's design ensures that heat is directed precisely where it's needed. This focused heating reduces overall cooking time and energy usage, making it an environmentally friendly choice.

Consistency and Precision

Achieving consistent results can be challenging with traditional cooking methods, especially for complex recipes. The Blackstone griddle excels in this area by providing an even cooking surface with precise temperature control. Whether you're searing steaks to perfection or cooking delicate crepes, the griddle ensures uniform heat distribution, eliminating hot spots and ensuring that every dish is cooked to perfection. This consistency is crucial for recipes that require exact temperatures and timing.

Versatility

The versatility of the Blackstone griddle is unmatched. It can replace multiple kitchen tools and gadgets, making it a multifunctional investment. The griddle is perfect for a wide range of meals:

Breakfast: Pancakes, bacon, eggs, hash browns, and French toast.

Lunch: Burgers, grilled cheese sandwiches, quesadillas, and stir-fried vegetables.

Dinner: Steak, seafood, chicken, and grilled vegetables.

Its ability to handle different ingredients and cooking styles means you can use it for everything from quick weekday meals to elaborate weekend feasts.

Health Benefits

Cooking on the Blackstone griddle can contribute to healthier meals. The griddle's design allows excess grease and fat to drain away from the food, reducing overall fat content. This makes it easier to prepare lean proteins and vegetables without the added oils and fats typically used in frying or traditional grilling. The even heating also ensures that food is cooked thoroughly and evenly, reducing the risk of undercooked or overcooked portions.

Ease of Use and Safety Features

The Blackstone griddle is equipped with user-friendly features that simplify cooking tasks, making it suitable for cooks of all skill levels. Features such as adjustable burners, easy-to-use ignition systems, and built-in grease management systems make cooking and cleaning a breeze. Safety features like stable legs, heat-resistant handles, and automatic shut-offs ensure that cooking is safe and hassle-free. These elements combine to create a griddle that is not only efficient but also enjoyable to use.

Tips for outdoor Gas Griddle's success

The Blackstone Outdoor Gas Griddle is a powerful and versatile cooking appliance designed to elevate your outdoor cooking experience. Known for its large, flat cooking surface and efficient heat distribution, the Blackstone griddle is perfect for preparing a wide range of dishes, from breakfast favorites to gourmet dinners. By mastering the use of this griddle, you can enhance your culinary skills and enjoy more efficient and flavorful meals. This article provides practical tips and tricks to help you get the most out of your Blackstone Outdoor Gas Griddle.

Essential Tips for Optimal Use:

Setup and Initial Use:

Unboxing and Assembly: Carefully unbox your Blackstone griddle and check for all components. Follow the manufacturer's instructions to assemble the appliance. Make sure to tighten all screws and bolts securely.

Washing: Before using the griddle for the first time, wash the cooking surface with warm, soapy water and a non-abrasive sponge. Rinse thoroughly and dry completely.

Seasoning: Seasoning the griddle is crucial for creating a non-stick surface. Apply a thin layer of cooking oil to the griddle surface and heat it until the oil begins to smoke. Let it cool and repeat this process 2-3 times. This creates a durable, non-stick layer that improves with each use.

Safety Check: Ensure the propane tank is connected securely and there are no gas leaks. Use soapy water to check for leaks around the connections; if bubbles form, tighten the connections and retest.

Efficient Operation:

Preheating: Always preheat the griddle for 10-15 minutes before cooking. This ensures even heat distribution and helps achieve better cooking results.

Temperature Control: Utilize the independent burner controls to create different cooking zones. Use higher heat for searing meats and lower heat for cooking delicate items like vegetables and eggs.

Oil Management: Use a squeeze bottle to apply oil evenly on the griddle surface. This prevents food from sticking and ensures even cooking.

Cook in Batches: To avoid overcrowding, cook in batches if necessary. Overcrowding can lead to uneven cooking and longer cooking times.

Advanced Techniques

Expert Cooking Tips:

Searing: To achieve a perfect sear on steaks and burgers, ensure the griddle is extremely hot before placing the meat. Press down gently with a spatula to ensure full contact with the cooking surface.

Caramelizing Onions: Use the medium heat setting to slowly cook onions in oil or butter, stirring frequently until they turn a rich, golden brown. This technique adds a sweet, deep flavor to your dishes.

Stir-Frying: Use high heat and constant motion to stir-fry vegetables and proteins. This method cooks food quickly and retains the natural flavors and textures.

Maintenance and Cleaning

Consistent cleaning and maintenance prevent food residue buildup, rust, and wear and tear on your Blackstone griddle. These practices help maintain the appliance's efficiency and extend its lifespan, ensuring you can continue to create fantastic meals without interruptions.

Step-by-Step Cleaning Guide:

Cool Down: Allow the griddle to cool slightly after use. Cleaning a warm surface is more effective than waiting until it is completely cold.

Scrape Off Residue: Use a griddle scraper to remove food particles and excess grease, pushing debris towards the grease trap.

Wipe Down: Use a damp paper towel or cloth with warm water to wipe down the surface. For stubborn spots, a mild dish soap solution can be used.

Rinse and Dry: Rinse with clean water using a damp cloth and dry thoroughly with paper towels or a soft cloth.

Re-season: Apply a thin layer of cooking oil to the griddle surface to maintain its seasoning and protect it from rust.

Maintenance and Care Tips:

Routine Checks: Regularly inspect seals, hoses, and connections for wear and tear. Replace any damaged parts promptly to ensure safe and efficient operation.
Lubrication: Apply lubricant to moving parts if necessary, following the manufacturer's recommendations.
Software Updates: For smart griddles, ensure the software is up-to-date to benefit from the latest features and improvements.
Common Issues: Address issues such as uneven heating or ignition problems by consulting the troubleshooting section of the user manual or contacting Blackstone support for assistance.
Professional Help: Seek professional repair services for persistent or complex problems to avoid further damage and ensure safety.

Choosing the Right Oils and Fats

The type of oil or fat you use can affect the flavor, texture, and healthfulness of your food, as well as the ease of cooking and cleaning. This guide will help you choose the best oils and fats for different cooking scenarios on your Blackstone griddle.

Best Oils and Fats for the Blackstone Griddle

Canola Oil: Smoke Point: 400°F (204°C) Benefits: Canola oil is a versatile and affordable option with a relatively high smoke point, making it suitable for a variety of cooking methods on the griddle. It has a neutral flavor, which allows the natural taste of your food to shine.
Vegetable Oil: Smoke Point: 400°F (204°C) Benefits: Similar to canola oil, vegetable oil is another budget-friendly option with a high smoke point. It's a good all-purpose oil for frying, searing, and sautéing.
Avocado Oil: Smoke Point: 520°F (271°C) Benefits: Avocado oil boasts one of the highest smoke points of any cooking oil, making it ideal for high-heat cooking. It has a mild, slightly nutty flavor that can enhance the taste of your dishes.
Grapeseed Oil: Smoke Point: 420°F (216°C) Benefits: Grapeseed oil is a light, neutral oil with a high smoke point. It's excellent for sautéing and stir-frying, and it also contains healthy fats that are good for your heart.
Sunflower Oil: Smoke Point: 450°F (232°C) Benefits: Sunflower oil is another high-smoke-point option that's perfect for griddle cooking. It has a mild flavor and is rich in vitamin E, an antioxidant.
Peanut Oil: Smoke Point: 450°F (232°C) Benefits: Peanut oil has a distinct flavor that pairs well with fried foods and Asian cuisine. Its high smoke point makes it suitable for frying, searing, and stir-frying.

Specialty Fats

Butter: Smoke Point: 350°F (177°C) Benefits: Butter adds a rich, creamy flavor to your food but has a lower smoke point. It's best used for low to medium-heat cooking or in combination with high-smoke-point oils to prevent burning.
Clarified Butter (Ghee): Smoke Point: 485°F (252°C) Benefits: Ghee is a butter with the milk solids removed, giving it a higher smoke point and making it suitable for higher-heat cooking. It imparts a nutty, buttery flavor to dishes.
Coconut Oil: Smoke Point: 350°F (177°C) to 450°F (232°C) (depending on refinement) Benefits: Coconut oil adds a subtle, tropical flavor to food. Refined coconut oil has a higher smoke point, suitable for higher-heat cooking, while unrefined (virgin) coconut oil is best for medium-heat cooking.

Tips for Using Oils and Fats on Your Griddle

Preheat the Griddle: Always preheat your griddle before adding oil. This helps the oil spread evenly and prevents food from sticking.
Use Squeeze Bottles: Store your oils in squeeze bottles for easy application. This allows you to control the amount of oil used and prevents spills.
Mix Oils and Fats: Combine oils with higher smoke points with flavorful fats like butter for the best of both worlds—high-heat cooking with great taste.
Re-season the Griddle: Regularly season your griddle with a high-smoke-point oil to maintain its non-stick surface and prevent rust.

Elevating flavors: Marinades, Rubs and Sauces

This guide will help you master the use of marinades, rubs, and sauces on your Blackstone griddle to create truly unforgettable meals.

Marinades

How to Use Marinades:

1. **Select Ingredients:** Choose an acid to help tenderize, oil to keep the food moist, and seasonings to add flavor. Popular choices include soy sauce, lime juice, olive oil, garlic, and fresh herbs.
2. **Marinate Correctly:** Place the food in a resealable plastic bag or a shallow dish. Pour the marinade over the food, ensuring it is fully coated. Seal or cover and refrigerate. Marinate for at least 30 minutes up to overnight, depending on the type of food and desired flavor intensity.
3. **Preheat the Griddle:** Preheat your Blackstone griddle to the desired temperature before cooking. This ensures even cooking and a nice sear.
4. **Cook the Marinated Food:** Remove the food from the marinade and pat it dry with paper towels to remove excess liquid, which helps achieve a good sear. Cook on the griddle, flipping as necessary, until the food reaches the desired doneness.

Recommended Marinade Recipe:
Asian Soy-Ginger Marinade:

- 1/4 cup soy sauce
- 2 tablespoons sesame oil
- 2 tablespoons rice vinegar
- 1 tablespoon fresh ginger, grated
- 2 cloves garlic, minced
- 1 tablespoon honey

Mix all ingredients and marinate chicken, beef, or vegetables for at least 30 minutes before cooking.

How to Use Rubs:

1. **Choose Your Rub:** Select a blend of spices and herbs that complement your dish. Common ingredients include paprika, cumin, brown sugar, garlic powder, and black pepper.
2. **Apply Generously:** Pat the food dry with paper towels. Apply the rub generously to all sides, pressing it into the surface to ensure it adheres well.
3. **Let It Sit:** Allow the food to rest with the rub applied for at least 15-30 minutes. This helps the flavors to penetrate the food.
4. **Cook on the Griddle:** Preheat your Blackstone griddle and cook the food as usual. The rub will form a flavorful crust as it cooks.

Recommended Rub Recipe:
Smoky BBQ Rub:

- 2 tablespoons smoked paprika
- 1 tablespoon brown sugar
- 1 tablespoon chili powder
- 1 tablespoon garlic powder
- 1 tablespoon onion powder
- 1 teaspoon cumin
- 1 teaspoon salt
- 1/2 teaspoon black pepper

Mix all ingredients and rub onto pork, chicken, or beef before grilling.

Sauces
How to Use Sauces:

1. **Prepare the Sauce:** Make your sauce ahead of time or while the food is cooking. Popular types include BBQ sauce, teriyaki sauce, chimichurri, and garlic butter.
2. **Apply During Cooking:** If applying during cooking, brush the sauce onto the food in the last few minutes of cooking. This prevents burning and allows the sauce to caramelize and create a glaze.
3. **Serve on the Side:** Alternatively, serve the sauce on the side for dipping or drizzling. This is particularly good for dishes like grilled vegetables or seared meats.

Recommended Sauce Recipe:
Classic Chimichurri Sauce:

- 1/2 cup fresh parsley, finely chopped
- 1/4 cup fresh cilantro, finely chopped
- 1/4 cup red wine vinegar
- 3 cloves garlic, minced
- 1/2 cup olive oil
- 1 teaspoon red pepper flakes
- Salt and pepper to taste

Mix all ingredients and use as a finishing sauce for steaks, chicken, or vegetables.

Breakfast

Crispy Bacon and Cheddar Hash Browns

Yield: 4 servings **Preparation Time:** 20 minutes. **Cooking Time:** 20 minutes

Ingredients:

- 4 large russet potatoes, peeled and grated
- 8 slices of bacon
- 1 cup shredded cheddar cheese
- 1 small onion, finely chopped
- 2 cloves garlic, minced
- 2 tablespoons unsalted butter, melted
- 2 tablespoons olive oil
- Salt and pepper to taste
- 2 tablespoons chopped fresh chives (optional, for garnish)
- 1/4 cup sour cream (optional, for serving)

Nutritional Information (per serving):

- Calories: 450
- Protein: 14g
- Carbohydrates: 30g
- Fats: 30g
- Fiber: 3g

Instructions:

1. **Grate the Potatoes:** Peel and grate the potatoes using a box grater. Place the grated potatoes in a bowl of cold water to remove excess starch. Drain and squeeze out as much moisture as possible using a clean kitchen towel or cheesecloth.
2. **Cook the Bacon:** Preheat the gas griddle to medium heat. Place the bacon slices on the griddle and cook until crispy, about 5-7 minutes. Transfer the cooked bacon to a paper towel-lined plate to drain. Once cooled, crumble the bacon into small pieces and set aside.
3. **Prepare the Hash Brown Mixture:** In a large mixing bowl, combine the grated potatoes, finely chopped onion, minced garlic, crumbled bacon, shredded cheddar cheese, melted butter, salt, and pepper. Mix well to ensure even distribution of all ingredients.
4. **Preheat the Griddle:** Set the gas griddle to medium-high heat and let it preheat for about 5 minutes. Apply a thin layer of olive oil to the griddle surface to prevent sticking.
5. **Form the Hash Browns:** Scoop the potato mixture onto the griddle, forming 4 equal-sized mounds. Use a spatula to press each mound down into a flat patty, about 1/2 inch thick.
6. **Cook the Hash Browns:** Cook the hash browns for about 6-8 minutes on each side or until golden brown and crispy. Use the spatula to carefully flip the hash browns halfway through cooking. For even cooking, use a press lid or another heavy object to press down on the hash browns during cooking.
7. **Ensure Even Cooking:** Check for even browning and adjust the heat if necessary. If parts of the hash browns are cooking faster than others, move them to a cooler zone on the griddle.
8. **Prevent Sticking:** Periodically check and reapply a thin layer of olive oil if the griddle surface starts to dry out.
9. **Serve Immediately:** Transfer the crispy bacon and cheddar hash browns to a serving platter. Garnish with chopped fresh chives and a dollop of sour cream if desired.

Classic Eggs Benedict with Hollandaise Sauce

Yield: 4 servings **Preparation Time:** 20 minutes **Cooking Time:** 20 minutes

Ingredients:

For the Eggs Benedict:

- 4 English muffins, split
- 8 slices of Canadian bacon
- 8 large eggs
- 2 tablespoons butter, melted
- 1 tablespoon white vinegar
- Salt and pepper to taste
- Chopped fresh chives (optional, for garnish)
- 3 large egg yolks
- 1 tablespoon lemon juice
- 1/2 cup unsalted butter, melted and hot
- 1/2 teaspoon salt
- 1/4 teaspoon cayenne pepper (optional)

Nutritional Information (per serving):

- Calories: 550
- Protein: 23g
- Carbohydrates: 30g
- Fats: 40g
- Fiber: 2g

Instructions:

1. **Prepare the English Muffins:** Split the English muffins in half and set aside. These will be toasted on the griddle.
2. **Prepare the Canadian Bacon:** Set the Canadian bacon slices aside. These will be cooked on the griddle as well.
3. **Preheat the Griddle:** Preheat the gas griddle to medium heat. Let it heat up for about 5 minutes.
4. **Toast the English Muffins:** Lightly butter the griddle surface and place the English muffin halves cut side down on the griddle. Toast for about 2-3 minutes or until golden brown. Remove from the griddle and set aside.
5. **Cook the Canadian Bacon:** Place the Canadian bacon slices on the griddle. Cook for about 2-3 minutes per side until heated through and slightly browned. Remove from the griddle and set aside.
6. **Poach the Eggs: Prepare Poaching Water:** Place a large skillet or saucepan filled with water on the griddle. Add 1 tablespoon of white vinegar to the water and bring it to a simmer. **Poach the Eggs:** Crack each egg into a small bowl and gently slide it into the simmering water. Cook the eggs for about 3-4 minutes until the whites are set but the yolks are still runny. Remove the eggs with a slotted spoon and set aside.
7. **Melt the Butter:** While the eggs are poaching, melt the butter in a small saucepan on the griddle over low heat.
8. **Blend the Sauce:** In a blender, combine the egg yolks, lemon juice, salt, and cayenne pepper. Blend for about 10 seconds to combine.
9. **Add the Butter:** With the blender running on low speed, slowly pour in the hot melted butter in a thin stream until the sauce is thick and emulsified. This should take about 30 seconds. Transfer the sauce to a bowl and keep warm.
10. **Assemble the Eggs Benedict:** Place two toasted English muffin halves on each plate. Top each half with a slice of Canadian bacon, a poached egg, and a generous spoonful of Hollandaise sauce.

Fluffy Griddle Pancakes with Berries

Yield: 4 servings **Preparation Time:** 15 minutes **Cooking Time:** 15 minutes

Ingredients:

- 2 cups all-purpose flour
- 2 tablespoons sugar
- 2 teaspoons baking powder
- 1/2 teaspoon baking soda
- 1/2 teaspoon salt
- 2 large eggs
- 2 cups buttermilk
- 1/4 cup unsalted butter, melted
- 1 teaspoon vanilla extract
- 1 cup mixed fresh berries (blueberries, strawberries, raspberries)
- Additional butter or oil for greasing the griddle
- Maple syrup, for serving

Nutritional Information (per serving):

- Calories: 450
- Protein: 10g
- Carbohydrates: 60g
- Fats: 18g
- Fiber: 3g

Instructions:

1. **Prepare the Batter:** In a large mixing bowl, whisk together the flour, sugar, baking powder, baking soda, and salt. In a separate bowl, beat the eggs and then mix in the buttermilk, melted butter, and vanilla extract. Pour the wet ingredients into the dry ingredients and stir until just combined. Be careful not to overmix; some lumps are fine.
2. **Prepare the Berries:** Wash and dry the berries. If using strawberries, hull and slice them. Set aside.
3. **Preheat the Griddle:** Preheat the gas griddle to medium heat. Let it heat up for about 5 minutes until evenly hot.
4. **Grease the Griddle:** Lightly grease the griddle surface with additional butter or oil to prevent sticking. Use a heat-resistant brush or paper towel to spread it evenly.
5. **Cook the Pancakes:**
6. **Pour the Batter:** Use a ladle or measuring cup to pour about 1/4 cup of batter per pancake onto the griddle. Leave enough space between pancakes for easy flipping.
7. **Add Berries:** Immediately sprinkle a few mixed berries onto each pancake while the batter is still wet.
8. **Cook Until Bubbles Form:** Cook the pancakes for about 2-3 minutes, or until bubbles form on the surface and the edges look set.

9. **Flip the Pancakes:** Use a spatula to gently flip the pancakes. Cook for another 2-3 minutes, or until golden brown and cooked through.
10. **Maintain Even Heat:** If the griddle has different heat zones, adjust as needed to ensure even cooking. Reduce heat slightly if pancakes are browning too quickly.
11. **Serve Warm:** Transfer the cooked pancakes to a plate and keep warm. Repeat the process with the remaining batter, greasing the griddle as needed.
12. **Garnish and Serve:** Stack the pancakes on serving plates, drizzle with maple syrup, and top with additional fresh berries if desired.

Blueberry Griddle Muffins

Yield: 12 muffins **Preparation Time:** 15 minutes **Cooking Time:** 20 minutes

Ingredients:

- 1 1/2 cups all-purpose flour
- 1/2 cup granulated sugar
- 2 teaspoons baking powder
- 1/2 teaspoon baking soda
- 1/4 teaspoon salt
- 1/2 cup buttermilk
- 1/4 cup unsalted butter, melted
- 1 large egg
- 1 teaspoon vanilla extract
- 1 cup fresh blueberries
- Additional butter or oil for greasing the griddle
- Powdered sugar (optional, for dusting)

Nutritional Information (per serving):

- Calories: 150
- Protein: 3g
- Carbohydrates: 25g
- Fats: 5g
- Fiber: 1g

Instructions:

1. **Prepare the Batter:** In a large mixing bowl, whisk together the flour, sugar, baking powder, baking soda, and salt. In a separate bowl, whisk together the buttermilk, melted butter, egg, and vanilla extract. Pour the wet ingredients into the dry ingredients and stir until just combined. Gently fold in the blueberries. Be careful not to overmix.
2. **Preheat the Griddle:** Preheat the gas griddle to medium heat. Allow it to heat up for about 5 minutes until evenly hot.
3. **Grease the Griddle:** Lightly grease the griddle surface with butter or oil to prevent sticking. Use a heat-resistant brush or paper towel to spread it evenly.
4. **Form the Muffins:** Using a ladle or large spoon, scoop about 1/4 cup of batter for each muffin onto the griddle. Leave enough space between each scoop of batter for spreading.
5. **Cook the Muffins:**
    a. **Initial Cooking:** Cook the muffins for about 4-5 minutes on the first side, until bubbles form on the surface and the edges start to look set.
    b. **Flip the Muffins:** Carefully flip each muffin using a spatula. Cook for an additional 3-4 minutes on the other side until golden brown and cooked through.
6. **Ensure Even Cooking:** If parts of the muffins are cooking faster than others, move them to a cooler zone on the griddle to ensure even cooking.
7. **Prevent Sticking:** Periodically check and reapply a thin layer of butter or oil if the griddle surface starts to dry out.
8. **Serve Warm:** Transfer the cooked muffins to a plate and let them cool slightly. Dust with powdered sugar if desired.

Griddled French Toast with Cinnamon Sugar

Yield: 4 servings **Preparation Time:** 10 minutes **Cooking Time:** 15 minutes

Ingredients:

- 8 slices of thick-cut bread (such as brioche or challah)
- 4 large eggs
- 1 cup whole milk
- 1/2 cup heavy cream
- 1 tablespoon vanilla extract
- 2 teaspoons ground cinnamon
- 1/4 teaspoon ground nutmeg
- 1/4 teaspoon salt
- 4 tablespoons unsalted butter, divided
- 1/4 cup granulated sugar

- 2 teaspoons ground cinnamon (for topping)

Nutritional Information (per serving):

- Calories: 450
- Protein: 12g
- Carbohydrates: 45g
- Fats: 25g
- Fiber: 2g

Instructions:

1. **Prepare the Egg Mixture:** In a large mixing bowl, whisk together the eggs, milk, heavy cream, vanilla extract, 2 teaspoons ground cinnamon, nutmeg, and salt until well combined.
2. **Prepare the Cinnamon Sugar:** In a small bowl, mix together the granulated sugar and 2 teaspoons of ground cinnamon. Set aside.
3. **Preheat the Griddle:** Preheat the gas griddle to medium heat. Allow it to heat up for about 5 minutes until evenly hot.
4. **Grease the Griddle:** Add 2 tablespoons of butter to the griddle and spread it around using a spatula or a heat-resistant brush to ensure even coverage.
5. **Dip the Bread:** Dip each slice of bread into the egg mixture, allowing it to soak for about 10 seconds on each side. Ensure the bread is fully coated but not overly saturated.
6. **Cook the French Toast:**
    a. **Place on Griddle:** Place the soaked bread slices onto the hot, greased griddle.
    b. **Cook Until Golden:** Cook for about 3-4 minutes on the first side until golden brown. Adjust the heat as needed to prevent burning.
    c. **Flip and Cook:** Add the remaining 2 tablespoons of butter to the griddle. Carefully flip the bread slices and cook for an additional 3-4 minutes on the other side until golden brown and cooked through.
7. **Ensure Even Cooking:** If some slices are cooking faster than others, move them to a cooler zone on the griddle to ensure even cooking.
8. **Prevent Sticking:** Periodically check and reapply a thin layer of butter if the griddle surface starts to dry out.
9. **Top with Cinnamon Sugar:** Immediately sprinkle the cooked French toast with the prepared cinnamon sugar mixture while still hot, ensuring an even coating.
10. **Serve Warm:** Transfer the French toast to a serving platter.

Cheesy Breakfast Burritos

Yield: 4 servings **Preparation Time:** 15 minutes **Cooking Time:** 20 minutes

Ingredients:

- 8 large eggs
- 1/4 cup milk
- Salt and pepper to taste
- 1 tablespoon unsalted butter
- 1 cup shredded cheddar cheese
- 1 cup cooked breakfast sausage or bacon, crumbled
- 1 cup diced bell peppers (any color)
- 1 small onion, finely chopped
- 4 large flour tortillas (10 inches)
- 1/2 cup salsa (optional, for serving)
- 1/4 cup chopped fresh cilantro (optional, for garnish)
- Additional butter or oil for greasing the griddle

Nutritional Information (per serving):

- Calories: 520
- Protein: 25g
- Carbohydrates: 35g
- Fats: 30g
- Fiber: 4g

Instructions:

1. **Prepare the Egg Mixture:** In a large mixing bowl, whisk together the eggs, milk, salt, and pepper until well combined.
2. **Prepare the Fillings:** Cook the breakfast sausage or bacon if not already done. Dice the bell peppers and chop the onion.
3. **Preheat the Griddle:** Preheat the gas griddle to medium heat. Allow it to heat up for about 5 minutes until evenly hot.
4. **Grease the Griddle:** Lightly grease the griddle surface with butter or oil to prevent sticking. Use a heat-resistant brush or paper towel to spread it evenly.
5. **Cook the Vegetables:** Place the diced bell peppers and chopped onion on the griddle. Cook for about 5 minutes, stirring occasionally, until the vegetables are tender and slightly charred. Move the vegetables to a cooler zone on the griddle to keep warm.

6. **Scramble the Eggs:**
    a. **Add Butter:** Add 1 tablespoon of butter to the griddle and let it melt.
    b. **Cook Eggs:** Pour the egg mixture onto the griddle. Use a spatula to gently scramble the eggs, cooking until they are just set, about 3-5 minutes. Move the scrambled eggs to a cooler zone on the griddle.
7. **Heat the Tortillas:** Place the flour tortillas on the griddle for about 30 seconds on each side to warm them up and make them pliable.
8. **Assemble the Burritos:**
    a. **Layer the Ingredients:** Lay each tortilla flat and evenly distribute the scrambled eggs, cooked vegetables, crumbled sausage or bacon, and shredded cheddar cheese.
    b. **Roll the Burritos:** Fold in the sides of each tortilla and then roll them up tightly to form burritos.
9. **Grill the Burritos:**
    a. **Add Butter:** Lightly grease the griddle with additional butter or oil.
    b. **Grill Burritos:** Place the burritos seam-side down on the griddle. Cook for about 2-3 minutes on each side until the tortillas are golden brown and crispy, and the cheese inside is melted.
10. **Serve Warm:** Transfer the grilled burritos to a serving platter. Serve with salsa and garnish with chopped fresh cilantro if desired.

Sausage and Egg Griddle Sandwiches

Yield: 4 servings **Preparation Time:** 10 minutes **Cooking Time:** 20 minutes

Ingredients:

- 4 English muffins, split
- 4 sausage patties
- 4 large eggs
- 4 slices of cheddar cheese
- 2 tablespoons unsalted butter
- Salt and pepper to taste
- 1 tablespoon vegetable oil (for greasing the griddle)
- Optional: 1/4 cup chopped fresh chives for garnish

Nutritional Information (per serving):

- Calories: 550
- Protein: 28g
- Carbohydrates: 30g
- Fats: 35g
- Fiber: 2g

Instructions:

1. **Prepare the English Muffins:** Split the English muffins in half and set aside.
2. **Shape the Sausage Patties:** If using bulk sausage, shape it into 4 equal-sized patties. Ensure they are slightly larger than the English muffin halves as they will shrink when cooked.
3. **Preheat the Griddle:** Preheat the gas griddle to medium heat. Allow it to heat up for about 5 minutes until evenly hot.
4. **Cook the Sausage Patties:** Lightly grease the griddle with vegetable oil. Place the sausage patties on the griddle and cook for about 5-6 minutes per side, or until fully cooked through and browned. Use a spatula to press them down slightly for even cooking. Once cooked, move the patties to a cooler zone on the griddle or keep warm on a plate.
5. **Toast the English Muffins:** Add a small amount of butter to the griddle and place the English muffin halves cut side down. Toast for about 2-3 minutes until golden brown. Remove and set aside.
6. **Cook the Eggs:**
    a. **Butter the Griddle:** Add 1 tablespoon of butter to the griddle and let it melt.
    b. **Cook Eggs:** Crack the eggs onto the griddle. Cook to your desired doneness. For over-easy or over-medium eggs, flip them carefully after a few minutes. Season with salt and pepper to taste.
7. **Assemble the Sandwiches:**
    a. **Layer the Ingredients:** Place a sausage patty on the bottom half of each toasted English muffin. Top with a slice of cheddar cheese, then an egg, and cover with the top half of the English muffin.
    b. **Melt the Cheese:** Optionally, you can place the assembled sandwiches back on the griddle and cover them with a press lid or another heavy object for about 1 minute to help melt the cheese and warm the sandwich through.
8. **Serve Immediately:** Transfer the assembled sandwiches to serving plates. Garnish with chopped fresh chives if desired.

Banana Nut Griddle Cakes

Yield: 4 servings **Preparation Time:** 15 minutes **Cooking Time:** 20 minutes

Ingredients:

- 1 1/2 cups all-purpose flour
- 2 tablespoons sugar
- 2 teaspoons baking powder
- 1/2 teaspoon baking soda
- 1/2 teaspoon salt
- 1/2 teaspoon ground cinnamon
- 1 cup buttermilk
- 2 large eggs
- 1 teaspoon vanilla extract
- 3 tablespoons unsalted butter, melted
- 2 ripe bananas, mashed
- 1/2 cup chopped walnuts
- Additional butter or oil for greasing the griddle
- Maple syrup, for serving

Nutritional Information (per serving):

- Calories: 450
- Protein: 10g
- Carbohydrates: 55g
- Fats: 20g
- Fiber: 4g

Instructions:

1. **Mix the Dry Ingredients:** In a large mixing bowl, whisk together the flour, sugar, baking powder, baking soda, salt, and ground cinnamon.
2. **Combine Wet Ingredients:** In a separate bowl, whisk together the buttermilk, eggs, vanilla extract, and melted butter. Stir in the mashed bananas until well combined.
3. **Combine Wet and Dry Ingredients:** Pour the wet ingredients into the dry ingredients and stir until just combined. Fold in the chopped walnuts. Be careful not to overmix; some lumps are fine.
4. **Preheat the Griddle:** Preheat the gas griddle to medium heat. Allow it to heat up for about 5 minutes until evenly hot.
5. **Grease the Griddle:** Lightly grease the griddle surface with butter or oil to prevent sticking. Use a heat-resistant brush or paper towel to spread it evenly.
6. **Cook the Griddle Cakes:**
    a. **Pour the Batter:** Use a ladle or measuring cup to pour about 1/4 cup of batter for each griddle cake onto the griddle. Leave enough space between each griddle cake for spreading.
    b. **Cook Until Bubbles Form:** Cook the griddle cakes for about 2-3 minutes on the first side, or until bubbles form on the surface and the edges look set.
    c. **Flip the Griddle Cakes:** Use a spatula to gently flip the griddle cakes. Cook for another 2-3 minutes, or until golden brown and cooked through.
    d. **Ensure Even Cooking:** If parts of the griddle cakes are cooking faster than others, move them to a cooler zone on the griddle to ensure even cooking.
    e. **Prevent Sticking:** Periodically check and reapply a thin layer of butter or oil if the griddle surface starts to dry out.
7. **Serve Warm:** Transfer the cooked griddle cakes to a plate and keep warm. Repeat the process with the remaining batter, greasing the griddle as needed.
8. **Garnish and Serve:** Stack the griddle cakes on serving plates, drizzle with maple syrup, and top with additional sliced bananas and chopped walnuts if desired.

Cinnamon Roll Pancakes

Yield: 4 servings **Preparation Time:** 15 minutes **Cooking Time:** 20 minutes

Ingredients:

Pancake Batter:

- 2 cups all-purpose flour
- 2 tablespoons sugar
- 2 teaspoons baking powder
- 1/2 teaspoon baking soda
- 1/2 teaspoon salt
- 1 1/2 cups buttermilk
- 2 large eggs
- 1 teaspoon vanilla extract
- 1/4 cup unsalted butter, melted

Cinnamon Swirl:

- 1/2 cup unsalted butter, melted

- 3/4 cup brown sugar, packed
- 1 tablespoon ground cinnamon

Cream Cheese Glaze:

- 4 oz cream cheese, softened
- 1/4 cup unsalted butter, softened
- 1 cup powdered sugar
- 1/2 teaspoon vanilla extract
- 2-3 tablespoons milk (as needed for consistency)

Nutritional Information (per serving):

- Calories: 650
- Protein: 9g
- Carbohydrates: 85g
- Fats: 32g
- Fiber: 2g

Instructions:

1. **Prepare the Pancake Batter:** In a large mixing bowl, whisk together the flour, sugar, baking powder, baking soda, and salt. In a separate bowl, whisk together the buttermilk, eggs, vanilla extract, and melted butter. Pour the wet ingredients into the dry ingredients and stir until just combined. Be careful not to overmix.
2. **Prepare the Cinnamon Swirl:** In a medium bowl, mix together the melted butter, brown sugar, and ground cinnamon until well combined. Transfer the mixture to a squeeze bottle or a plastic zip-top bag with a small corner cut off for piping.
3. **Prepare the Cream Cheese Glaze:** In a medium bowl, beat the cream cheese and butter together until smooth. Add the powdered sugar and vanilla extract, and beat until well combined. Add milk, one tablespoon at a time, until the glaze reaches a pourable consistency.
4. **Preheat the Griddle:** Preheat the gas griddle to medium heat. Allow it to heat up for about 5 minutes until evenly hot.
5. **Grease the Griddle:** Lightly grease the griddle surface with butter or oil to prevent sticking. Use a heat-resistant brush or paper towel to spread it evenly.
6. **Cook the Pancakes:**
   a. **Pour the Batter:** Use a ladle or measuring cup to pour about 1/4 cup of batter for each pancake onto the griddle. Leave enough space between each pancake for spreading.
   b. **Add the Cinnamon Swirl:** When the pancakes start to set but are still slightly wet on top (about 1-2 minutes), pipe a swirl of the cinnamon mixture onto each pancake, starting from the center and spiraling outwards.
   c. **Cook Until Bubbles Form:** Cook the pancakes for about 2-3 minutes on the first side, or until bubbles form on the surface and the edges look set.
   d. **Flip the Pancakes:** Use a spatula to gently flip the pancakes. Cook for another 2-3 minutes, or until golden brown and cooked through.
   e. **Ensure Even Cooking:** If parts of the pancakes are cooking faster than others, move them to a cooler zone on the griddle to ensure even cooking.
   f. **Prevent Sticking:** Periodically check and reapply a thin layer of butter or oil if the griddle surface starts to dry out.
7. **Serve Warm:** Transfer the cooked pancakes to a plate and keep warm. Repeat the process with the remaining batter and cinnamon swirl mixture, greasing the griddle as needed.
8. **Top with Cream Cheese Glaze:** Drizzle the cream cheese glaze over the warm pancakes before serving.

Veggie Omelet with Grilled Tomatoes

Yield: 4 servings **Preparation Time:** 10 minutes **Cooking Time:** 15 minutes

Ingredients:

- 8 large eggs
- 1/4 cup whole milk
- Salt and pepper to taste
- 2 tablespoons olive oil, divided
- 1 cup baby spinach, chopped
- 1/2 cup bell peppers, diced (any color)
- 1/2 cup mushrooms, sliced
- 1/4 cup red onion, finely chopped
- 1 cup cherry tomatoes, halved
- 1 cup shredded cheddar cheese
- 2 tablespoons fresh basil, chopped (optional, for garnish)

Nutritional Information (per serving):

- Calories: 300
- Protein: 18g
- Carbohydrates: 10g
- Fats: 20g
- Fiber: 2g

Instructions:

1. **Prepare the Egg Mixture:** In a large mixing bowl, whisk together the eggs, milk, salt, and pepper until well combined.
2. **Chop the Vegetables:** Prepare the baby spinach, bell peppers, mushrooms, and red onion. Halve the cherry tomatoes.
3. **Preheat the Griddle:** Preheat the gas griddle to medium heat. Allow it to heat up for about 5 minutes until evenly hot.
4. **Grease the Griddle:** Add 1 tablespoon of olive oil to the griddle and spread it around using a spatula or a heat-resistant brush to ensure even coverage.
5. **Grill the Tomatoes:**
    a. **Place the Tomatoes:** Arrange the cherry tomato halves on the griddle, cut side down. Grill for about 3-4 minutes until they are slightly charred and softened. Move them to a cooler zone on the griddle to keep warm.
6. **Cook the Vegetables:**
    a. **Add Vegetables to Griddle:** Add the chopped spinach, bell peppers, mushrooms, and red onion to the griddle. Cook for about 5 minutes, stirring occasionally, until the vegetables are tender and slightly caramelized.
    b. **Move to Cooler Zone:** Move the cooked vegetables to a cooler zone on the griddle to keep warm.
7. **Cook the Omelets:**
    a. **Add Oil:** Add the remaining 1 tablespoon of olive oil to the griddle.
    b. **Pour Egg Mixture:** Pour a quarter of the egg mixture onto the griddle, spreading it out with a spatula to form a round omelet.
    c. **Add Filling:** Once the edges start to set (about 1-2 minutes), add a quarter of the cooked vegetables and a quarter of the shredded cheddar cheese to one-half of the omelet.
8. **Fold the Omelet:** Use a spatula to carefully fold the other half of the omelet over the filling. Cook for another 1-2 minutes until the cheese is melted and the eggs are fully cooked. Repeat the process for the remaining omelets.
9. **Ensure Even Cooking:** If parts of the omelet are cooking faster than others, move them to a cooler zone on the griddle to ensure even cooking.
10. **Prevent Sticking:** Periodically check and reapply a thin layer of olive oil if the griddle surface starts to dry out.
11. **Serve Warm:** Transfer the cooked omelets to a serving platter. Top with the grilled tomatoes and garnish with fresh basil if desired.

Griddled Avocado Toast

Yield: 4 servings **Preparation Time:** 10 minutes **Cooking Time:** 10 minutes

Ingredients:

- 4 large slices of sourdough bread
- 2 ripe avocados
- 1 tablespoon lemon juice
- 1/4 teaspoon salt
- 1/4 teaspoon black pepper
- 2 tablespoons olive oil
- 1/4 cup cherry tomatoes, halved
- 1/4 cup crumbled feta cheese
- 1/4 cup radish slices (optional)
- 2 tablespoons fresh cilantro or parsley, chopped (optional)
- Red pepper flakes (optional)

Nutritional Information (per serving):

- Calories: 350
- Protein: 7g
- Carbohydrates: 30g
- Fats: 25g
- Fiber: 8g

Instructions:

1. **Prepare the Avocado Mixture:** In a medium bowl, mash the avocados with a fork until smooth. Stir in the lemon juice, salt, and black pepper. Set aside.
2. **Prepare the Toppings:** Halve the cherry tomatoes, crumble the feta cheese, and slice the radishes if using.
3. **Preheat the Griddle:** Preheat the gas griddle to medium heat. Allow it to heat up for about 5 minutes until evenly hot.
4. **Grease the Griddle:** Lightly grease the griddle surface with olive oil to prevent sticking. Use a heat-resistant brush or paper towel to spread it evenly.
5. **Toast the Bread:**
    a. **Place the Bread:** Arrange the slices of sourdough bread on the griddle. Toast for about 2-3 minutes on each side, or until golden brown and crispy. Move the toasted bread to a cooler zone on the griddle to keep warm.
6. **Grill the Tomatoes:**
    a. **Add the Tomatoes:** Place the cherry tomato halves on the griddle, and cut side down. Grill for about 2-3 minutes until they are slightly charred and softened. Move them to a cooler zone on the griddle to keep warm.

7. **Assemble the Avocado Toast:**
    a. **Spread the Avocado Mixture:** Evenly spread the mashed avocado mixture over each slice of toasted sourdough bread.
8. **Add Toppings:** Top with the grilled cherry tomatoes, crumbled feta cheese, and radish slices. Garnish with fresh cilantro or parsley and a sprinkle of red pepper flakes if desired.
9. **Serve Immediately:** Transfer the assembled avocado toast to serving plates.

Grilled Breakfast Quesadillas

Yield: 4 servings **Preparation Time:** 15 minutes **Cooking Time:** 20 minutes

Ingredients:

- 8 large flour tortillas
- 8 large eggs
- 1/4 cup whole milk
- Salt and pepper to taste
- 1 cup cooked breakfast sausage or bacon, crumbled
- 1 cup shredded cheddar cheese
- 1/2 cup diced bell peppers (any color)
- 1/2 cup diced onions
- 1/4 cup chopped fresh cilantro (optional)
- 2 tablespoons unsalted butter
- 2 tablespoons vegetable oil (for greasing the griddle)
- Salsa, sour cream, and guacamole for serving (optional)

Nutritional Information (per serving):

- Calories: 500
- Protein: 22g
- Carbohydrates: 40g
- Fats: 28g
- Fiber: 3g

Instructions:

1. **Prepare the Egg Mixture:** In a large mixing bowl, whisk together the eggs, milk, salt, and pepper until well combined.
2. **Prepare the Fillings:** Cook and crumble the breakfast sausage or bacon if not already done. Dice the bell peppers and onions.
3. **Preheat the Griddle:** Preheat the gas griddle to medium heat. Allow it to heat up for about 5 minutes until evenly hot.
4. **Grease the Griddle:** Lightly grease the griddle surface with vegetable oil to prevent sticking. Use a heat-resistant brush or paper towel to spread it evenly.
5. **Cook the Vegetables:**
    a. **Add Vegetables to Griddle:** Place the diced bell peppers and onions on the griddle. Cook for about 5 minutes, stirring occasionally, until the vegetables are tender and slightly caramelized. Move the vegetables to a cooler zone on the griddle to keep warm.
6. **Scramble the Eggs:**
    a. **Add Butter:** Add 1 tablespoon of butter to the griddle and let it melt.
    b. **Cook Eggs:** Pour the egg mixture onto the griddle. Use a spatula to gently scramble the eggs, cooking until they are just set, about 3-5 minutes. Move the scrambled eggs to a cooler zone on the griddle.
7. **Assemble the Quesadillas:**
    a. **Lay Out Tortillas:** Place four tortillas on the griddle.
    b. **Layer the Fillings:** Evenly distribute the scrambled eggs, cooked vegetables, crumbled sausage or bacon, and shredded cheddar cheese on each tortilla. Top with the remaining tortillas.
    c. **Press and Cook:** Use a spatula or press lid to press down on each quesadilla. Cook for about 3-4 minutes on the first side until golden brown and crispy. Carefully flip and cook for another 3-4 minutes on the other side.
8. **Ensure Even Cooking:** If parts of the quesadillas are cooking faster than others, move them to a cooler zone on the griddle to ensure even cooking.
9. **Prevent Sticking:** Periodically check and reapply a thin layer of vegetable oil if the griddle surface starts to dry out.
10. **Serve Warm:** Transfer the cooked quesadillas to a cutting board. Let them cool slightly before cutting them into wedges.
11. **Garnish and Serve:** Serve the quesadilla wedges with salsa, sour cream, guacamole, and fresh cilantro if desired.

Strawberry and Cream Cheese Stuffed French Toast

Yield: 4 servings **Preparation Time:** 15 minutes **Cooking Time:** 15 minutes

Ingredients:

- 8 slices of thick-cut brioche or challah bread
- 1 cup fresh strawberries, sliced
- 8 oz cream cheese, softened
- 2 tablespoons powdered sugar
- 1 teaspoon vanilla extract
- 4 large eggs
- 1 cup whole milk
- 1/2 teaspoon ground cinnamon
- 1/4 teaspoon salt
- 2 tablespoons unsalted butter
- Additional butter or oil for greasing the griddle
- Maple syrup, for serving
- Additional powdered sugar, for dusting

Nutritional Information (per serving):

- Calories: 480
- Protein: 14g
- Carbohydrates: 50g
- Fats: 24g
- Fiber: 3g

Instructions:

1. **Prepare the Filling:** In a medium bowl, combine the softened cream cheese, powdered sugar, and vanilla extract. Mix until smooth. Gently fold in the sliced strawberries.
2. **Prepare the Egg Mixture:** In a large mixing bowl, whisk together the eggs, milk, ground cinnamon, and salt until well combined.
3. **Preheat the Griddle:** Preheat the gas griddle to medium heat. Allow it to heat up for about 5 minutes until evenly hot.
4. **Assemble the French Toast:** Spread the cream cheese and strawberry mixture evenly on four slices of bread. Top each with another slice of bread to form a sandwich.
5. **Dip the Sandwiches:** Carefully dip each sandwich into the egg mixture, making sure both sides are well coated. Allow any excess egg mixture to drip off.
6. **Grease the Griddle:** Lightly grease the griddle surface with additional butter or oil to prevent sticking. Use a heat-resistant brush or paper towel to spread it evenly.
7. **Cook the French Toast:**
   a. **Place the Sandwiches:** Arrange the dipped sandwiches on the griddle.
   b. **Cook Until Golden:** Cook for about 3-4 minutes on the first side until golden brown and crisp. Carefully flip with a spatula and cook for another 3-4 minutes on the other side until golden brown and the filling is warmed through.
8. **Ensure Even Cooking:** If parts of the French toast are cooking faster than others, move them to a cooler zone on the griddle to ensure even cooking.
9. **Prevent Sticking:** Periodically check and reapply a thin layer of butter or oil if the griddle surface starts to dry out.
10. **Serve Warm:** Transfer the cooked stuffed French toast to a plate. Dust with additional powdered sugar if desired.

Breakfast Tacos with Chorizo

Yield: 4 servings **Preparation Time:** 10 minutes **Cooking Time:** 20 minutes

Ingredients:

- 8 small flour tortillas
- 8 oz chorizo sausage, casing removed
- 8 large eggs
- 1/4 cup whole milk
- Salt and pepper to taste
- 1 cup shredded cheddar cheese
- 1/2 cup diced bell peppers (any color)
- 1/2 cup diced onions
- 1/4 cup chopped fresh cilantro (optional)
- 1 avocado, sliced
- Salsa, for serving
- 2 tablespoons vegetable oil (for greasing the griddle)

Nutritional Information (per serving):

- Calories: 450
- Protein: 22g
- Carbohydrates: 30g
- Fats: 26g
- Fiber: 4g

Instructions:

1. **Prepare the Egg Mixture:** In a large mixing bowl, whisk together the eggs, milk, salt, and pepper until well combined.
2. **Chop the Vegetables:** Dice the bell peppers and onions.

3. **Preheat the Griddle:** Preheat the gas griddle to medium heat. Allow it to heat up for about 5 minutes until evenly hot.
4. **Add Chorizo to Griddle:** Lightly grease the griddle with vegetable oil. Place the chorizo on the griddle and cook, breaking it up with a spatula, until fully cooked and browned, about 5-7 minutes. Move the cooked chorizo to a cooler zone on the griddle to keep warm.
5. **Add Vegetables to Griddle:** Add the diced bell peppers and onions to the griddle. Cook for about 5 minutes, stirring occasionally, until the vegetables are tender and slightly caramelized. Move the cooked vegetables to a cooler zone on the griddle to keep warm.
6. **Scramble the Eggs:**
    a. **Add Oil:** Add a small amount of oil to the griddle if needed. Pour the egg mixture onto the griddle. Use a spatula to gently scramble the eggs, cooking until they are just set, about 3-5 minutes. Move the scrambled eggs to a cooler zone on the griddle to keep warm.
7. **Warm the Tortillas:**
    a. **Warm Tortillas on Griddle:** Place the tortillas on the griddle and warm for about 30 seconds on each side until they are pliable and lightly toasted.
8. **Assemble the Tacos:**
    a. **Layer the Ingredients:** Place some of the scrambled eggs, chorizo, and cooked vegetables on each tortilla.
    b. **Add Cheese:** Sprinkle with shredded cheddar cheese. Let it melt slightly from the heat of the other ingredients.
    c. **Add Toppings:** Top with avocado slices and chopped fresh cilantro if desired.
9. **Serve Warm:** Transfer the assembled breakfast tacos to serving plates. Serve with salsa on the side.

Grilled Breakfast Pizza

Yield: 4 servings **Preparation Time:** 15 minutes **Cooking Time:** 20 minutes

Ingredients:

- 1 pound pizza dough (store-bought or homemade)
- 8 large eggs
- 1/4 cup whole milk
- Salt and pepper to taste
- 1 cup shredded mozzarella cheese
- 1/2 cup cooked breakfast sausage, crumbled
- 1/2 cup diced bell peppers (any color)
- 1/4 cup diced onions
- 1 cup fresh spinach, chopped
- 1/4 cup grated Parmesan cheese
- 2 tablespoons olive oil, divided
- Fresh basil leaves (optional, for garnish)
- Red pepper flakes (optional, for garnish)

Nutritional Information (per serving):

- Calories: 480
- Protein: 25g
- Carbohydrates: 45g
- Fats: 20g
- Fiber: 3g

Instructions:

1. **Prepare the Egg Mixture:** In a large mixing bowl, whisk together the eggs, milk, salt, and pepper until well combined.
2. **Chop the Vegetables:** Dice the bell peppers and onions. Chop the fresh spinach.
3. **Roll Out the Dough:** On a lightly floured surface, roll out the pizza dough into a large round or rectangular shape, about 1/4 inch thick.
4. **Preheat the Griddle:** Preheat the gas griddle to medium heat. Allow it to heat up for about 5 minutes until evenly hot.
5. **Grease the Griddle:** Lightly grease the griddle surface with 1 tablespoon of olive oil to prevent sticking. Use a heat-resistant brush or paper towel to spread it evenly.
6. **Cook the Pizza Crust:**
7. **Place the Dough on the Griddle:** Carefully transfer the rolled-out dough onto the griddle. Cook for about 3-4 minutes until the bottom is golden brown and the dough starts to bubble. Use a spatula to check the underside.
8. **Flip the Dough:** Carefully flip the dough to cook the other side for another 3-4 minutes until golden brown.
9. **Cook the Vegetables and Sausage:**
    a. **Add to Griddle:** While the dough is cooking, add the diced bell peppers, onions, and crumbled breakfast sausage to another section of the griddle. Cook for about 5 minutes until the vegetables are tender and the sausage is heated through. Move to a cooler zone to keep warm.
10. **Scramble the Eggs:**
    a. **Add Oil:** Add the remaining 1 tablespoon of olive oil to the griddle if needed. Pour the egg mixture onto the griddle. Use a spatula to gently scramble the eggs, cooking until they are just set, about 3-5 minutes. Move to a cooler zone to keep warm.

11. **Assemble the Pizza:**
    a. **Layer the Ingredients:** Spread the scrambled eggs evenly over the cooked pizza crust. Sprinkle with shredded mozzarella cheese, cooked vegetables, sausage, and chopped spinach.
    b. **Melt the Cheese:** Cover the pizza with a large lid or aluminum foil to help melt the cheese. Cook for an additional 2-3 minutes until the cheese is melted and bubbly.
12. **Garnish and Serve:** Transfer the grilled breakfast pizza to a cutting board. Sprinkle with grated Parmesan cheese and garnish with fresh basil leaves and red pepper flakes if desired. Slice and serve immediately.

Smoked Salmon and Cream Cheese Bagels

Yield: 4 servings **Preparation Time:** 10 minutes **Cooking Time:** 10 minutes

Ingredients:

- 4 plain or everything bagels, halved
- 8 oz smoked salmon, thinly sliced
- 8 oz cream cheese, softened
- 1/4 cup red onion, thinly sliced
- 1/4 cup capers, drained
- 1/4 cup fresh dill, chopped
- 1 medium tomato, thinly sliced
- 1 cucumber, thinly sliced
- 1 tablespoon olive oil (for greasing the griddle)
- Lemon wedges, for serving

Nutritional Information (per serving):

- Calories: 450
- Protein: 20g
- Carbohydrates: 45g
- Fats: 20g
- Fiber: 3g

Instructions:

1. **Prepare the Ingredients:** Slice the red onion, tomato, and cucumber thinly. Drain the capers and chop the fresh dill.
2. **Preheat the Griddle:** Preheat the gas griddle to medium heat. Allow it to heat up for about 5 minutes until evenly hot.
3. **Grease the Griddle:** Lightly grease the griddle surface with olive oil to prevent sticking. Use a heat-resistant brush or paper towel to spread it evenly.
4. **Toast the Bagels:**
    a. **Place Bagel Halves:** Arrange the bagel halves, cut side down, on the griddle.
    b. **Toast Until Golden:** Toast for about 2-3 minutes until the bagels are golden brown and crispy. Use a spatula to check the underside. Flip and toast the other side for an additional 1-2 minutes if desired. Remove from the griddle and set aside.
5. **Spread Cream Cheese:** Generously spread the softened cream cheese on each toasted bagel half.
6. **Add Smoked Salmon:** Layer the smoked salmon evenly over the cream cheese on each bagel half.
7. **Add Toppings:** Top with thinly sliced red onion, capers, tomato, cucumber, and chopped fresh dill.
8. **Serve Immediately:** Transfer the assembled bagels to serving plates. Serve with lemon wedges on the side for squeezing over the top.

Griddled Ham and Cheese Croissants

Yield: 4 servings **Preparation Time:** 10 minutes **Cooking Time:** 10 minutes

Ingredients:

- 4 large croissants, sliced in half horizontally
- 8 slices of deli ham
- 8 slices of Swiss cheese
- 2 tablespoons Dijon mustard
- 2 tablespoons unsalted butter, divided
- 1 tablespoon olive oil (for greasing the griddle)
- Fresh arugula or baby spinach (optional, for serving)

Nutritional Information (per serving):

- Calories: 550
- Protein: 25g
- Carbohydrates: 35g
- Fats: 35g
- Fiber: 2g

Instructions:

1. **Prepare the Croissants:** Slice the croissants in half horizontally.
2. **Assemble the Sandwiches:** Spread Dijon mustard on the inside of each croissant half. Layer two slices of ham and two slices of Swiss cheese on the bottom half of each croissant. Top with the other half of the croissant.
3. **Preheat the Griddle:** Preheat the gas griddle to medium heat. Allow it to heat up for about 5 minutes until evenly hot.
4. **Grease the Griddle:** Lightly grease the griddle surface with olive oil to prevent sticking. Use a heat-resistant brush or paper towel to spread it evenly.
5. **Cook the Croissants:**
    a. **Add Butter:** Melt 1 tablespoon of butter on the griddle.
    b. **Place the Sandwiches:** Place the assembled croissant sandwiches on the griddle. Press down gently with a spatula or press the lid.
    c. **Cook Until Golden:** Cook for about 3-4 minutes on the first side until the croissants are golden brown and crispy. Carefully flip the sandwiches and add the remaining butter. Cook for another 3-4 minutes until the other side is golden brown and the cheese is melted.
6. **Ensure Even Cooking:** If parts of the sandwiches are cooking faster than others, move them to a cooler zone on the griddle to ensure even cooking.
7. **Prevent Sticking:** Periodically check and reapply a thin layer of olive oil if the griddle surface starts to dry out.
8. **Serve Warm:** Transfer the cooked ham and cheese croissants to serving plates. Optionally, add fresh arugula or baby spinach inside the croissants for a fresh touch.

Grilled Breakfast Sausage Patties

Yield: 4 servings **Preparation Time:** 10 minutes **Cooking Time:** 10 minutes

Ingredients:

- 1 pound ground pork
- 1 tablespoon maple syrup
- 1 teaspoon salt
- 1/2 teaspoon black pepper
- 1/2 teaspoon dried sage
- 1/2 teaspoon dried thyme
- 1/4 teaspoon garlic powder
- 1/4 teaspoon onion powder
- 1/4 teaspoon crushed red pepper flakes (optional, for heat)
- 1 tablespoon olive oil (for greasing the griddle)

Nutritional Information (per serving):

- Calories: 250
- Protein: 20g
- Carbohydrates: 1g
- Fats: 18g
- Fiber: 0g

Instructions:

1. **Prepare the Sausage Mixture:** In a large mixing bowl, combine the ground pork, maple syrup, salt, black pepper, dried sage, dried thyme, garlic powder, onion powder, and crushed red pepper flakes (if using). Mix until well combined.
2. **Form the Patties:** Divide the sausage mixture into 8 equal portions and shape each portion into a patty, about 1/2 inch thick.
3. **Preheat the Griddle:** Preheat the gas griddle to medium heat. Allow it to heat up for about 5 minutes until evenly hot.
4. **Grease the Griddle:** Lightly grease the griddle surface with olive oil to prevent sticking. Use a heat-resistant brush or paper towel to spread it evenly.
5. **Cook the Sausage Patties:**
    a. **Place Patties on Griddle:** Arrange the sausage patties on the griddle.
    b. **Cook Until Golden:** Cook for about 4-5 minutes on the first side until golden brown and crispy. Use a spatula to carefully flip the patties and cook for another 4-5 minutes on the other side until fully cooked through (internal temperature of 160°F/71°C).
6. **Ensure Even Cooking:** If parts of the patties are cooking faster than others, move them to a cooler zone on the griddle to ensure even cooking.
7. **Prevent Sticking:** Periodically check and reapply a thin layer of olive oil if the griddle surface starts to dry out.
8. **Serve Warm:** Transfer the cooked sausage patties to a serving platter.

Apple Cinnamon Griddle Pancakes

Yield: 4 servings **Preparation Time:** 15 minutes **Cooking Time:** 15 minutes

Ingredients:

- 1 1/2 cups all-purpose flour
- 2 tablespoons sugar
- 2 teaspoons baking powder
- 1/2 teaspoon baking soda
- 1/2 teaspoon salt
- 1 teaspoon ground cinnamon
- 1/4 teaspoon ground nutmeg
- 1 1/4 cups buttermilk
- 2 large eggs
- 1 teaspoon vanilla extract
- 3 tablespoons unsalted butter, melted
- 1 cup grated apple (about 1 large apple, peeled and cored)
- Additional butter or oil for greasing the griddle

Nutritional Information (per serving):

- Calories: 320
- Protein: 8g
- Carbohydrates: 45g
- Fats: 12g
- Fiber: 3g

Instructions:

1. **Mix Dry Ingredients:** In a large mixing bowl, whisk together the flour, sugar, baking powder, baking soda, salt, ground cinnamon, and ground nutmeg.
2. **Mix Wet Ingredients:** In a separate bowl, whisk together the buttermilk, eggs, vanilla extract, and melted butter.
3. **Combine Wet and Dry Ingredients:** Pour the wet ingredients into the dry ingredients and stir until just combined. Gently fold in the grated apple. Be careful not to overmix; some lumps are fine.
4. **Preheat the Griddle:** Preheat the gas griddle to medium heat. Allow it to heat up for about 5 minutes until evenly hot.
5. **Grease the Griddle:** Lightly grease the griddle surface with butter or oil to prevent sticking. Use a heat-resistant brush or paper towel to spread it evenly.
6. **Cook the Pancakes:**
   a. **Pour the Batter:** Use a ladle or measuring cup to pour about 1/4 cup of batter for each pancake onto the griddle. Leave enough space between each pancake for spreading.
   b. **Cook Until Bubbles Form:** Cook the pancakes for about 2-3 minutes on the first side, or until bubbles form on the surface and the edges look set.
   c. **Flip the Pancakes:** Use a spatula to gently flip the pancakes. Cook for another 2-3 minutes, or until golden brown and cooked through.
7. **Ensure Even Cooking:** If parts of the pancakes are cooking faster than others, move them to a cooler zone on the griddle to ensure even cooking.
8. **Prevent Sticking:** Periodically check and reapply a thin layer of butter or oil if the griddle surface starts to dry out.
9. **Serve Warm:** Transfer the cooked pancakes to a plate and keep warm. Repeat the process with the remaining batter, greasing the griddle as needed.
10. **Garnish and Serve:** Stack the pancakes on serving plates and serve with maple syrup, additional grated apple, and a sprinkle of ground cinnamon if desired.

Griddled Breakfast Hash

Yield: 4 servings **Preparation Time:** 15 minutes **Cooking Time:** 25 minutes

Ingredients:

- 4 large russet potatoes, peeled and diced
- 1 medium onion, diced
- 1 bell pepper, diced (any color)
- 1 cup cooked ham or sausage, diced
- 1 cup mushrooms, sliced
- 4 large eggs
- 1/2 cup shredded cheddar cheese
- 2 tablespoons olive oil
- 2 tablespoons unsalted butter
- Salt and pepper to taste
- 1/2 teaspoon smoked paprika
- 1/4 cup chopped fresh parsley (optional, for garnish)
- Hot sauce (optional, for serving)

Nutritional Information (per serving):

- Calories: 450

- Protein: 22g
- Carbohydrates: 45g
- Fats: 20g
- Fiber: 5g

Instructions:

1. **Prepare the Ingredients:** Dice the potatoes, onion, bell pepper, and cooked ham or sausage. Slice the mushrooms.
2. **Preheat the Griddle:** Preheat the gas griddle to medium-high heat. Allow it to heat up for about 5 minutes until evenly hot.
3. **Grease the Griddle:** Add 1 tablespoon of olive oil and 1 tablespoon of butter to the griddle. Spread it evenly using a spatula or a heat-resistant brush.
4. **Cook the Potatoes:**
   a. **Add Potatoes to Griddle:** Place the diced potatoes on the griddle. Spread them out into an even layer. Cook for about 10-12 minutes, turning occasionally with a spatula, until the potatoes are golden brown and crispy.
5. **Add Vegetables and Meat:**
   a. **Add Onion, Bell Pepper, and Mushrooms:** Add the diced onion, bell pepper, and sliced mushrooms to the griddle. Cook for about 5 minutes until the vegetables are tender.
   b. **Add Cooked Ham or Sausage:** Add the diced ham or sausage to the griddle and cook for another 3-4 minutes until heated through.
6. **Season with Salt, Pepper, and Smoked Paprika:** Sprinkle salt, pepper, and smoked paprika over the hash. Stir to combine and cook for an additional 2 minutes.
7. **Cook the Eggs:**
   a. **Move Hash to Cooler Zone:** Move the hash to a cooler zone on the griddle to keep warm.
   b. **Add Remaining Butter:** Add the remaining 1 tablespoon of butter to the griddle.
   c. **Cook Eggs:** Crack the eggs directly onto the griddle. Cook to your desired doneness. For sunny-side-up eggs, cook for about 3-4 minutes until the whites are set. For over-easy eggs, flip after 2 minutes and cook for an additional minute.
8. **Combine and Melt Cheese:**
   a. **Combine Hash and Eggs:** Move the cooked eggs on top of the hash. Sprinkle shredded cheddar cheese over the entire mixture. Cover with a large lid or aluminum foil for about 2 minutes to melt the cheese.
9. **Serve Warm:** Transfer the griddled breakfast hash to serving plates. Garnish with chopped fresh parsley and serve with hot sauce if desired.

Grilled Belgian Waffles with Fresh Fruit

Yield: 4 servings **Preparation Time:** 20 minutes **Cooking Time:** 15 minutes

Ingredients:

- **For the Waffles:**
- 2 cups all-purpose flour
- 1/4 cup granulated sugar
- 1 tablespoon baking powder
- 1/2 teaspoon salt
- 1 3/4 cups whole milk
- 2 large eggs
- 1/2 cup unsalted butter, melted and cooled
- 1 teaspoon vanilla extract

For the Topping:

- 1 cup fresh strawberries, sliced
- 1 cup fresh blueberries
- 1 cup fresh raspberries
- 1/2 cup maple syrup
- Whipped cream (optional)

Nutritional Information (per serving):

- Calories: 450
- Protein: 10g
- Carbohydrates: 65g
- Fats: 18g
- Fiber: 5g

Instructions:

1. **Prepare the Waffle Batter:** In a large mixing bowl, whisk together the flour, sugar, baking powder, and salt. In a separate bowl, whisk together the milk, eggs, melted butter, and vanilla extract. Pour the wet ingredients into the dry ingredients and stir until just combined. Be careful not to overmix; some lumps are fine.
2. **Prepare the Fresh Fruit:** Wash and slice the strawberries. Wash the blueberries and raspberries. Set aside.
3. **Preheat the Griddle:** Preheat the gas griddle to medium heat. Allow it to heat up for about 5 minutes until evenly hot.

4. **Grease the Griddle:** Lightly grease the griddle surface with butter or oil to prevent sticking. Use a heat-resistant brush or paper towel to spread it evenly.
5. **Cook the Waffles:**
   a. **Pour the Batter:** Use a ladle or measuring cup to pour about 1/2 cup of batter for each waffle onto the griddle. Spread the batter into a round shape using the back of the ladle or a spatula.
   b. **Cook Until Golden:** Cook the waffles for about 3-4 minutes on the first side, or until bubbles form on the surface and the edges look set. Use a spatula to carefully flip the waffles and cook for another 3-4 minutes on the other side until golden brown and cooked through.
6. **Ensure Even Cooking:** If parts of the waffles are cooking faster than others, move them to a cooler zone on the griddle to ensure even cooking.
7. **Prevent Sticking:** Periodically check and reapply a thin layer of butter or oil if the griddle surface starts to dry out.
8. **Serve Warm:** Transfer the cooked waffles to a plate and keep warm. Repeat the process with the remaining batter, greasing the griddle as needed.
9. **Top with Fresh Fruit:** Arrange the sliced strawberries, blueberries, and raspberries on top of the waffles.
10. **Garnish and Serve:** Drizzle with maple syrup and add a dollop of whipped cream if desired.

Breakfast Griddled Potatoes with Peppers

Yield: 4 servings **Preparation Time:** 15 minutes **Cooking Time:** 20 minutes

Ingredients:

- 4 large russet potatoes, peeled and diced
- 1 red bell pepper, diced
- 1 green bell pepper, diced
- 1 yellow bell pepper, diced
- 1 medium onion, diced
- 3 tablespoons olive oil, divided
- 1 teaspoon smoked paprika
- 1 teaspoon garlic powder
- 1/2 teaspoon onion powder
- Salt and pepper to taste
- Fresh parsley, chopped (optional, for garnish)

Nutritional Information (per serving):

- Calories: 280
- Protein: 5g
- Carbohydrates: 45g
- Fats: 10g
- Fiber: 6g

Instructions:

1. **Prepare the Vegetables:** Peel and dice the potatoes. Dice the red, green, and yellow bell peppers. Dice the onion.
2. **Preheat the Griddle:** Preheat the gas griddle to medium-high heat. Allow it to heat up for about 5 minutes until evenly hot.
3. **Grease the Griddle:** Add 2 tablespoons of olive oil to the griddle and spread it evenly using a heat-resistant brush or paper towel.
4. **Cook the Potatoes:**
   a. **Add Potatoes to Griddle:** Place the diced potatoes on the griddle. Spread them out into an even layer.
   b. **Season and Cook:** Sprinkle the potatoes with smoked paprika, garlic powder, onion powder, salt, and pepper. Cook for about 10-12 minutes, turning occasionally with a spatula, until the potatoes are golden brown and crispy.
5. **Cook the Vegetables:**
   a. **Add Remaining Oil:** Add the remaining 1 tablespoon of olive oil to the griddle.
   b. **Add Bell Peppers and Onion:** Add the diced bell peppers and onion to the griddle. Cook for about 5-7 minutes, stirring occasionally, until the vegetables are tender and slightly caramelized.
6. **Mix Potatoes and Vegetables:** Combine the cooked potatoes with the bell peppers and onions on the griddle. Cook for an additional 3-5 minutes, stirring occasionally, to blend the flavors together.
7. **Ensure Even Cooking:** If parts of the mixture are cooking faster than others, move them to a cooler zone on the griddle to ensure even cooking.
8. **Prevent Sticking:** Periodically check and reapply a thin layer of olive oil if the griddle surface starts to dry out.
9. **Serve Warm:** Transfer the griddled potatoes and peppers to a serving platter. Garnish with chopped fresh parsley if desired.

Grilled Canadian Bacon and Eggs

Yield: 4 servings **Preparation Time:** 10 minutes **Cooking Time:** 10 minutes

Ingredients:

- 8 slices of Canadian bacon
- 8 large eggs
- 1 tablespoon unsalted butter
- Salt and pepper to taste
- 1 tablespoon olive oil (for greasing the griddle)
- Fresh parsley, chopped (optional, for garnish)
- Hot sauce (optional, for serving)

Nutritional Information (per serving):

- Calories: 250
- Protein: 20g
- Carbohydrates: 2g
- Fats: 17g
- Fiber: 0g

Instructions:

1. **Prepare the Ingredients:** Gather the Canadian bacon, eggs, butter, salt, and pepper. Chop the fresh parsley if using for garnish.
2. **Preheat the Griddle:** Preheat the gas griddle to medium heat. Allow it to heat up for about 5 minutes until evenly hot.
3. **Grease the Griddle:** Lightly grease the griddle surface with olive oil to prevent sticking. Use a heat-resistant brush or paper towel to spread it evenly.
4. **Cook the Canadian Bacon:**
   a. **Add Canadian Bacon to Griddle:** Place the Canadian bacon slices on the griddle. Cook for about 2-3 minutes on each side until they are lightly browned and heated through.
   b. **Move to Cooler Zone:** Once cooked, move the Canadian bacon slices to a cooler zone on the griddle to keep warm.
5. **Cook the Eggs:**
   a. **Add Butter:** Add the unsalted butter to the griddle and let it melt.
   b. **Cook Eggs:** Crack the eggs directly onto the griddle. Season with salt and pepper. Cook to your desired doneness. For sunny-side-up eggs, cook for about 3-4 minutes until the whites are set. For over-easy eggs, flip after 2-3 minutes and cook for an additional minute.
6. **Ensure Even Cooking:** If parts of the eggs or Canadian bacon are cooking faster than others, move them to a cooler zone on the griddle to ensure even cooking.
7. **Prevent Sticking:** Periodically check and reapply a thin layer of olive oil if the griddle surface starts to dry out.
8. **Serve Warm:** Transfer the cooked Canadian bacon and eggs to serving plates. Garnish with chopped fresh parsley if desired.

Griddled Breakfast Frittata

Yield: 4 servings **Preparation Time:** 10 minutes **Cooking Time:** 15 minutes

Ingredients:

- 8 large eggs
- 1/4 cup whole milk
- Salt and pepper to taste
- 1/2 cup shredded cheddar cheese
- 1/2 cup diced bell peppers (any color)
- 1/2 cup diced onions
- 1 cup fresh spinach, chopped
- 1/2 cup diced cooked ham or cooked sausage
- 2 tablespoons olive oil
- 2 tablespoons unsalted butter
- Fresh parsley, chopped (optional, for garnish)

Nutritional Information (per serving):

- Calories: 350
- Protein: 20g
- Carbohydrates: 8g
- Fats: 25g
- Fiber: 2g

Instructions:

1. **Prepare the Egg Mixture:** In a large mixing bowl, whisk together the eggs, milk, salt, and pepper until well combined.

2. **Prepare the Vegetables and Meat:** Dice the bell peppers, onions, and cooked ham or sausage. Chop the fresh spinach.
3. **Preheat the Griddle:** Preheat the gas griddle to medium heat. Allow it to heat up for about 5 minutes until evenly hot.
4. **Grease the Griddle:** Add 1 tablespoon of olive oil and 1 tablespoon of unsalted butter to the griddle. Spread it evenly using a heat-resistant brush or paper towel.
5. **Cook the Vegetables:**
    a. **Add Vegetables to Griddle:** Place the diced bell peppers and onions on the griddle. Cook for about 5 minutes, stirring occasionally, until the vegetables are tender and slightly caramelized.
    b. **Add Spinach:** Add the chopped spinach to the griddle and cook for an additional 1-2 minutes until wilted. Move the cooked vegetables to a cooler zone on the griddle to keep warm.
6. **Add Cooked Ham or Sausage:** Add the diced cooked ham or sausage to the griddle. Cook for about 3-4 minutes until heated through. Move the cooked meat to a cooler zone on the griddle to keep warm.
7. **Cook the Frittata:**
    a. **Add Remaining Oil:** Add the remaining 1 tablespoon of olive oil and 1 tablespoon of butter to the griddle.
    b. **Pour Egg Mixture:** Pour the egg mixture onto the griddle. Use a spatula to gently scramble the eggs for about 2-3 minutes until they start to set but are still slightly runny.
    c. **Add Fillings:** Evenly distribute the cooked vegetables and meat over the egg mixture. Sprinkle the shredded cheddar cheese on top.
8. **Finish Cooking:** Use a press lid or large spatula to cover the frittata. Cook for an additional 3-4 minutes until the eggs are fully set and the cheese is melted.
9. **Ensure Even Cooking:** If parts of the frittata are cooking faster than others, move them to a cooler zone on the griddle to ensure even cooking.
10. **Prevent Sticking:** Periodically check and reapply a thin layer of olive oil or butter if the griddle surface starts to dry out.
11. **Serve Warm:** Transfer the cooked frittata to a serving platter. Garnish with chopped fresh parsley if desired.

Grilled Bacon and Egg Stuffed Bell Peppers

Yield: 4 servings **Preparation Time:** 15 minutes **Cooking Time:** 20 minutes

Ingredients:

- 4 large bell peppers (any color)
- 8 slices of bacon
- 8 large eggs
- 1/2 cup shredded cheddar cheese
- 1/4 cup diced onions
- 1/4 cup diced tomatoes
- Salt and pepper to taste
- 2 tablespoons olive oil
- Fresh parsley, chopped (optional, for garnish)
- Hot sauce (optional, for serving)

Nutritional Information (per serving):

- Calories: 300
- Protein: 20g
- Carbohydrates: 10g
- Fats: 20g
- Fiber: 3g

Instructions:

1. **Prepare the Bell Peppers:** Cut the tops off the bell peppers and remove the seeds and membranes. Rinse and set aside.
2. **Cook the Bacon:** Preheat the gas griddle to medium heat. Place the bacon slices on the griddle and cook until crispy, about 5-7 minutes. Remove and drain on paper towels. Once cooled, crumble the bacon into small pieces.
3. **Prepare the Egg Mixture:** In a large mixing bowl, whisk together the eggs, shredded cheddar cheese, diced onions, diced tomatoes, salt, and pepper. Stir in the crumbled bacon.
4. **Preheat the Griddle:** Preheat the gas griddle to medium heat. Allow it to heat up for about 5 minutes until evenly hot.
5. **Grease the Griddle:** Lightly grease the griddle surface with olive oil to prevent sticking. Use a heat-resistant brush or paper towel to spread it evenly.
6. **Fill the Peppers:** Place the bell peppers on the griddle cut side up. Carefully pour the egg mixture into each bell pepper, filling them to the top.
7. **Cook the Stuffed Bell Peppers:**
    a. **Cover the Peppers:** Use a large lid or aluminum foil to cover the bell peppers. This helps to trap the heat and cook the eggs evenly.
    b. **Cook Until Set:** Cook for about 15-20 minutes, or until the eggs are set and fully cooked through. Check periodically to ensure even cooking and adjust the heat if necessary.

8. **Ensure Even Cooking:** If parts of the bell peppers are cooking faster than others, move them to a cooler zone on the griddle to ensure even cooking.
9. **Prevent Sticking:** Periodically check and reapply a thin layer of olive oil if the griddle surface starts to dry out.
10. **Serve Warm:** Transfer the grilled bacon and egg-stuffed bell peppers to serving plates. Garnish with chopped fresh parsley if desired.

Griddled Pancake Tacos with Syrup

Yield: 4 servings **Preparation Time:** 15 minutes **Cooking Time:** 20 minutes

Ingredients:

Pancakes:

- 2 cups all-purpose flour
- 2 tablespoons sugar
- 2 teaspoons baking powder
- 1/2 teaspoon baking soda
- 1/2 teaspoon salt
- 1 1/2 cups buttermilk
- 2 large eggs
- 1/4 cup unsalted butter, melted
- 1 teaspoon vanilla extract
- Additional butter or oil for greasing the griddle

Filling:

- 8 slices of bacon, cooked and crumbled
- 4 large eggs
- 1/4 cup whole milk
- Salt and pepper to taste
- 1 cup shredded cheddar cheese
- 1 cup fresh berries (strawberries, blueberries, raspberries)
- Maple syrup for drizzling

Nutritional Information (per serving):

- Calories: 450
- Protein: 20g
- Carbohydrates: 50g
- Fats: 20g
- Fiber: 3g

Instructions:

1. **Prepare the Pancake Batter:** In a large mixing bowl, whisk together the flour, sugar, baking powder, baking soda, and salt. In a separate bowl, whisk together the buttermilk, eggs, melted butter, and vanilla extract. Pour the wet ingredients into the dry ingredients and stir until just combined. Be careful not to overmix; some lumps are fine.
2. **Prepare the Filling Ingredients:** Cook and crumble the bacon. In a bowl, whisk together the eggs, milk, salt, and pepper.
3. **Preheat the Griddle:** Preheat the gas griddle to medium heat. Allow it to heat up for about 5 minutes until evenly hot.
4. **Cook the Pancakes:**
   a. **Grease the Griddle:** Lightly grease the griddle surface with butter or oil to prevent sticking. Use a heat-resistant brush or paper towel to spread it evenly.
   b. **Pour the Batter:** Use a ladle or measuring cup to pour about 1/4 cup of batter for each pancake onto the griddle. Spread the batter into a round shape using the back of the ladle or a spatula.
   c. **Cook Until Bubbles Form:** Cook the pancakes for about 2-3 minutes on the first side, or until bubbles form on the surface and the edges look set. Use a spatula to carefully flip the pancakes and cook for another 2-3 minutes on the other side until golden brown and cooked through.
5. **Cook the Scrambled Eggs:**
   a. **Add Butter:** Add 1 tablespoon of butter to the griddle and let it melt.
   b. **Cook Eggs:** Pour the egg mixture onto the griddle. Use a spatula to gently scramble the eggs, cooking until they are just set, about 3-5 minutes. Move to a cooler zone on the griddle to keep warm.
6. **Ensure Even Cooking:** If parts of the pancakes or eggs are cooking faster than others, move them to a cooler zone on the griddle to ensure even cooking.
7. **Prevent Sticking:** Periodically check and reapply a thin layer of butter or oil if the griddle surface starts to dry out.
8. **Assemble the Pancake Tacos:**
   a. **Layer the Ingredients:** Place a small amount of scrambled eggs and crumbled bacon on each pancake. Sprinkle with shredded cheddar cheese and a few fresh berries.
9. **Fold the Pancakes:** Fold each pancake in half to create a taco shape.
10. **Serve Warm:** Transfer the pancake tacos to serving plates. Drizzle with maple syrup before serving.

Grilled Sweet Potato and Chorizo Hash

Yield: 4 servings **Preparation Time:** 15 minutes **Cooking Time:** 20 minutes

Ingredients:

- 2 large sweet potatoes, peeled and diced
- 1 red bell pepper, diced
- 1 green bell pepper, diced
- 1 medium onion, diced
- 8 oz chorizo sausage, casing removed
- 2 tablespoons olive oil
- 1 teaspoon smoked paprika
- 1/2 teaspoon garlic powder
- Salt and pepper to taste
- 2 tablespoons fresh cilantro, chopped (optional, for garnish)
- 4 large eggs (optional, for serving)
- Additional olive oil or butter for greasing the griddle

Nutritional Information (per serving):

- Calories: 400
- Protein: 16g
- Carbohydrates: 35g
- Fats: 22g
- Fiber: 6g

Instructions:

1. **Prepare the Ingredients:** Peel and dice the sweet potatoes. Dice the red and green bell peppers. Dice the onion. Remove the casing from the chorizo sausage.
2. **Preheat the Griddle:** Preheat the gas griddle to medium-high heat. Allow it to heat up for about 5 minutes until evenly hot.
3. **Grease the Griddle:** Add 1 tablespoon of olive oil to the griddle and spread it evenly using a heat-resistant brush or paper towel.
4. **Cook the Sweet Potatoes:**
   a. **Add Sweet Potatoes to Griddle:** Place the diced sweet potatoes on the griddle. Spread them out into an even layer.
   b. **Season and Cook:** Sprinkle the sweet potatoes with smoked paprika, garlic powder, salt, and pepper. Cook for about 10-12 minutes, turning occasionally with a spatula, until the sweet potatoes are golden brown and tender.
5. **Cook the Chorizo:**
   a. **Add Chorizo to the Griddle:** Move the sweet potatoes to one side of the griddle. Add the chorizo to the other side and cook, breaking it up with a spatula, until fully cooked and browned, about 5-7 minutes.
   b. **Combine with Sweet Potatoes:** Mix the cooked chorizo with the sweet potatoes on the griddle.
6. **Cook the Vegetables:**
   a. **Add Remaining Oil:** Add the remaining 1 tablespoon of olive oil to the griddle.
   b. **Add Bell Peppers and Onion:** Add the diced bell peppers and onion to the griddle. Cook for about 5 minutes, stirring occasionally, until the vegetables are tender and slightly caramelized.
7. **Mix All Ingredients:** Combine the cooked sweet potatoes, chorizo, bell peppers, and onion on the griddle. Cook for an additional 3-5 minutes, stirring occasionally, to blend the flavors together.
8. **Optional: Cook the Eggs:**
   a. **Add Butter:** If desired, add a small amount of butter or olive oil to the griddle.
   b. **Cook Eggs:** Crack the eggs directly onto the griddle. Cook to your desired doneness. For sunny-side-up eggs, cook for about 3-4 minutes until the whites are set. For over-easy eggs, flip after 2 minutes and cook for an additional minute.
9. **Serve Warm:** Transfer the grilled sweet potato and chorizo hash to serving plates. Top with cooked eggs if desired. Garnish with chopped fresh cilantro.

Grilled Breakfast Flatbread with Spinach and Feta

Yield: 4 servings **Preparation Time:** 15 minutes **Cooking Time:** 20 minutes

Ingredients:

- 2 large flatbreads or naan
- 8 large eggs
- 1/4 cup whole milk
- Salt and pepper to taste
- 1 tablespoon olive oil
- 1 cup fresh spinach, chopped

- 1/2 cup crumbled feta cheese
- 1/2 cup cherry tomatoes, halved
- 1/4 cup red onion, thinly sliced
- 2 tablespoons fresh dill, chopped (optional)
- 2 tablespoons unsalted butter
- Additional olive oil for greasing the griddle

Nutritional Information (per serving):

- Calories: 350
- Protein: 18g
- Carbohydrates: 25g
- Fats: 20g
- Fiber: 3g

Instructions:

1. **Prepare the Egg Mixture:** In a large mixing bowl, whisk together the eggs, milk, salt, and pepper until well combined.
2. **Prepare the Vegetables:** Chop the spinach, halve the cherry tomatoes, and thinly slice the red onion.
3. **Preheat the Griddle:** Preheat the gas griddle to medium heat. Allow it to heat up for about 5 minutes until evenly hot.
4. **Grease the Griddle:** Lightly grease the griddle surface with olive oil to prevent sticking. Use a heat-resistant brush or paper towel to spread it evenly.
5. **Cook the Vegetables:**
   a. **Add Vegetables to Griddle:** Place the chopped spinach, cherry tomatoes, and red onion on the griddle. Cook for about 3-4 minutes, stirring occasionally, until the vegetables are tender. Move the cooked vegetables to a cooler zone on the griddle to keep warm.
6. **Scramble the Eggs:**
   a. **Add Butter:** Add the unsalted butter to the griddle and let it melt.
   b. **Cook Eggs:** Pour the egg mixture onto the griddle. Use a spatula to gently scramble the eggs, cooking until they are just set, about 3-5 minutes. Move the scrambled eggs to a cooler zone on the griddle to keep warm.
7. **Grill the Flatbreads:**
   a. **Place Flatbreads on Griddle:** Lightly brush the flatbreads with olive oil and place them on the griddle.
   b. **Cook Until Warm:** Cook for about 2-3 minutes on each side until they are warmed through and slightly crispy.
8. **Assemble the Flatbreads:**
   a. **Layer the Ingredients:** Evenly distribute the scrambled eggs over the grilled flatbreads. Top with the cooked spinach, cherry tomatoes, and red onion. Sprinkle with crumbled feta cheese and chopped fresh dill if desired.
9. **Melt the Cheese (Optional):** If you prefer the feta cheese slightly melted, cover the assembled flatbreads with a large lid or aluminum foil for about 1-2 minutes.
10. **Serve Warm:** Transfer the grilled breakfast flatbreads to serving plates. Cut into slices for easy serving.

Griddled Breakfast Panini

Yield: 4 servings **Preparation Time:** 15 minutes **Cooking Time:** 10 minutes

Ingredients:

- 8 slices of sourdough or ciabatta bread
- 8 large eggs
- 1/4 cup whole milk
- Salt and pepper to taste
- 8 slices of bacon, cooked and crumbled
- 8 slices of deli ham
- 8 slices of cheddar cheese
- 1/2 cup baby spinach
- 2 tablespoons unsalted butter, melted
- 2 tablespoons olive oil (for greasing the griddle)

Nutritional Information (per serving):

- Calories: 520
- Protein: 25g
- Carbohydrates: 40g
- Fats: 30g
- Fiber: 2g

Instructions:

1. **Prepare the Egg Mixture:** In a large mixing bowl, whisk together the eggs, milk, salt, and pepper until well combined.
2. **Cook the Bacon:** Cook the bacon on the griddle until crispy. Remove and crumble the bacon. Set aside.
3. **Cook the Eggs:**
   a. Preheat the griddle to medium heat.
   b. Lightly grease the griddle with olive oil.
   c. Pour the egg mixture onto the griddle and scramble until just set. Remove from heat and set aside.
4. **Prepare the Bread:** Spread a thin layer of melted butter on one side of each slice of bread.

5. **Assemble the Panini:**
    a. Place four slices of bread butter-side down.
    b. Layer each with scrambled eggs, crumbled bacon, a slice of ham, a slice of cheddar cheese, and baby spinach.
    c. Top with the remaining slices of bread, butter-side up.
6. **Griddle the Panini:**
    a. **Preheat the Griddle:** Preheat the gas griddle to medium heat. Allow it to heat up for about 5 minutes until evenly hot.
    b. **Grease the Griddle:** Lightly grease the griddle surface with olive oil to prevent sticking.
    c. **Cook the Panini:** Place the assembled panini on the griddle. Use a spatula or press lid to press down on each sandwich. Cook for about 3-4 minutes on the first side until golden brown and crispy. Carefully flip and cook for another 3-4 minutes on the other side until golden brown and the cheese is melted.
7. **Serve Warm:** Transfer the cooked breakfast panini to serving plates. Slice in half and serve immediately.

Appetizer and Sides

Grilled Garlic Parmesan Wings

Yield: 4 servings **Preparation Time:** 15 minutes **Cooking Time:** 20 minutes

Ingredients:

- 2 pounds chicken wings, separated into drumettes and flats
- 2 tablespoons olive oil
- 1 teaspoon salt
- 1/2 teaspoon black pepper
- 1 teaspoon garlic powder
- 1 teaspoon onion powder
- 1/2 teaspoon smoked paprika
- 4 tablespoons unsalted butter, melted
- 3 cloves garlic, minced
- 1/4 cup grated Parmesan cheese
- 2 tablespoons chopped fresh parsley (optional, for garnish)

Nutritional Information (per serving):

- Calories: 400
- Protein: 30g
- Carbohydrates: 2g
- Fats: 30g
- Fiber: 0

Instructions:

1. **Season the Wings:** In a large mixing bowl, toss the chicken wings with olive oil, salt, black pepper, garlic powder, onion powder, and smoked paprika until evenly coated.
2. **Preheat the Griddle:** Preheat the gas griddle to medium-high heat. Allow it to heat up for about 5 minutes until evenly hot.
3. **Grease the Griddle:** Lightly grease the griddle surface with a thin layer of olive oil to prevent sticking. Use a heat-resistant brush or paper towel to spread it evenly.
4. **Cook the Wings:**
    a. **Place Wings on Griddle:** Arrange the seasoned wings on the griddle in a single layer.
    b. **Cook Until Golden:** Cook the wings for about 10-12 minutes, turning occasionally with a spatula, until they are golden brown and crispy on all sides.
    c. **Ensure Even Cooking:** If parts of the wings are cooking faster than others, move them to a cooler zone on the griddle to ensure even cooking.
5. **Prepare Garlic Parmesan Sauce:**
    a. **Melt Butter:** In a small saucepan on the griddle, melt the unsalted butter.
    b. **Add Garlic:** Add the minced garlic to the melted butter and cook for 1-2 minutes until fragrant. Remove from heat.
6. **Coat the Wings:**
    a. **Combine with Sauce:** Transfer the cooked wings to a large mixing bowl. Pour the garlic butter over the wings and toss to coat evenly.
    b. **Add Parmesan:** Sprinkle the grated Parmesan cheese over the wings and toss again to coat.
7. **Serve Warm:** Transfer the garlic Parmesan wings to a serving platter. Garnish with chopped fresh parsley if desired.

Grilled Mozzarella Sticks

Yield: 4 servings **Preparation Time:** 15 minutes **Cooking Time:** 10 minutes

Ingredients:

- 12 mozzarella string cheese sticks
- 1 cup all-purpose flour
- 2 large eggs
- 2 tablespoons milk
- 1 1/2 cups panko breadcrumbs
- 1 teaspoon garlic powder
- 1 teaspoon onion powder
- 1 teaspoon dried oregano
- 1/2 teaspoon salt
- 1/2 teaspoon black pepper
- 1/4 cup grated Parmesan cheese
- 1/4 cup vegetable oil (for greasing the griddle)
- Marinara sauce for dipping

Nutritional Information (per serving):

- Calories: 380
- Protein: 20g
- Carbohydrates: 25g
- Fats: 22g
- Fiber: 2g

Instructions:

1. **Prepare the Cheese Sticks:** Unwrap the mozzarella string cheese sticks and cut them in half to create 24 pieces. Place them in the freezer for about 30 minutes to firm up.
2. **Set Up Breading Stations:**
3. **Flour Mixture:** In a shallow bowl, place the all-purpose flour.
4. **Egg Mixture:** In another shallow bowl, whisk together the eggs and milk.
5. **Breadcrumb Mixture:** In a third shallow bowl, combine the panko breadcrumbs, garlic powder, onion powder, dried oregano, salt, black pepper, and grated Parmesan cheese.
6. **Preheat the Griddle:** Preheat the gas griddle to medium heat. Allow it to heat up for about 5 minutes until evenly hot.
7. **Bread the Cheese Sticks:**
8. **Dredge in Flour:** Coat each mozzarella stick in the flour, shaking off any excess.
9. **Dip in Egg:** Dip the floured cheese sticks into the egg mixture, ensuring they are fully coated.
10. **Coat with Breadcrumbs:** Dredge the egg-coated cheese sticks in the breadcrumb mixture, pressing lightly to adhere to the coating. For a thicker coating, repeat the egg and breadcrumb steps. Set the breaded cheese sticks aside on a plate.
11. **Cook the Mozzarella Sticks:**
    a. **Grease the Griddle:** Add the vegetable oil to the griddle and spread it evenly using a heat-resistant brush or paper towel.
    b. **Place Cheese Sticks on the Griddle:** Arrange the breaded mozzarella sticks on the griddle in a single layer.
    c. **Cook Until Golden:** Cook the mozzarella sticks for about 1-2 minutes on each side, or until golden brown and crispy. Use a spatula to carefully flip the sticks.
    d. **Ensure Even Cooking:** If parts of the mozzarella sticks are cooking faster than others, move them to a cooler zone on the griddle to ensure even cooking.
12. **Prevent Sticking:** Periodically check and reapply a thin layer of vegetable oil if the griddle surface starts to dry out.
13. **Serve Warm:** Transfer the cooked mozzarella sticks to a serving platter. Serve immediately with marinara sauce for dipping.

Spicy Griddled Jalapeño Poppers

Yield: 4 servings **Preparation Time:** 20 minutes **Cooking Time:** 15 minutes

Ingredients:

- 12 large jalapeño peppers
- 8 oz cream cheese, softened
- 1 cup shredded cheddar cheese
- 1/2 teaspoon garlic powder
- 1/2 teaspoon onion powder
- 1/2 teaspoon smoked paprika
- 1/2 teaspoon salt
- 1/4 teaspoon black pepper
- 12 slices bacon, halved
- 1/4 cup vegetable oil (for greasing the griddle)

- Fresh cilantro, chopped (optional, for garnish)

Nutritional Information (per serving):

- Calories: 350
- Protein: 12g
- Carbohydrates: 8g
- Fats: 30g
- Fiber: 2g

Instructions:

1. **Prepare the Jalapeños:** Cut the jalapeños in half lengthwise and remove the seeds and membranes using a small spoon or knife. Set aside.
2. **Prepare the Filling:** In a medium mixing bowl, combine the cream cheese, shredded cheddar cheese, garlic powder, onion powder, smoked paprika, salt, and black pepper. Mix until well combined.
3. **Stuff the Jalapeños:** Fill each jalapeño half with the cream cheese mixture. Use a small spoon to press the filling into the jalapeños evenly.
4. **Wrap with Bacon:** Wrap each stuffed jalapeño half with a half slice of bacon, securing it with a toothpick if needed.
5. **Preheat the Griddle:** Preheat the gas griddle to medium heat. Allow it to heat up for about 5 minutes until evenly hot.
6. **Grease the Griddle:** Add the vegetable oil to the griddle and spread it evenly using a heat-resistant brush or paper towel.
7. **Cook the Jalapeño Poppers:**
   a. **Place Poppers on Griddle:** Arrange the bacon-wrapped jalapeño peppers on the griddle in a single layer.
   b. **Cook Until Crispy:** Cook for about 7-8 minutes on each side, or until the bacon is crispy and the jalapeños are tender. Use a spatula to carefully flip the poppers halfway through cooking.
   c. **Ensure Even Cooking:** If parts of the poppers are cooking faster than others, move them to a cooler zone on the griddle to ensure even cooking.
8. **Prevent Sticking:** Periodically check and reapply a thin layer of vegetable oil if the griddle surface starts to dry out.
9. **Serve Warm:** Transfer the cooked jalapeño peppers to a serving platter. Garnish with chopped fresh cilantro if desired.

BBQ Griddled Shrimp Skewers

Yield: 4 servings **Preparation Time:** 20 minutes **Cooking Time:** 10 minutes

Ingredients:

- 1 1/2 pounds large shrimp, peeled and deveined
- 1/4 cup olive oil
- 1/4 cup BBQ sauce
- 2 tablespoons honey
- 2 tablespoons soy sauce
- 2 cloves garlic, minced
- 1 teaspoon smoked paprika
- 1 teaspoon onion powder
- 1/2 teaspoon salt
- 1/2 teaspoon black pepper
- 2 tablespoons fresh parsley, chopped (optional, for garnish)
- Lemon wedges (optional, for serving)
- Skewers (if using wooden skewers, soak in water for 30 minutes)

Nutritional Information (per serving):

- Calories: 280
- Protein: 24g
- Carbohydrates: 10g
- Fats: 15g
- Fiber: 1g

Instructions:

1. **Prepare the Marinade:** In a large mixing bowl, whisk together the olive oil, BBQ sauce, honey, soy sauce, minced garlic, smoked paprika, onion powder, salt, and black pepper.
2. **Marinate the Shrimp:** Add the peeled and deveined shrimp to the marinade. Toss to coat evenly. Cover and refrigerate for at least 15 minutes, or up to 1 hour for more flavor.
3. **Preheat the Griddle:** Preheat the gas griddle to medium-high heat. Allow it to heat up for about 5 minutes until evenly hot.
4. **Skewer the Shrimp:** Thread the marinated shrimp onto skewers, leaving a little space between each shrimp to ensure even cooking.
5. **Grease the Griddle:** Lightly grease the griddle surface with a thin layer of olive oil to prevent sticking. Use a heat-resistant brush or paper towel to spread it evenly.
6. **Cook the Shrimp Skewers:**
   a. **Place Skewers on Griddle:** Arrange the shrimp skewers on the griddle in a single layer.

    b. **Cook Until Opaque:** Cook the shrimp for about 2-3 minutes on each side, or until they are opaque and slightly charred. Use a spatula to carefully flip the skewers halfway through cooking.
    c. **Ensure Even Cooking:** If parts of the skewers are cooking faster than others, move them to a cooler zone on the griddle to ensure even cooking.
7. **Prevent Sticking:** Periodically check and reapply a thin layer of olive oil if the griddle surface starts to dry out.
8. **Serve Warm:** Transfer the cooked shrimp skewers to a serving platter. Garnish with chopped fresh parsley and serve with lemon wedges if desired.

Cheesy Griddle Nachos

Yield: 4 servings **Preparation Time:** 15 minutes **Cooking Time:** 15 minutes

Ingredients:

- 1 bag (10 oz) tortilla chips
- 2 cups shredded cheddar cheese
- 1 cup shredded Monterey Jack cheese
- 1/2 pound ground beef or chicken
- 1 tablespoon olive oil
- 1 small onion, diced
- 1 jalapeño, sliced (optional)
- 1/2 cup black beans, drained and rinsed
- 1/2 cup corn kernels (fresh, frozen, or canned)
- 1/4 cup sliced black olives
- 1/4 cup diced tomatoes
- 2 tablespoons taco seasoning
- 1/4 cup water
- Fresh cilantro, chopped (optional, for garnish)
- Sour cream, guacamole, and salsa (for serving)

Nutritional Information (per serving):

- Calories: 450
- Protein: 20g
- Carbohydrates: 40g
- Fats: 25g
- Fiber: 6g

Instructions:

1. **Prepare the Ingredients:** Dice the onion, slice the jalapeño, and dice the tomatoes. Drain and rinse the black beans.
2. **Preheat the Griddle:** Preheat the gas griddle to medium heat. Allow it to heat up for about 5 minutes until evenly hot.
3. **Cook the Ground Beef or Chicken:**
    a. **Add Olive Oil:** Add the olive oil to the griddle and spread it evenly using a heat-resistant brush or paper towel.
    b. **Cook Meat and Onion:** Add the ground beef or chicken and diced onion to the griddle. Cook for about 5-7 minutes, breaking up the meat with a spatula, until it is fully cooked and browned.
    c. **Season the Meat:** Sprinkle the taco seasoning over the meat and add the water. Stir to combine and cook for an additional 2 minutes until the seasoning is well incorporated. Move the cooked meat to a cooler zone on the griddle to keep warm.
4. **Add Jalapeño, Black Beans, and Corn:** Add the sliced jalapeño (if using), black beans, and corn kernels to the griddle. Cook for about 3-4 minutes, stirring occasionally, until they are heated through. Move the cooked vegetables to the cooler zone with the meat.
5. **Assemble the Nachos:**
    a. **Spread Tortilla Chips:** Spread the tortilla chips in an even layer directly on the griddle.
    b. **Add Cheese:** Sprinkle the shredded cheddar and Monterey Jack cheese evenly over the tortilla chips.
    c. **Add Toppings:** Distribute the cooked meat, vegetables, black olives, and diced tomatoes evenly over the cheese-covered chips.
6. **Cover and Cook:** Use a large lid or aluminum foil to cover the nachos on the griddle. Cook for about 3-5 minutes until the cheese is melted and bubbly.
7. **Ensure Even Cooking:** If parts of the nachos are cooking faster than others, move them to a cooler zone on the griddle to ensure even cooking.
8. **Serve Warm:** Transfer the griddled nachos to a serving platter. Garnish with chopped fresh cilantro if desired.

Grilled Veggie Platter with Hummus

Yield: 4 servings **Preparation Time:** 20 minutes **Cooking Time:** 15 minutes

Ingredients:

Vegetables:

- 1 large zucchini, sliced into rounds
- 1 large yellow squash, sliced into rounds
- 1 red bell pepper, cut into strips
- 1 yellow bell pepper, cut into strips
- 1 red onion, sliced into rings

- 1 bunch asparagus, trimmed
- 1/4 cup olive oil
- 1 teaspoon garlic powder
- 1 teaspoon onion powder
- 1 teaspoon smoked paprika
- Salt and pepper to taste

Hummus:

- 1 can (15 oz) chickpeas, drained and rinsed
- 1/4 cup tahini
- 2 tablespoons olive oil
- 2 tablespoons lemon juice
- 2 cloves garlic, minced
- 1/2 teaspoon cumin
- Salt and pepper to taste
- Water as needed for desired consistency

Nutritional Information (per serving):

- Calories: 300
- Protein: 8g
- Carbohydrates: 28g
- Fats: 18g
- Fiber: 8g

Instructions:

1. **Prepare the Vegetables:** Slice the zucchini and yellow squash into rounds. Cut the red and yellow bell peppers into strips. Slice the red onion into rings. Trim the asparagus.
2. **Season the Vegetables:**
3. In a large bowl, toss the vegetables with olive oil, garlic powder, onion powder, smoked paprika, salt, and pepper until evenly coated.
4. **Prepare the Hummus:** In a food processor, combine the chickpeas, tahini, olive oil, lemon juice, minced garlic, cumin, salt, and pepper. Process until smooth, adding water as needed to reach the desired consistency. Transfer the hummus to a serving bowl and drizzle with a bit of olive oil if desired. Set aside.
5. **Preheat the Griddle:** Preheat the gas griddle to medium-high heat. Allow it to heat up for about 5 minutes until evenly hot.
6. **Grease the Griddle:** Lightly grease the griddle surface with olive oil to prevent sticking. Use a heat-resistant brush or paper towel to spread it evenly.
7. **Zucchini and Yellow Squash:** Place the zucchini and yellow squash rounds on the griddle. Cook for about 3-4 minutes on each side until tender and slightly charred.
8. **Bell Peppers and Onions:** Place the bell pepper strips and onion rings on the griddle. Cook for about 5-6 minutes, turning occasionally, until tender and slightly caramelized.
9. **Asparagus:** Place the asparagus on the griddle. Cook for about 5-6 minutes, turning occasionally, until tender and slightly charred.
10. **Ensure Even Cooking:** If parts of the vegetables are cooking faster than others, move them to a cooler zone on the griddle to ensure even cooking.
11. **Prevent Sticking:** Periodically check and reapply a thin layer of olive oil if the griddle surface starts to dry out.
12. **Assemble the Platter:** Arrange the grilled vegetables on a large serving platter. Serve with the prepared hummus in the center.
13. **Serve Warm:** Serve the grilled veggie platter warm, with the hummus on the side for dipping.

Griddled Mini Crab Cakes

Yield: 4 servings (12 mini crab cakes) **Preparation Time:** 20 minutes **Cooking Time:** 10 minutes

Ingredients:

- 1 pound lump crab meat
- 1/4 cup mayonnaise
- 1 large egg, beaten
- 1 tablespoon Dijon mustard
- 1 tablespoon Worcestershire sauce
- 1 teaspoon Old Bay seasoning
- 1/2 teaspoon garlic powder
- 1/2 teaspoon onion powder
- 1 tablespoon fresh lemon juice
- 1/4 cup finely chopped green onions
- 1/4 cup finely chopped red bell pepper
- 1/2 cup panko breadcrumbs
- 2 tablespoons fresh parsley, chopped
- Salt and pepper to taste
- 1/4 cup vegetable oil (for greasing the griddle)
- Lemon wedges (for serving)

Nutritional Information (per serving):

- Calories: 250
- Protein: 20g
- Carbohydrates: 10g
- Fats: 15g
- Fiber: 1g

Instructions:

1. **Prepare the Crab Cake Mixture:** In a large mixing bowl, combine the mayonnaise, beaten egg, Dijon mustard, Worcestershire sauce, Old Bay seasoning, garlic powder, onion powder, and lemon juice. Mix until well combined. Gently fold in the lump crab meat, green onions, red bell pepper, panko breadcrumbs, and chopped parsley. Season with salt and pepper to taste. Form the mixture into 12 small patties, about 2 inches in diameter. Place the patties on a baking sheet and refrigerate for at least 15 minutes to firm up.
2. **Preheat the Griddle:** Preheat the gas griddle to medium heat. Allow it to heat up for about 5 minutes until evenly hot.
3. **Grease the Griddle:** Add the vegetable oil to the griddle and spread it evenly using a heat-resistant brush or paper towel.
4. **Cook the Crab Cakes:**
   a. **Place Crab Cakes on Griddle:** Carefully place the crab cakes on the griddle in a single layer.
   b. **Cook Until Golden:** Cook for about 3-4 minutes on the first side, or until golden brown and crispy. Use a spatula to carefully flip the crab cakes and cook for another 3-4 minutes on the other side until golden brown and heated through.
5. **Ensure Even Cooking:** If parts of the crab cakes are cooking faster than others, move them to a cooler zone on the griddle to ensure even cooking.
6. **Prevent Sticking:** Periodically check and reapply a thin layer of vegetable oil if the griddle surface starts to dry out.
7. **Serve Warm:** Transfer the cooked mini crab cakes to a serving platter. Serve immediately with lemon wedges on the side.

Griddled Stuffed Mushrooms

Yield: 4 servings (16 stuffed mushrooms) **Preparation Time:** 20 minutes **Cooking Time:** 15 minutes

Ingredients:

- 16 large white or cremini mushrooms
- 1/2 cup cream cheese, softened
- 1/4 cup grated Parmesan cheese
- 1/4 cup finely chopped spinach
- 2 tablespoons finely chopped sun-dried tomatoes
- 2 tablespoons finely chopped green onions
- 1 garlic clove, minced
- 1/2 teaspoon dried oregano
- 1/2 teaspoon salt
- 1/4 teaspoon black pepper
- 1/4 cup panko breadcrumbs
- 2 tablespoons olive oil (for greasing the griddle)
- Fresh parsley, chopped (optional, for garnish)

Nutritional Information (per serving):

- Calories: 160
- Protein: 5g
- Carbohydrates: 8g
- Fats: 12g
- Fiber: 2g

Instructions:

1. **Prepare the Mushrooms:** Remove the stems from the mushrooms and set the caps aside. Finely chop the stems.
2. **Prepare the Filling:** In a medium bowl, combine the chopped mushroom stems, cream cheese, grated Parmesan cheese, chopped spinach, sun-dried tomatoes, green onions, minced garlic, dried oregano, salt, and black pepper. Mix until well combined.
3. **Stuff the Mushrooms:** Spoon the filling into each mushroom cap, pressing slightly to pack the filling. Sprinkle the tops with panko breadcrumbs.
4. **Preheat the Griddle:** Preheat the gas griddle to medium heat. Allow it to heat up for about 5 minutes until evenly hot.
5. **Grease the Griddle:** Add the olive oil to the griddle and spread it evenly using a heat-resistant brush or paper towel.
6. **Cook the Stuffed Mushrooms:**
   a. **Place Mushrooms on Griddle:** Carefully place the stuffed mushrooms, filling side up, on the griddle.
   b. **Cover and Cook:** Cover the mushrooms with a large lid or aluminum foil to help trap the heat. Cook for about 10-12 minutes, or until the mushrooms are tender and the filling is heated through.
   c. **Crisp the Breadcrumbs:** During the last 2-3 minutes of cooking, uncover the mushrooms to allow the breadcrumbs to crisp up.
7. **Ensure Even Cooking:** If parts of the mushrooms are cooking faster than others, move them to a cooler zone on the griddle to ensure even cooking.
8. **Serve Warm:** Transfer the cooked stuffed mushrooms to a serving platter. Garnish with chopped fresh parsley if desired.

Sweet and Spicy Griddled Meatballs

Yield: 4 servings (16 meatballs) **Preparation Time:** 15 minutes **Cooking Time:** 15 minutes

Ingredients:

Meatballs:

- 1 pound ground beef (or a mix of beef and pork)
- 1/4 cup breadcrumbs
- 1/4 cup grated Parmesan cheese
- 1 large egg
- 2 cloves garlic, minced
- 1/4 cup finely chopped onion
- 1 tablespoon soy sauce
- 1 tablespoon Worcestershire sauce
- 1 teaspoon dried oregano
- 1/2 teaspoon red pepper flakes
- 1/2 teaspoon salt
- 1/4 teaspoon black pepper

Sweet and Spicy Sauce:

- 1/4 cup honey
- 1/4 cup soy sauce
- 2 tablespoons sriracha sauce (adjust to taste)
- 1 tablespoon rice vinegar
- 1 tablespoon cornstarch mixed with 2 tablespoons water (slurry)
- 2 tablespoons olive oil (for greasing the griddle)

Nutritional Information (per serving):

- Calories: 350
- Protein: 20g
- Carbohydrates: 25g
- Fats: 20g
- Fiber: 1g

Instructions:

1. **Prepare the Meatballs:** In a large mixing bowl, combine the ground beef, breadcrumbs, grated Parmesan cheese, egg, minced garlic, chopped onion, soy sauce, Worcestershire sauce, dried oregano, red pepper flakes, salt, and black pepper. Mix until well combined. Form the mixture into 16 evenly-sized meatballs.
2. **Prepare the Sweet and Spicy Sauce:** In a small bowl, whisk together the honey, soy sauce, sriracha sauce, and rice vinegar. Set aside.
3. **Preheat the Griddle:** Preheat the gas griddle to medium heat. Allow it to heat up for about 5 minutes until evenly hot.
4. **Grease the Griddle:** Add the olive oil to the griddle and spread it evenly using a heat-resistant brush or paper towel.
5. **Cook the Meatballs:**
   a. **Place Meatballs on Griddle:** Arrange the meatballs on the griddle in a single layer.
   b. **Cook Until Browned:** Cook the meatballs for about 8-10 minutes, turning occasionally with a spatula, until they are browned on all sides and cooked through. Move the meatballs to a cooler zone on the griddle to keep warm.
6. **Cook the Sauce:**
   a. **Pour Sauce on Griddle:** Pour the sweet and spicy sauce mixture onto the griddle.
   b. **Add Slurry:** Add the cornstarch slurry to the sauce and stir continuously until the sauce thickens about 2-3 minutes.
7. **Coat the Meatballs:** Return the meatballs to the sauce on the griddle, turning them to coat evenly.
8. **Serve Warm:** Transfer the glazed meatballs to a serving platter. Garnish with chopped green onions or sesame seeds if desired.

Grilled Bruschetta with Tomato and Basil

Yield: 4 servings **Preparation Time:** 15 minutes **Cooking Time:** 10 minutes

Ingredients:

- 1 baguette, sliced into 1/2-inch thick slices
- 4 large tomatoes, diced
- 1/4 cup fresh basil leaves, chopped
- 2 cloves garlic, minced
- 1/4 cup extra virgin olive oil, divided
- 1 tablespoon balsamic vinegar
- Salt and pepper to taste
- 1/4 cup grated Parmesan cheese (optional)
- Olive oil spray or additional olive oil for greasing the griddle

Nutritional Information (per serving):

- Calories: 250
- Protein: 6g
- Carbohydrates: 30g
- Fats: 12g
- Fiber: 2g

Instructions:

1. **Prepare the Tomato and Basil Topping:** In a medium mixing bowl, combine the diced tomatoes, chopped basil leaves, minced garlic, 2 tablespoons of olive oil, balsamic vinegar, salt, and pepper. Mix well and set aside to marinate while preparing the bread.
2. **Prepare the Bread:** Slice the baguette into 1/2-inch thick slices. Brush each slice on both sides with the remaining 2 tablespoons of olive oil.
3. **Preheat the Griddle:** Preheat the gas griddle to medium-high heat. Allow it to heat up for about 5 minutes until evenly hot.
4. **Grease the Griddle:** Lightly spray or brush the griddle surface with olive oil to prevent sticking.
5. **Grill the Bread:**
    a. **Place Bread on Griddle:** Arrange the baguette slices on the griddle in a single layer.
    b. **Cook Until Golden:** Grill for about 2-3 minutes on each side, or until the bread is golden brown and crispy. Use a spatula to carefully flip the slices halfway through cooking.
6. **Ensure Even Cooking:** If parts of the bread are toasting faster than others, move them to a cooler zone on the griddle to ensure even cooking.
7. **Assemble the Bruschetta:**
    a. **Top with Tomato Mixture:** Once the bread slices are toasted, remove them from the griddle and place them on a serving platter. Spoon the tomato and basil mixture evenly over each slice.
8. **Optional Parmesan:** Sprinkle with grated Parmesan cheese if desired.
9. **Serve Immediately:** Serve the grilled bruschetta warm or at room temperature. Garnish with additional fresh basil leaves if desired.

Griddled Zucchini Fritters

Yield: 4 servings (8-10 fritters) **Preparation Time:** 15 minutes **Cooking Time:** 15 minutes

Ingredients:

- 4 medium zucchini (about 1.5 pounds), grated
- 1 teaspoon salt
- 1/2 cup all-purpose flour
- 1/4 cup grated Parmesan cheese
- 2 large eggs, beaten
- 2 cloves garlic, minced
- 1/4 cup chopped green onions
- 1/4 teaspoon black pepper
- 1/4 teaspoon baking powder
- 1/4 teaspoon smoked paprika (optional)
- 2 tablespoons olive oil (for greasing the griddle)
- Sour cream or Greek yogurt (for serving)
- Fresh chopped dill or parsley (optional, for garnish)

Nutritional Information (per serving):

- Calories: 150
- Protein: 6g
- Carbohydrates: 12g
- Fats: 9g
- Fiber: 2g

Instructions:

1. **Prepare the Zucchini:** Grate the zucchini and place it in a colander. Sprinkle with 1 teaspoon of salt and let it sit for 10 minutes to draw out the moisture.
2. After 10 minutes, squeeze out as much liquid as possible from the zucchini using a clean kitchen towel or cheesecloth.
3. **Prepare the Batter:** In a large mixing bowl, combine the drained zucchini, all-purpose flour, grated Parmesan cheese, beaten eggs, minced garlic, chopped green onions, black pepper, baking powder, and smoked paprika (if using). Mix until well combined.
4. **Preheat the Griddle:** Preheat the gas griddle to medium heat. Allow it to heat up for about 5 minutes until evenly hot.
    a. **Grease the Griddle:** Add the olive oil to the griddle and spread it evenly using a heat-resistant brush or paper towel.
5. **Cook the Fritters:**
    a. **Scoop the Batter:** Using a spoon or a small scoop, drop spoonfuls of the zucchini batter onto the griddle. Flatten each mound slightly with the back of the spoon to form fritters.
    b. **Cook Until Golden:** Cook the fritters for about 3-4 minutes on each side, or until golden brown and crispy. Use a spatula to carefully flip the fritters halfway through cooking.
    c. **Ensure Even Cooking:** If parts of the fritters are cooking faster than others, move them to a cooler zone on the griddle to ensure even cooking.
    d. **Prevent Sticking:** Periodically check and reapply a thin layer of olive oil if the griddle surface starts to dry out.

6. **Serve Warm:** Transfer the cooked zucchini fritters to a serving platter. Serve immediately with a dollop of sour cream or Greek yogurt on top.
7. **Optional Garnish:** Garnish with fresh chopped dill or parsley if desired.

Grilled Artichoke Hearts with Lemon Aioli

Yield: 4 servings **Preparation Time:** 20 minutes **Cooking Time:** 15 minutes

Ingredients:

For the Artichoke Hearts:

- 2 cans (14 oz each) of artichoke hearts, drained and halved
- 2 tablespoons olive oil
- 1 teaspoon garlic powder
- 1 teaspoon dried oregano
- 1/2 teaspoon salt
- 1/4 teaspoon black pepper

For the Lemon Aioli:

- 1/2 cup mayonnaise
- 1 tablespoon lemon juice
- 1 teaspoon lemon zest
- 1 clove garlic, minced
- Salt and pepper to taste

Nutritional Information (per serving):

- Calories: 200
- Protein: 2g
- Carbohydrates: 5g
- Fats: 18g
- Fiber: 3g

Instructions:

1. **Prepare the Artichoke Hearts:** Drain the artichoke hearts and cut them in half. Pat them dry with paper towels to remove excess moisture.
2. **Season the Artichoke Hearts:** In a mixing bowl, toss the artichoke hearts with olive oil, garlic powder, dried oregano, salt, and black pepper until evenly coated.
3. **Prepare the Lemon Aioli:** In a small bowl, combine the mayonnaise, lemon juice, lemon zest, minced garlic, salt, and pepper. Mix well until smooth. Refrigerate until ready to serve.
4. **Preheat the Griddle:** Preheat the gas griddle to medium-high heat. Allow it to heat up for about 5 minutes until evenly hot.
5. **Grease the Griddle:** Lightly grease the griddle surface with a thin layer of olive oil to prevent sticking. Use a heat-resistant brush or paper towel to spread it evenly.
6. **Grill the Artichoke Hearts:**
   a. **Place Artichoke Hearts on Griddle:** Arrange the seasoned artichoke hearts on the griddle in a single layer.
   b. **Cook Until Golden:** Grill for about 4-5 minutes on each side, or until they are golden brown and slightly crispy. Use a spatula to carefully flip the artichoke hearts halfway through cooking.
   c. **Ensure Even Cooking:** If parts of the artichoke hearts are cooking faster than others, move them to a cooler zone on the griddle to ensure even cooking.
7. **Prevent Sticking:** Periodically check and reapply a thin layer of olive oil if the griddle surface starts to dry out.
8. **Serve Warm:** Transfer the grilled artichoke hearts to a serving platter.
9. **Serve with Lemon Aioli:** Serve the grilled artichoke hearts warm with the lemon aioli on the side for dipping.

Grilled Asparagus with Balsamic Glaze

Yield: 4 servings **Preparation Time:** 10 minutes **Cooking Time:** 10 minutes

Ingredients:

- 1 pound fresh asparagus, trimmed
- 2 tablespoons olive oil
- 1/2 teaspoon salt
- 1/4 teaspoon black pepper
- 1/4 cup balsamic vinegar
- 1 tablespoon honey
- 1 clove garlic, minced
- 1 tablespoon fresh lemon juice
- Olive oil spray or additional olive oil for greasing the griddle

Nutritional Information (per serving):

- Calories: 90
- Protein: 2g
- Carbohydrates: 10g
- Fats: 5g
- Fiber: 3g

Instructions:

1. **Prepare the Asparagus:** Trim the tough ends off the asparagus spears.
2. **Season the Asparagus:** In a large bowl, toss the asparagus with olive oil, salt, and black pepper until evenly coated.
3. **Prepare the Balsamic Glaze:** In a small saucepan, combine the balsamic vinegar, honey, minced garlic, and lemon juice. Bring to a simmer over medium heat and cook until the mixture is reduced by half and has a syrupy consistency, about 5-7 minutes. Set aside.
4. **Preheat the Griddle:** Preheat the gas griddle to medium-high heat. Allow it to heat up for about 5 minutes until evenly hot.
5. **Grease the Griddle:** Lightly spray or brush the griddle surface with olive oil to prevent sticking.
6. **Grill the Asparagus:**
    a. **Place Asparagus on Griddle:** Arrange the asparagus spears on the griddle in a single layer.
    b. **Cook Until Tender:** Grill the asparagus for about 5-7 minutes, turning occasionally with tongs, until they are tender and slightly charred.
    c. **Ensure Even Cooking:** If parts of the asparagus are cooking faster than others, move them to a cooler zone on the griddle to ensure even cooking.
7. **Prevent Sticking:** Periodically check and reapply a thin layer of olive oil if the griddle surface starts to dry out.
8. **Serve Warm:** Transfer the grilled asparagus to a serving platter.
9. **Drizzle with Balsamic Glaze:** Drizzle the balsamic glaze over the grilled asparagus before serving.

Grilled Avocado with Salsa

Yield: 4 servings **Preparation Time:** 10 minutes **Cooking Time:** 10 minutes

Ingredients:

- 2 ripe avocados, halved and pitted
- 1 tablespoon olive oil
- 1/2 teaspoon salt
- 1/4 teaspoon black pepper
- 1 cup cherry tomatoes, quartered
- 1/4 cup red onion, finely chopped
- 1 small jalapeño, seeded and finely chopped
- 1/4 cup fresh cilantro, chopped
- 1 tablespoon fresh lime juice
- Salt and pepper to taste
- Olive oil spray or additional olive oil for greasing the griddle

Nutritional Information (per serving):

- Calories: 180
- Protein: 2g
- Carbohydrates: 10g
- Fats: 15g
- Fiber: 7g

Instructions:

1. **Prepare the Avocados:** Cut the avocados in half and remove the pits. Brush the cut sides with olive oil and season with salt and black pepper.
2. **Prepare the Salsa:** In a medium bowl, combine the cherry tomatoes, red onion, jalapeño, cilantro, and lime juice. Season with salt and pepper to taste. Mix well and set aside.
3. **Preheat the Griddle:** Preheat the gas griddle to medium-high heat. Allow it to heat up for about 5 minutes until evenly hot.
4. **Grease the Griddle:** Lightly spray or brush the griddle surface with olive oil to prevent sticking.
5. **Grill the Avocados:**
    a. **Place Avocados on Griddle:** Place the avocado halves cut side down on the griddle.
    b. **Cook Until Charred:** Grill the avocados for about 3-4 minutes, or until they have nice grill marks and are slightly charred.
6. **Ensure Even Cooking:** If parts of the avocados are cooking faster than others, move them to a cooler zone on the griddle to ensure even cooking.
7. **Serve Warm:** Remove the grilled avocados from the griddle and place them on a serving platter.
8. **Top with Salsa:** Spoon the prepared salsa into the cavities of the grilled avocado halves.

Grilled prosciutto-wrapped Wrapped Asparagus

Yield: 4 servings **Preparation Time:** 10 minutes **Cooking Time:** 10 minutes

Ingredients:

- 1 pound fresh asparagus, trimmed
- 8 slices of prosciutto, cut in half lengthwise
- 2 tablespoons olive oil
- 1/2 teaspoon garlic powder
- 1/2 teaspoon black pepper
- Olive oil spray or additional olive oil for greasing the griddle

Nutritional Information (per serving):

- Calories: 140
- Protein: 8g
- Carbohydrates: 5g
- Fats: 10g
- Fiber: 2g

Instructions:

1. **Prepare the Asparagus:** Trim the tough ends off the asparagus spears.
2. **Wrap the Asparagus:** Wrap each asparagus spear with a half slice of prosciutto, starting at the bottom and spiraling up to the top. The prosciutto should stick to itself, holding the asparagus tightly.
3. **Season the Asparagus:** In a small bowl, mix the olive oil, garlic powder, and black pepper. Brush this mixture over the prosciutto-wrapped asparagus.
4. **Preheat the Griddle:** Preheat the gas griddle to medium-high heat. Allow it to heat up for about 5 minutes until evenly hot.
5. **Grease the Griddle:** Lightly spray or brush the griddle surface with olive oil to prevent sticking.
   a. **Grill the Asparagus:**
   b. **Place Asparagus on Griddle:** Arrange the wrapped asparagus spears on the griddle in a single layer.
   c. **Cook Until Crispy:** Grill the asparagus for about 4-5 minutes, turning occasionally, until the prosciutto is crispy and the asparagus is tender.
6. **Ensure Even Cooking:** If parts of the asparagus are cooking faster than others, move them to a cooler zone on the griddle to ensure even cooking.
7. **Serve Warm:** Transfer the grilled prosciutto-wrapped asparagus to a serving platter.

Griddled Smoked Salmon Crostini

Yield: 4 servings (16 crostini) **Preparation Time:** 10 minutes **Cooking Time:** 10 minutes

Ingredients:

- 1 baguette, sliced into 1/2-inch thick slices
- 4 oz smoked salmon, thinly sliced
- 1/2 cup cream cheese, softened
- 1 tablespoon capers, drained
- 1 tablespoon fresh dill, chopped
- 1 teaspoon lemon zest
- 2 tablespoons olive oil
- Freshly ground black pepper, to taste
- Lemon wedges (for garnish)
- Olive oil spray or additional olive oil for greasing the griddle

Nutritional Information (per serving):

- Calories: 200
- Protein: 8g
- Carbohydrates: 20g
- Fats: 10g
- Fiber: 2g

Instructions:

1. **Prepare the Crostini Base:** Slice the baguette into 1/2-inch thick slices. Brush each slice on both sides with olive oil.
2. **Prepare the Cream Cheese Mixture:** In a small bowl, mix the softened cream cheese with the capers, fresh dill, and lemon zest until well combined.
3. **Preheat the Griddle:** Preheat the gas griddle to medium-high heat. Allow it to heat up for about 5 minutes until evenly hot.
4. **Grease the Griddle:** Lightly spray or brush the griddle surface with olive oil to prevent sticking.
5. **Grill the Baguette Slices:**
   a. **Place Baguette Slices on the Griddle:** Arrange the baguette slices on the griddle in a single layer.
   b. **Cook Until Golden:** Grill the bread for about 2-3 minutes on each side or until golden brown and crispy. Use a spatula to carefully flip the slices halfway through cooking.
6. **Ensure Even Cooking:** If parts of the bread are toasting faster than others, move them to a cooler zone on the griddle to ensure even cooking.
7. **Assemble the Crostini:** Spread a generous layer of the cream cheese mixture onto each grilled baguette slice. Top each with a slice of smoked salmon. Sprinkle freshly ground black pepper over the top.

8. **Garnish:** Garnish with extra dill and serve with lemon wedges on the side for squeezing over the top.

Griddled Eggplant Rollatini

Yield: 4 servings (8 rollatini) **Preparation Time:** 20 minutes **Cooking Time:** 15 minutes

Ingredients:

- 2 medium eggplants, sliced lengthwise into 1/4-inch thick slices
- 2 tablespoons olive oil
- 1 teaspoon salt
- 1/2 teaspoon black pepper
- 1 cup ricotta cheese
- 1/2 cup grated Parmesan cheese
- 1/2 cup shredded mozzarella cheese
- 1 large egg, beaten
- 2 cloves garlic, minced
- 1/4 cup fresh basil, chopped
- 1/4 cup fresh parsley, chopped
- 1 cup marinara sauce
- Olive oil spray or additional olive oil for greasing the griddle

Nutritional Information (per serving):

- Calories: 280
- Protein: 15g
- Carbohydrates: 15g
- Fats: 18g
- Fiber: 6g

Instructions:

1. **Prepare the Eggplants:** Slice the eggplants lengthwise into 1/4-inch thick slices. Lightly sprinkle both sides with salt and let them sit for 10 minutes to draw out excess moisture. Pat dry with paper towels.
2. **Season the Eggplant:** Brush both sides of the eggplant slices with olive oil and season with black pepper.
3. **Prepare the Filling:** In a medium bowl, combine the ricotta cheese, grated Parmesan cheese, shredded mozzarella cheese, beaten egg, minced garlic, chopped basil, and chopped parsley. Mix well until smooth.
4. **Preheat the Griddle:** Preheat the gas griddle to medium heat. Allow it to heat up for about 5 minutes until evenly hot.
5. **Grease the Griddle:** Lightly spray or brush the griddle surface with olive oil to prevent sticking.
6. **Grill the Eggplant:**
   a. **Place Eggplant Slices on the Griddle:** Arrange the eggplant slices on the griddle in a single layer.
   b. **Cook Until Tender:** Grill the eggplant slices for about 3-4 minutes on each side, or until they are tender and have nice grill marks. Use a spatula to carefully flip the slices halfway through cooking.
   c. **Ensure Even Cooking:** If parts of the eggplant slices are cooking faster than others, move them to a cooler zone on the griddle to ensure even cooking.
7. **Assemble the Rollatini:**
   a. **Add Filling:** Place a tablespoon of the ricotta mixture on one end of each grilled eggplant slice.
   b. **Roll Up:** Roll up the eggplant slices around the filling and place them seam-side down.
8. **Heat the Marinara Sauce:** Pour the marinara sauce into a small saucepan and heat it on the griddle or stovetop until warmed through.
9. **Serve Warm:** Spoon some of the warmed marinara sauce onto a serving platter. Place the eggplant rollatini on top of the sauce and drizzle with additional sauce. Garnish with extra grated Parmesan cheese and fresh basil if desired.

Vegetables

Smoky Grilled Eggplant Slices

Yield: 4 servings **Preparation Time:** 10 minutes **Cooking Time:** 15 minutes

Ingredients:

- 2 medium eggplants, sliced into 1/2-inch thick rounds
- 3 tablespoons olive oil
- 1 teaspoon smoked paprika
- 1 teaspoon garlic powder
- 1/2 teaspoon onion powder
- 1/2 teaspoon salt
- 1/4 teaspoon black pepper
- Fresh parsley, chopped (optional, for garnish)
- Lemon wedges (optional, for serving)

- Olive oil spray or additional olive oil for greasing the griddle

Nutritional Information (per serving):

- Calories: 120
- Protein: 2g
- Carbohydrates: 10g
- Fats: 9g
- Fiber: 4g

Instructions:

1. **Prepare the Eggplants:** Slice the eggplants into 1/2-inch thick rounds. Pat dry with paper towels to remove excess moisture.
2. **Season the Eggplants:** In a small bowl, combine the olive oil, smoked paprika, garlic powder, onion powder, salt, and black pepper. Brush both sides of the eggplant slices with the mixture.
3. **Preheat the Griddle:** Preheat the gas griddle to medium-high heat. Allow it to heat up for about 5 minutes until evenly hot.
4. **Grease the Griddle:** Lightly spray or brush the griddle surface with olive oil to prevent sticking.
5. **Grill the Eggplant Slices:**
    a. **Place Eggplant Slices on the Griddle:** Arrange the eggplant slices on the griddle in a single layer.
    b. **Cook Until Tender:** Grill the eggplant slices for about 4-5 minutes on each side, or until they are tender and have nice grill marks. Use a spatula to carefully flip the slices halfway through cooking.
6. **Ensure Even Cooking:** If parts of the eggplant slices are cooking faster than others, move them to a cooler zone on the griddle to ensure even cooking.
7. **Serve Warm:** Transfer the grilled eggplant slices to a serving platter. Garnish with chopped fresh parsley if desired.
8. **Optional Garnish:** Serve with lemon wedges for squeezing over the top.

Griddled Brussels Sprouts with Bacon

Yield: 4 servings **Preparation Time:** 10 minutes **Cooking Time:** 15 minutes

Ingredients:

- 1 pound Brussels sprouts, trimmed and halved
- 4 slices bacon, chopped
- 2 tablespoons olive oil
- 1/2 teaspoon salt
- 1/4 teaspoon black pepper
- 1 tablespoon balsamic vinegar
- 1 tablespoon honey
- Olive oil spray or additional olive oil for greasing the griddle

Nutritional Information (per serving):

- Calories: 180
- Protein: 6g
- Carbohydrates: 14g
- Fats: 12g
- Fiber: 5g

Instructions:

1. **Prepare the Brussels Sprouts:** Trim the ends and remove any yellow or damaged outer leaves. Cut the Brussels sprouts in half.
2. **Prepare the Bacon:** Chop the bacon into small pieces.
3. **Preheat the Griddle:** Preheat the gas griddle to medium heat. Allow it to heat up for about 5 minutes until evenly hot.
4. **Cook the Bacon:**
    a. **Add Bacon to Griddle:** Place the chopped bacon on the griddle. Cook for about 5 minutes, stirring occasionally, until the bacon is crispy. Use a spatula to transfer the bacon to a paper towel-lined plate to drain, leaving the bacon grease on the griddle.
    b. **Grease the Griddle:** If needed, add a bit more olive oil to the bacon grease on the griddle to ensure there is enough fat for cooking the Brussels sprouts.
5. **Cook the Brussels Sprouts:**
    a. **Add Brussels Sprouts to Griddle:** Place the halved Brussels sprouts on the griddle, cut side down.
    b. **Season:** Sprinkle with salt and black pepper.
    c. **Cook Until Tender:** Cook for about 7-10 minutes, turning occasionally, until the Brussels sprouts are tender and caramelized. If necessary, move them to a cooler zone on the griddle to prevent burning.

   d. **Add Balsamic Glaze:** In a small bowl, mix the balsamic vinegar and honey. Drizzle this mixture over the Brussels sprouts during the last 2 minutes of cooking and toss to coat evenly.
6. **Combine with Bacon:** Add the cooked bacon back to the griddle and mix with the Brussels sprouts until everything is well combined and heated through.
7. **Serve Warm:** Transfer the griddled Brussels sprouts with bacon to a serving platter.

Grilled Corn Salad with Avocado

Yield: 4 servings **Preparation Time:** 15 minutes **Cooking Time:** 15 minutes

Ingredients:

- 4 ears of corn, husked
- 1 red bell pepper, diced
- 1/2 red onion, finely chopped
- 1 avocado, diced
- 1/4 cup fresh cilantro, chopped
- 2 tablespoons olive oil
- 1 tablespoon lime juice
- 1 teaspoon ground cumin
- 1/2 teaspoon smoked paprika
- 1/2 teaspoon salt
- 1/4 teaspoon black pepper
- Olive oil spray or additional olive oil for greasing the griddle

Nutritional Information (per serving):

- Calories: 210
- Protein: 4g
- Carbohydrates: 24g
- Fats: 12g
- Fiber: 6g

Instructions:

1. **Prepare the Corn:** Husk the corn and remove any remaining silk. Brush each ear of corn with 1 tablespoon of olive oil.
2. **Prepare the Dressing:** In a small bowl, whisk together the lime juice, ground cumin, smoked paprika, salt, black pepper, and the remaining 1 tablespoon of olive oil. Set aside.
3. **Preheat the Griddle:** Preheat the gas griddle to medium-high heat. Allow it to heat up for about 5 minutes until evenly hot.
4. **Grease the Griddle:** Lightly spray or brush the griddle surface with olive oil to prevent sticking.
5. **Grill the Corn:**
   a. **Place Corn on Griddle:** Place the ears of corn on the griddle.
   b. **Cook Until Charred:** Grill the corn for about 10-12 minutes, turning occasionally, until the corn is tender and charred in spots. Use tongs to rotate the corn for even cooking.
6. **Prepare the Vegetables:** While the corn is grilling, dice the red bell pepper and avocado, and finely chop the red onion and cilantro.
7. **Remove Corn Kernels:** Once the corn is cooked, remove it from the griddle and let it cool slightly. Use a sharp knife to carefully cut the kernels off the cob into a large mixing bowl.
8. **Assemble the Salad:** Add the diced red bell pepper, chopped red onion, diced avocado, and chopped cilantro to the bowl with the corn kernels.
9. **Add Dressing:** Pour the prepared dressing over the salad and toss gently to combine all ingredients.
10. **Serve Immediately:** Transfer the grilled corn salad to a serving platter or bowl. Serve immediately for the best flavor and texture.

Griddled Sweet Potato Fries

Yield: 4 servings **Preparation Time:** 15 minutes **Cooking Time:** 20 minutes

Ingredients:

- 2 large sweet potatoes, peeled and cut into 1/4-inch thick fries
- 3 tablespoons olive oil
- 1 teaspoon smoked paprika
- 1 teaspoon garlic powder
- 1/2 teaspoon onion powder
- 1/2 teaspoon salt
- 1/4 teaspoon black pepper
- Fresh parsley, chopped (optional, for garnish)

Nutritional Information (per serving):

- Calories: 200
- Protein: 2g
- Carbohydrates: 30g

- Fats: 9g
- Fiber: 5g

Instructions:

1. **Prepare the Sweet Potatoes:** Peel the sweet potatoes and cut them into 1/4-inch thick fries.
2. **Season the Sweet Potatoes:** In a large bowl, toss the sweet potato fries with olive oil, smoked paprika, garlic powder, onion powder, salt, and black pepper until evenly coated.
3. **Preheat the Griddle:** Preheat the gas griddle to medium heat. Allow it to heat up for about 5 minutes until evenly hot.
4. **Grease the Griddle:** Lightly spray or brush the griddle surface with olive oil to prevent sticking.
5. **Cook the Sweet Potato Fries:**
6. **Place Fries on Griddle:** Arrange the sweet potato fries on the griddle in a single layer, ensuring they are not overcrowded.
7. **Cook Until Crispy:** Cook the fries for about 10 minutes on each side, turning occasionally with a spatula, until they are crispy and cooked through. Total cooking time should be around 20 minutes.
8. **Ensure Even Cooking:** If parts of the sweet potato fries are cooking faster than others, move them to a cooler zone on the griddle to ensure even cooking.
9. **Prevent Sticking:** Periodically check and reapply a thin layer of olive oil if the griddle surface starts to dry out.
10. **Serve Warm:** Transfer the griddled sweet potato fries to a serving platter. Garnish with chopped fresh parsley if desired.

Grilled Cauliflower Steaks

Yield: 4 servings **Preparation Time:** 10 minutes **Cooking Time:** 20 minutes

Ingredients:

- 1 large head of cauliflower
- 3 tablespoons olive oil
- 1 teaspoon smoked paprika
- 1 teaspoon garlic powder
- 1/2 teaspoon onion powder
- 1/2 teaspoon salt
- 1/4 teaspoon black pepper
- 1 tablespoon fresh lemon juice
- Fresh parsley, chopped (optional, for garnish)
- Olive oil spray or additional olive oil for greasing the griddle

Nutritional Information (per serving):

- Calories: 120
- Protein: 3g
- Carbohydrates: 10g
- Fats: 9g
- Fiber: 4g

Instructions:

1. **Prepare the Cauliflower:** Remove the outer leaves and trim the stem of the cauliflower, leaving the core intact.
2. Cut the cauliflower into 3/4-inch thick slices to create "steaks." You should get about 4-6 steaks from one head of cauliflower.
3. **Season the Cauliflower:** In a small bowl, mix the olive oil, smoked paprika, garlic powder, onion powder, salt, and black pepper. Brush both sides of the cauliflower steaks with the seasoned olive oil mixture.
4. **Preheat the Griddle:** Preheat the gas griddle to medium heat. Allow it to heat up for about 5 minutes until evenly hot.
5. **Grease the Griddle:** Lightly spray or brush the griddle surface with olive oil to prevent sticking.
6. **Cook the Cauliflower Steaks:**
   a. **Place Cauliflower Steaks on the Griddle:** Arrange the cauliflower steaks on the griddle in a single layer.
   b. **Cook Until Tender:** Grill the steaks for about 7-8 minutes on each side, or until they are tender and have nice char marks. Use a spatula to carefully flip the steaks halfway through cooking.
   c. **Ensure Even Cooking:** If parts of the cauliflower steaks are cooking faster than others, move them to a cooler zone on the griddle to ensure even cooking.
7. **Add Lemon Juice:** During the last minute of cooking, drizzle the cauliflower steaks with fresh lemon juice for added flavor.
8. **Serve Warm:** Transfer the grilled cauliflower steaks to a serving platter. Garnish with chopped fresh parsley if desired.

Grilled Tomato and Mozzarella Skewers

Yield: 4 servings (8 skewers) **Preparation Time:** 10 minutes **Cooking Time:** 10 minutes

Ingredients:

- 16 cherry tomatoes
- 16 small mozzarella balls (bocconcini)
- 16 fresh basil leaves
- 2 tablespoons olive oil
- 1 tablespoon balsamic vinegar
- 1 teaspoon garlic powder
- 1/2 teaspoon salt
- 1/4 teaspoon black pepper
- Olive oil spray or additional olive oil for greasing the griddle
- Skewers (if using wooden skewers, soak in water for 30 minutes)

Nutritional Information (per serving):

- Calories: 150
- Protein: 7g
- Carbohydrates: 4g
- Fats: 11g
- Fiber: 1g

Instructions:

1. **Prepare the Ingredients:** Thread the cherry tomatoes, mozzarella balls, and fresh basil leaves alternately onto the skewers, starting and ending with a cherry tomato. In a small bowl, whisk together the olive oil, balsamic vinegar, garlic powder, salt, and black pepper.
2. **Season the Skewers:** Brush the prepared skewers with the olive oil and balsamic mixture on all sides.
3. **Preheat the Griddle:** Preheat the gas griddle to medium heat. Allow it to heat up for about 5 minutes until evenly hot.
4. **Grease the Griddle:** Lightly spray or brush the griddle surface with olive oil to prevent sticking.
5. **Cook the Skewers:**
    a. **Place Skewers on Griddle:** Arrange the skewers on the griddle in a single layer.
    b. **Cook Until Charred:** Grill the skewers for about 2-3 minutes on each side, or until the tomatoes are slightly charred and the mozzarella is beginning to melt. Use tongs to carefully turn the skewers to ensure even cooking.
    c. **Ensure Even Cooking:** If parts of the skewers are cooking faster than others, move them to a cooler zone on the griddle to ensure even cooking.
6. **Serve Warm:** Transfer the grilled tomato and mozzarella skewers to a serving platter.

Grilled Artichoke Hearts with Herb Butter

Yield: 4 servings **Preparation Time:** 10 minutes **Cooking Time:** 15 minutes

Ingredients:

- 2 cans (14 oz each) of artichoke hearts, drained and halved
- 3 tablespoons olive oil
- 1 teaspoon garlic powder
- 1/2 teaspoon salt
- 1/4 teaspoon black pepper

Herb Butter:

- 4 tablespoons unsalted butter, softened
- 1 tablespoon fresh parsley, chopped
- 1 tablespoon fresh thyme, chopped
- 1 teaspoon fresh rosemary, chopped
- 1 teaspoon lemon zest
- 1 garlic clove, minced
- 1/4 teaspoon salt
- 1/4 teaspoon black pepper

Nutritional Information (per serving):

- Calories: 180
- Protein: 4g
- Carbohydrates: 10g
- Fats: 14g
- Fiber: 5g

Instructions:

1. **Prepare the Artichoke Hearts:** Drain the artichoke hearts and cut them in half if not already halved. Pat them dry with paper towels to remove excess moisture.
2. **Season the Artichoke Hearts:** In a mixing bowl, toss the artichoke hearts with olive oil, garlic powder, salt, and black pepper until evenly coated.
3. **Prepare the Herb Butter:** In a small bowl, combine the softened butter with chopped parsley, thyme, rosemary, lemon zest, minced garlic, salt, and black pepper. Mix until well combined.
4. **Preheat the Griddle:** Preheat the gas griddle to medium-high heat. Allow it to heat up for about 5 minutes until evenly hot.
5. **Grease the Griddle:** Lightly spray or brush the griddle surface with olive oil to prevent sticking.
6. **Grill the Artichoke Hearts:**

a. **Place Artichoke Hearts on Griddle:** Arrange the seasoned artichoke hearts on the griddle in a single layer, cut side down.
b. **Cook Until Golden:** Grill the artichoke hearts for about 5-7 minutes, turning occasionally, until they are golden brown and slightly crispy on the edges. Use a spatula to carefully flip the artichoke hearts halfway through cooking.
c. **Ensure Even Cooking:** If parts of the artichoke hearts are cooking faster than others, move them to a cooler zone on the griddle to ensure even cooking.

7. **Serve Warm:** Transfer the grilled artichoke hearts to a serving platter.
8. **Top with Herb Butter:** Immediately top the hot artichoke hearts with dollops of the herb butter, allowing it to melt over the artichokes.

Griddled Broccoli with Cheese Sauce

Yield: 4 servings **Preparation Time:** 10 minutes **Cooking Time:** 15 minutes

Ingredients:

For the Broccoli:

- 1 pound broccoli, cut into florets
- 2 tablespoons olive oil
- 1/2 teaspoon garlic powder
- 1/2 teaspoon onion powder
- 1/2 teaspoon salt
- 1/4 teaspoon black pepper

For the Cheese Sauce:

- 2 tablespoons butter
- 2 tablespoons all-purpose flour
- 1 cup milk
- 1 cup shredded cheddar cheese
- 1/2 teaspoon Dijon mustard
- Salt and pepper to taste

Nutritional Information (per serving):

- Calories: 220
- Protein: 9g
- Carbohydrates: 12g
- Fats: 15g
- Fiber: 4g

Instructions:

1. **Prepare the Broccoli:** Cut the broccoli into florets. In a mixing bowl, toss the broccoli florets with olive oil, garlic powder, onion powder, salt, and black pepper until evenly coated.
2. **Prepare the Cheese Sauce:**
   a. In a medium saucepan, melt the butter over medium heat. Add the flour and whisk continuously for about 2 minutes to make a roux.
   b. Gradually add the milk while whisking, ensuring there are no lumps. Continue to cook and whisk until the sauce thickens, about 3-4 minutes.
   c. Remove the saucepan from heat and stir in the shredded cheddar cheese and Dijon mustard. Season with salt and pepper to taste. Keep warm.
3. **Preheat the Griddle:** Preheat the gas griddle to medium-high heat. Allow it to heat up for about 5 minutes until evenly hot.
4. **Grease the Griddle:** Lightly spray or brush the griddle surface with olive oil to prevent sticking.
5. **Cook the Broccoli:**
   a. **Place Broccoli on Griddle:** Arrange the seasoned broccoli florets on the griddle in a single layer.
   b. **Cook Until Tender:** Grill the broccoli for about 10-12 minutes, turning occasionally, until the florets are tender and slightly charred. Use a spatula to turn the broccoli for even cooking.
   c. **Ensure Even Cooking:** If parts of the broccoli are cooking faster than others, move them to a cooler zone on the griddle to ensure even cooking.
6. **Serve Warm:** Transfer the grilled broccoli to a serving platter.
7. **Top with Cheese Sauce:** Drizzle the warm cheese sauce over the grilled broccoli before serving.

Grilled Vegetable Stir-Fry

Yield: 4 servings **Preparation Time:** 15 minutes **Cooking Time:** 15 minutes

Ingredients:

- 1 red bell pepper, sliced into strips
- 1 yellow bell pepper, sliced into strips
- 1 zucchini, sliced into half-moons
- 1 yellow squash, sliced into half-moons

- 1 red onion, sliced
- 1 cup broccoli florets
- 1 cup snap peas
- 1 carrot, julienned
- 2 tablespoons olive oil
- 2 tablespoons soy sauce
- 1 tablespoon hoisin sauce
- 1 tablespoon sesame oil
- 1 teaspoon garlic powder
- 1 teaspoon ginger powder
- 1/2 teaspoon red pepper flakes (optional)
- Salt and black pepper to taste
- 2 green onions, chopped (for garnish)
- Sesame seeds (for garnish)
- Olive oil spray or additional olive oil for greasing the griddle

Nutritional Information (per serving):

- Calories: 150
- Protein: 3g
- Carbohydrates: 16g
- Fats: 8g
- Fiber: 5g

Instructions:

1. **Prepare the Vegetables:**
    a. Slice the red and yellow bell peppers into strips.
    b. Slice the zucchini and yellow squash into half-moons.
    c. Slice the red onion.
    d. Cut the broccoli into small florets.
    e. Julienne the carrot.
    f. Trim the snap peas.
2. **Prepare the Sauce:** In a small bowl, whisk together the soy sauce, hoisin sauce, sesame oil, garlic powder, ginger powder, and red pepper flakes (if using). Set aside.
3. **Preheat the Griddle:** Preheat the gas griddle to medium-high heat. Allow it to heat up for about 5 minutes until evenly hot.
4. **Grease the Griddle:** Lightly spray or brush the griddle surface with olive oil to prevent sticking.
5. **Cook the Vegetables:**
    a. **Add Vegetables to Griddle:** Place the prepared vegetables on the griddle.
    b. **Season and Stir-Fry:** Drizzle the vegetables with olive oil, and season with salt and black pepper. Stir-fry the vegetables for about 10-12 minutes, using a spatula to toss and turn the vegetables occasionally until they are tender-crisp and slightly charred.
    c. **Add Sauce:** Drizzle the prepared sauce over the vegetables during the last 2-3 minutes of cooking. Toss to coat the vegetables evenly with the sauce.
    d. **Ensure Even Cooking:** If parts of the vegetables are cooking faster than others, move them to a cooler zone on the griddle to ensure even cooking.
6. **Serve Warm:** Transfer the grilled vegetable stir-fry to a serving platter.
7. **Garnish:** Garnish with chopped green onions and sesame seeds before serving.

Grilled Sweet Peppers with Feta

Yield: 4 servings **Preparation Time:** 10 minutes **Cooking Time:** 15 minutes

Ingredients:

- 4 sweet bell peppers (red, yellow, or orange), cut into quarters and seeds removed
- 2 tablespoons olive oil
- 1 teaspoon garlic powder
- 1/2 teaspoon dried oregano
- 1/2 teaspoon salt
- 1/4 teaspoon black pepper
- 1/2 cup crumbled feta cheese
- 2 tablespoons fresh parsley, chopped (optional for garnish)
- Olive oil spray or additional olive oil for greasing the griddle

Nutritional Information (per serving):

- Calories: 130
- Protein: 3g
- Carbohydrates: 8g
- Fats: 10g
- Fiber: 2g

Instructions:

1. **Prepare the Peppers:** Cut the sweet bell peppers into quarters and remove the seeds and membranes.
2. **Season the Peppers:** In a large bowl, toss the pepper quarters with olive oil, garlic powder, dried oregano, salt, and black pepper until evenly coated.
3. **Preheat the Griddle:** Preheat the gas griddle to medium-high heat. Allow it to heat up for about 5 minutes until evenly hot.
4. **Grease the Griddle:** Lightly spray or brush the griddle surface with olive oil to prevent sticking.
5. **Cook the Peppers:**
    a. **Place Peppers on Griddle:** Arrange the seasoned pepper quarters on the griddle in a single layer, skin-side down.
    b. **Cook Until Tender:** Grill the peppers for about 6-8 minutes, turning occasionally, until they are tender and slightly charred. Use a spatula to turn the peppers for even cooking.
    c. **Ensure Even Cooking:** If parts of the peppers are cooking faster than others, move them to a cooler zone on the griddle to ensure even cooking.
6. **Serve Warm:** Transfer the grilled sweet peppers to a serving platter.
7. **Top with Feta:** Sprinkle the crumbled feta cheese over the warm peppers. Garnish with chopped fresh parsley if desired.

Griddled Mushrooms with Soy Sauce

Yield: 4 servings **Preparation Time:** 10 minutes **Cooking Time:** 15 minutes

Ingredients:

- 1 pound mixed mushrooms (e.g., cremini, button, shiitake), cleaned and sliced
- 2 tablespoons olive oil
- 2 tablespoons soy sauce
- 1 tablespoon sesame oil
- 1 tablespoon rice vinegar
- 2 cloves garlic, minced
- 1 teaspoon fresh ginger, minced
- 1/2 teaspoon black pepper
- 1/4 cup green onions, chopped (for garnish)
- Sesame seeds (optional, for garnish)
- Olive oil spray or additional olive oil for greasing the griddle

Nutritional Information (per serving):

- Calories: 120
- Protein: 3g
- Carbohydrates: 8g
- Fats: 9g
- Fiber: 2g

Instructions:

1. **Prepare the Mushrooms:** Clean and slice the mushrooms if not pre-sliced.
2. **Prepare the Sauce:** In a small bowl, whisk together the soy sauce, sesame oil, rice vinegar, minced garlic, minced ginger, and black pepper. Set aside.
3. **Preheat the Griddle:** Preheat the gas griddle to medium-high heat. Allow it to heat up for about 5 minutes until evenly hot.
4. **Grease the Griddle:** Lightly spray or brush the griddle surface with olive oil to prevent sticking.
5. **Cook the Mushrooms:**
    a. **Place Mushrooms on Griddle:** Arrange the sliced mushrooms on the griddle in a single layer.
    b. **Cook Until Tender:** Grill the mushrooms for about 8-10 minutes, stirring occasionally, until they are tender and have released their moisture. Use a spatula to turn the mushrooms for even cooking.
    c. **Add the Sauce:** During the last 2-3 minutes of cooking, drizzle the prepared soy sauce mixture over the mushrooms. Toss to coat evenly and continue to cook until the sauce is absorbed and the mushrooms are caramelized.
    d. **Ensure Even Cooking:** If parts of the mushrooms are cooking faster than others, move them to a cooler zone on the griddle to ensure even cooking.
6. **Serve Warm:** Transfer the griddled mushrooms to a serving platter.
7. **Garnish:** Garnish with chopped green onions and sesame seeds if desired.

Griddled Fennel with Parmesan

Yield: 4 servings **Preparation Time:** 10 minutes **Cooking Time:** 15 minutes

Ingredients:

- 2 large fennel bulbs
- 3 tablespoons olive oil
- 1 teaspoon garlic powder
- 1 teaspoon dried thyme
- 1/2 teaspoon salt
- 1/4 teaspoon black pepper
- 1/2 cup grated Parmesan cheese
- 1 tablespoon fresh parsley, chopped (optional, for garnish)
- Lemon wedges (optional, for serving)
- Olive oil spray or additional olive oil for greasing the griddle

Nutritional Information (per serving):

- Calories: 150
- Protein: 4g
- Carbohydrates: 10g
- Fats: 10g
- Fiber: 5g

Instructions:

1. **Prepare the Fennel:** Trim the fennel bulbs, removing the stalks and fronds. Cut each bulb into 1/2-inch thick slices, keeping the core intact to hold the slices together.
2. **Season the Fennel:** In a large bowl, toss the fennel slices with olive oil, garlic powder, dried thyme, salt, and black pepper until evenly coated.
3. **Preheat the Griddle:** Preheat the gas griddle to medium heat. Allow it to heat up for about 5 minutes until evenly hot.
4. **Grease the Griddle:** Lightly spray or brush the griddle surface with olive oil to prevent sticking.
5. **Cook the Fennel:**
    a. **Place Fennel on Griddle:** Arrange the seasoned fennel slices on the griddle in a single layer.
    b. **Cook Until Tender:** Grill the fennel for about 7-8 minutes on each side or until tender and caramelized. Use a spatula to carefully flip the slices halfway through cooking.
    c. **Add Parmesan:** During the last 2 minutes of cooking, sprinkle the grated Parmesan cheese evenly over the fennel slices. Allow the cheese to melt and form a crispy crust.
6. **Ensure Even Cooking:** If parts of the fennel are cooking faster than others, move them to a cooler zone on the griddle to ensure even cooking.
7. **Serve Warm:** Transfer the griddled fennel slices to a serving platter.
8. **Garnish:** Garnish with chopped fresh parsley if desired and serve with lemon wedges for an extra burst of flavor.

Griddled Eggplant Parmesan

Yield: 4 servings **Preparation Time:** 20 minutes **Cooking Time:** 20 minutes

Ingredients:

- 2 medium eggplants, sliced into 1/2-inch thick rounds
- 1 cup all-purpose flour
- 2 large eggs, beaten
- 1 cup breadcrumbs
- 1/2 cup grated Parmesan cheese
- 1 teaspoon garlic powder
- 1 teaspoon dried oregano
- 1 teaspoon dried basil
- 1/2 teaspoon salt
- 1/4 teaspoon black pepper
- 2 cups marinara sauce, warmed
- 1 cup shredded mozzarella cheese
- 1/4 cup fresh basil leaves, chopped (optional, for garnish)
- Olive oil spray or additional olive oil for greasing the griddle

Nutritional Information (per serving):

- Calories: 350
- Protein: 15g
- Carbohydrates: 40g
- Fats: 15g
- Fiber: 8g

Instructions:

1. **Prepare the Eggplants:** Slice the eggplants into 1/2-inch thick rounds. Lay them out on a paper towel-lined baking sheet and sprinkle with salt. Let them sit for 10 minutes to draw out excess moisture. Pat dry with additional paper towels.
2. **Prepare the Breading Stations:** Set up three shallow bowls: one with flour, one with beaten eggs, and one with a mixture of breadcrumbs, grated Parmesan cheese, garlic powder, dried oregano, dried basil, salt, and black pepper.
3. **Bread the Eggplant Slices:** Dredge each eggplant slice in flour, shaking off excess, then dip in the beaten eggs, and finally coat with the breadcrumb mixture. Press the breadcrumbs onto the eggplant slices to ensure they adhere well.
4. **Preheat the Griddle:** Preheat the gas griddle to medium heat. Allow it to heat up for about 5 minutes until evenly hot.
5. **Grease the Griddle:** Lightly spray or brush the griddle surface with olive oil to prevent sticking.
6. **Cook the Eggplant Slices:**
    a. **Place Eggplant on Griddle:** Arrange the breaded eggplant slices on the griddle in a single layer.
    b. **Cook Until Golden:** Grill the eggplant for about 4-5 minutes on each side, or until golden brown and crispy. Use a spatula to carefully flip the slices halfway through cooking.
    c. **Ensure Even Cooking:** If parts of the eggplant are cooking faster than others, move them to a cooler zone on the griddle to ensure even cooking.
    d. **Add the Cheese:** During the last minute of cooking, sprinkle shredded mozzarella cheese on top of each eggplant slice. Close the griddle lid or use a press lid to melt the cheese.
7. **Assemble the Dish:** Transfer the cooked eggplant slices to a serving platter. Spoon warm marinara sauce over each slice.
8. **Serve Warm:** Garnish with fresh chopped basil if desired. Serve immediately.

Meat

Griddled Ribeye Steak with Garlic Butter

Yield: 4 servings **Preparation Time:** 10 minutes **Cooking Time:** 15 minutes

Ingredients:

- 4 ribeye steaks (about 1 inch thick)
- 2 tablespoons olive oil
- 1 teaspoon salt
- 1 teaspoon black pepper
- 1 teaspoon garlic powder

Garlic Butter:

- 1/2 cup unsalted butter, softened
- 4 cloves garlic, minced
- 2 tablespoons fresh parsley, chopped
- 1 teaspoon fresh thyme, chopped
- 1 tablespoon lemon juice
- 1/2 teaspoon salt
- 1/4 teaspoon black pepper

Nutritional Information (per serving):

- Calories: 580
- Protein: 38g
- Carbohydrates: 2g
- Fats: 47g
- Fiber: 0g

Instructions:

1. **Prepare the Steaks:** Pat the ribeye steaks dry with paper towels. Brush both sides with olive oil and season generously with salt, black pepper, and garlic powder.
2. **Prepare the Garlic Butter:** In a small bowl, combine the softened butter, minced garlic, chopped parsley, chopped thyme, lemon juice, salt, and black pepper. Mix well until all ingredients are evenly incorporated. Set aside.
3. **Preheat the Griddle:** Preheat the gas griddle to high heat. Allow it to heat up for about 5-10 minutes until it reaches a high temperature.
4. **Grease the Griddle:** Lightly spray or brush the griddle surface with olive oil to prevent sticking.
5. **Cook the Steaks:**
    a. **Place Steaks on Griddle:** Arrange the seasoned ribeye steaks on the griddle.
    b. **Sear the Steaks:** Sear the steaks for about 3-4 minutes on each side for medium-rare, or until they reach the desired level of doneness. Use a spatula to flip the steaks only once to ensure a good sear.
    c. **Baste with Garlic Butter:** During the last minute of cooking, add a dollop of the prepared garlic butter on top of each steak. Use a spoon to baste the steaks with the melted butter.

   d. **Ensure Even Cooking:** If parts of the steaks are cooking faster than others, move them to a cooler zone on the griddle to ensure even cooking.
6. **Rest the Steaks:** Remove the steaks from the griddle and let them rest for 5 minutes to allow the juices to redistribute.
7. **Serve Warm:** Transfer the steaks to a serving platter and drizzle with any remaining garlic butter from the griddle.

BBQ Grilled Pork Chops

Yield: 4 servings **Preparation Time:** 10 minutes **Cooking Time:** 20 minutes

Ingredients:

- 4 bone-in pork chops (about 1 inch thick)
- 2 tablespoons olive oil
- 1 teaspoon salt
- 1 teaspoon black pepper
- 1 teaspoon garlic powder
- 1 teaspoon onion powder
- 1 teaspoon smoked paprika
- 1 cup BBQ sauce (store-bought or homemade)
- Olive oil spray or additional olive oil for greasing the griddle

Nutritional Information (per serving):

- Calories: 400
- Protein: 32g
- Carbohydrates: 15g
- Fats: 22g
- Fiber: 1g

Instructions:

1. **Prepare the Pork Chops:** Pat the pork chops dry with paper towels. Brush both sides with olive oil.
2. **Season the Pork Chops:** In a small bowl, mix together the salt, black pepper, garlic powder, onion powder, and smoked paprika. Rub the spice mixture evenly over both sides of the pork chops.
3. **Preheat the Griddle:** Preheat the gas griddle to medium-high heat. Allow it to heat up for about 5-10 minutes until it reaches a high temperature.
4. **Grease the Griddle:** Lightly spray or brush the griddle surface with olive oil to prevent sticking.
5. **Cook the Pork Chops:**
   a. **Place Pork Chops on Griddle:** Arrange the seasoned pork chops on the griddle.
   b. **Sear the Pork Chops:** Sear the pork chops for about 4-5 minutes on each side to develop a nice crust.
   c. **Apply BBQ Sauce:** After the initial sear, brush BBQ sauce on the top side of the pork chops. Flip and cook for an additional 4-5 minutes, then brush more BBQ sauce on the other side. Continue cooking until the internal temperature reaches 145°F (63°C), basting with BBQ sauce occasionally.
   d. **Ensure Even Cooking:** If parts of the pork chops are cooking faster than others, move them to a cooler zone on the griddle to ensure even cooking.
6. **Rest the Pork Chops:** Remove the pork chops from the griddle and let them rest for 5 minutes to allow the juices to redistribute.
7. **Serve Warm:** Transfer the pork chops to a serving platter and drizzle with any remaining BBQ sauce.

Grilled Lamb Chops with Rosemary

Yield: 4 servings **Preparation Time:** 15 minutes **Cooking Time:** 15 minutes

Ingredients:

- 8 lamb chops (about 1 inch thick)
- 3 tablespoons olive oil
- 4 cloves garlic, minced
- 2 tablespoons fresh rosemary, chopped
- 1 teaspoon salt
- 1/2 teaspoon black pepper
- 1 tablespoon fresh lemon juice
- Olive oil spray or additional olive oil for greasing the griddle

Nutritional Information (per serving):

- Calories: 450
- Protein: 28g
- Carbohydrates: 2g
- Fats: 36g
- Fiber: 0g

Instructions:

1. **Marinate the Lamb Chops:** In a small bowl, mix together the olive oil, minced garlic, chopped rosemary, salt, black pepper, and lemon juice. Rub this mixture evenly over both sides of the lamb chops. Let the lamb chops marinate at room temperature for at least 15 minutes.
2. **Preheat the Griddle:** Preheat the gas griddle to medium-high heat. Allow it to heat up for about 5-10 minutes until it reaches a high temperature.
3. **Grease the Griddle:** Lightly spray or brush the griddle surface with olive oil to prevent sticking.
4. **Cook the Lamb Chops:**
   a. **Place Lamb Chops on Griddle:** Arrange the marinated lamb chops on the griddle.
   b. **Sear the Lamb Chops:** Sear the lamb chops for about 4-5 minutes on each side for medium-rare, or until they reach the desired level of doneness. Use a spatula to carefully flip the lamb chops only once to ensure a good sear.
5. **Ensure Even Cooking:** If parts of the lamb chops are cooking faster than others, move them to a cooler zone on the griddle to ensure even cooking.
6. **Rest the Lamb Chops:** Remove the lamb chops from the griddle and let them rest for 5 minutes to allow the juices to redistribute.
7. **Serve Warm:** Transfer the lamb chops to a serving platter. Garnish with additional fresh rosemary if desired.

Griddled BBQ Brisket

Yield: 6 servings **Preparation Time:** 15 minutes (plus marinating time) **Cooking Time:** 45 minutes to 1 hour

Ingredients:

- 2 pounds of beef brisket, trimmed of excess fat
- 2 tablespoons olive oil
- 1 cup BBQ sauce (store-bought or homemade)

Dry Rub:

- 2 tablespoons brown sugar
- 1 tablespoon smoked paprika
- 1 tablespoon garlic powder
- 1 tablespoon onion powder
- 1 teaspoon salt
- 1 teaspoon black pepper
- 1 teaspoon ground cumin
- 1/2 teaspoon cayenne pepper (optional, for heat)

Nutritional Information (per serving):

- Calories: 450
- Protein: 35g
- Carbohydrates: 15g
- Fats: 28g
- Fiber: 1g

Instructions:

1. **Prepare the Brisket:** Trim the brisket of excess fat, leaving a thin layer for flavor. Cut the brisket into smaller sections if necessary to fit on the griddle.
2. **Make the Dry Rub:** In a small bowl, mix together the brown sugar, smoked paprika, garlic powder, onion powder, salt, black pepper, ground cumin, and cayenne pepper (if using).
3. **Season the Brisket:** Rub the olive oil all over the brisket pieces. Generously coat the brisket with the dry rub, pressing it into the meat. Let the brisket marinate for at least 1 hour, or preferably overnight in the refrigerator.
4. **Preheat the Griddle:** Preheat the gas griddle to medium-high heat. Allow it to heat up for about 5-10 minutes until it reaches a high temperature.
5. **Grease the Griddle:** Lightly spray or brush the griddle surface with olive oil to prevent sticking.
6. **Sear the Brisket:**
   a. **Place Brisket on Griddle:** Arrange the brisket pieces on the griddle.
   b. **Sear Both Sides:** Sear the brisket for about 5-7 minutes on each side or until a nice crust forms.
7. Cook Through:
   a. **Lower Heat:** Reduce the heat to medium. Continue cooking the brisket, turning occasionally, for about 30-40 minutes, or until the internal temperature reaches at least 190°F (88°C) for tender brisket.
   b. **Apply BBQ Sauce:** During the last 10 minutes of cooking, brush the brisket with BBQ sauce. Turn and baste frequently to caramelize the sauce and form a sticky glaze.
   c. **Ensure Even Cooking:** If parts of the brisket are cooking faster than others, move them to a cooler zone on the griddle to ensure even cooking.
8. **Rest the Brisket:** Remove the brisket from the griddle and let it rest for 10 minutes to allow the juices to redistribute.
9. **Slice and Serve:** Slice the brisket against the grain into thin slices. Serve with additional BBQ sauce on the side if desired.

Smoky Grilled Beef Kebabs

Yield: 4 servings **Preparation Time:** 20 minutes (plus marinating time) **Cooking Time:** 15 minutes

Ingredients:

- 1.5 pounds beef sirloin or tenderloin, cut into 1-inch cubes
- 1 red bell pepper, cut into 1-inch pieces
- 1 yellow bell pepper, cut into 1-inch pieces
- 1 red onion, cut into 1-inch pieces
- 1 zucchini, sliced into thick rounds

Marinade:

- 1/4 cup olive oil
- 1/4 cup soy sauce
- 2 tablespoons lemon juice
- 2 tablespoons Worcestershire sauce
- 1 tablespoon smoked paprika
- 1 tablespoon garlic powder
- 1 teaspoon onion powder
- 1 teaspoon black pepper
- 1/2 teaspoon salt
- 1 teaspoon dried oregano

For Grilling:

- Olive oil spray or additional olive oil for greasing the griddle

Nutritional Information (per serving):

- Calories: 350
- Protein: 30g
- Carbohydrates: 12g
- Fats: 20g
- Fiber: 3g

Instructions:

1. **Prepare the Beef and Vegetables:**
   a. Cut the beef into 1-inch cubes.
   b. Cut the red and yellow bell peppers, red onion, and zucchini into 1-inch pieces.
2. **Make the Marinade:** In a large bowl, whisk together the olive oil, soy sauce, lemon juice, Worcestershire sauce, smoked paprika, garlic powder, onion powder, black pepper, salt, and dried oregano.
3. **Marinate the Beef:** Add the beef cubes to the marinade and toss to coat evenly. Cover and refrigerate for at least 1 hour, or preferably overnight for more flavor.
4. **Prepare the Skewers:** If using wooden skewers, soak them in water for at least 30 minutes to prevent burning.
5. Thread the marinated beef, bell peppers, red onion, and zucchini alternately onto the skewers.
6. **Preheat the Griddle:** Preheat the gas griddle to medium-high heat. Allow it to heat up for about 5-10 minutes until it reaches a high temperature.
7. **Grease the Griddle:** Lightly spray or brush the griddle surface with olive oil to prevent sticking.
8. **Cook the Kebabs:**
   a. **Place Kebabs on the Griddle:** Arrange the skewers on the griddle.
   b. **Cook Until Charred:** Grill the kebabs for about 10-15 minutes, turning occasionally, until the beef is cooked to your desired level of doneness and the vegetables are tender and slightly charred.
   c. **Ensure Even Cooking:** If parts of the kebabs are cooking faster than others, move them to a cooler zone on the griddle to ensure even cooking.
9. **Serve Warm:** Transfer the grilled beef kebabs to a serving platter. Serve immediately.

Teriyaki Griddled Beef Skewers

Yield: 4 servings **Preparation Time:** 20 minutes (plus marinating time) **Cooking Time:** 15 minutes

Ingredients:

- 1.5 pounds beef sirloin or tenderloin, cut into 1-inch cubes
- 1 red bell pepper, cut into 1-inch pieces
- 1 yellow bell pepper, cut into 1-inch pieces
- 1 red onion, cut into 1-inch pieces
- 1 zucchini, sliced into thick rounds

Teriyaki Marinade:

- 1/4 cup soy sauce
- 1/4 cup mirin (sweet rice wine)
- 1/4 cup sake (rice wine) or water
- 2 tablespoons brown sugar
- 2 cloves garlic, minced
- 1 tablespoon fresh ginger, grated
- 1 tablespoon sesame oil
- 1 tablespoon cornstarch (optional, for thickening)

For Grilling:

- Olive oil spray or additional olive oil for greasing the griddle

Nutritional Information (per serving):

- Calories: 320
- Protein: 30g
- Carbohydrates: 15g
- Fats: 15g
- Fiber: 2g

Instructions:

1. **Prepare the Beef and Vegetables:**
    a. Cut the beef into 1-inch cubes.
    b. Cut the red and yellow bell peppers, red onion, and zucchini into 1-inch pieces.
2. **Make the Teriyaki Marinade:** In a medium bowl, whisk together the soy sauce, mirin, sake (or water), brown sugar, minced garlic, grated ginger, and sesame oil. If a thicker sauce is desired, dissolve the cornstarch in 1 tablespoon of water and add it to the mixture.
3. **Marinate the Beef:** Add the beef cubes to the marinade and toss to coat evenly. Cover and refrigerate for at least 1 hour, or preferably overnight for more flavor.
4. **Prepare the Skewers:**
    a. If using wooden skewers, soak them in water for at least 30 minutes to prevent burning.
    b. Thread the marinated beef, bell peppers, red onion, and zucchini alternately onto the skewers.
5. **Preheat the Griddle:** Preheat the gas griddle to medium-high heat. Allow it to heat up for about 5-10 minutes until it reaches a high temperature.
6. **Grease the Griddle:** Lightly spray or brush the griddle surface with olive oil to prevent sticking.
7. **Cook the Skewers:**
    a. **Place Skewers on Griddle:** Arrange the skewers on the griddle.
    b. **Cook Until Charred:** Grill the skewers for about 10-15 minutes, turning occasionally, until the beef is cooked to your desired level of doneness and the vegetables are tender and slightly charred.
    c. **Baste with Marinade:** During the last few minutes of cooking, brush the skewers with any remaining marinade to enhance the flavor.
8. **Ensure Even Cooking:** If parts of the skewers are cooking faster than others, move them to a cooler zone on the griddle to ensure even cooking.
9. **Serve Warm:** Transfer the teriyaki beef skewers to a serving platter. Serve immediately.

Grilled Steak Fajitas

Yield: 4 servings **Preparation Time:** 15 minutes (plus marinating time) **Cooking Time:** 20 minutes

Ingredients:

- 1.5 pounds flank steak or skirt steak
- 2 tablespoons olive oil
- 1 large red bell pepper, sliced into strips
- 1 large green bell pepper, sliced into strips
- 1 large yellow bell pepper, sliced into strips
- 1 large onion, sliced into strips
- 8 small flour tortillas

Marinade:

- 1/4 cup olive oil
- 1/4 cup lime juice (about 2 limes)
- 3 cloves garlic, minced
- 1 tablespoon soy sauce
- 1 tablespoon Worcestershire sauce
- 1 tablespoon ground cumin
- 1 teaspoon smoked paprika
- 1 teaspoon chili powder
- 1/2 teaspoon black pepper
- 1/2 teaspoon salt

Nutritional Information (per serving):

- Calories: 450
- Protein: 30g
- Carbohydrates: 35g
- Fats: 20g
- Fiber: 5g

Instructions:

1. **Prepare the Marinade:** In a medium bowl, whisk together the olive oil, lime juice, minced garlic, soy sauce, Worcestershire sauce, ground cumin, smoked paprika, chili powder, black pepper, and salt.

2. **Marinate the Steak:** Place the steak in a resealable plastic bag or shallow dish. Pour the marinade over the steak, ensuring it is well coated. Seal the bag or cover the dish and refrigerate for at least 1 hour, or preferably overnight.
3. **Prepare the Vegetables:** Slice the red, green, and yellow bell peppers into strips. Slice the onion into strips.
4. **Preheat the Griddle:** Preheat the gas griddle to medium-high heat. Allow it to heat up for about 5-10 minutes until it reaches a high temperature.
5. **Grease the Griddle:** Lightly spray or brush the griddle surface with olive oil to prevent sticking.
6. **Cook the Vegetables:**
    a. **Place Vegetables on Griddle:** Arrange the bell pepper and onion strips on the griddle.
    b. **Cook Until Tender:** Cook the vegetables for about 8-10 minutes, stirring occasionally, until they are tender and slightly charred. Use a spatula to turn the vegetables for even cooking. Once done, move them to a cooler zone or a separate plate to keep them warm.
7. **Cook the Steak:**
    a. **Place Steak on Griddle:** Remove the steak from the marinade and let any excess marinade drip off. Place the steak on the hot griddle.
    b. **Sear the Steak:** Sear the steak for about 4-5 minutes on each side, or until it reaches the desired level of doneness. Use a meat thermometer to ensure the internal temperature reaches 130-135°F (54-57°C) for medium-rare.
    c. **Rest the Steak:** Remove the steak from the griddle and let it rest for 5 minutes to allow the juices to redistribute.
    d. **Slice the Steak:** Slice the steak against the grain into thin strips.
8. **Warm the Tortillas:** Place the flour tortillas on the griddle for about 30 seconds on each side to warm them up.
9. **Assemble the Fajitas:** Arrange the sliced steak and cooked vegetables on a serving platter. Serve with warm tortillas.

Korean BBQ Beef on the Griddle

Yield: 4 servings **Preparation Time:** 15 minutes (plus marinating time) **Cooking Time:** 15 minutes

Ingredients:

- 1.5 pounds beef sirloin or ribeye, thinly sliced
- 1 tablespoon vegetable oil (for greasing the griddle)

Marinade:

- 1/4 cup soy sauce
- 1/4 cup brown sugar
- 2 tablespoons sesame oil
- 4 cloves garlic, minced
- 1 tablespoon fresh ginger, grated
- 2 tablespoons rice vinegar
- 2 tablespoons gochujang (Korean chili paste)
- 1/4 teaspoon black pepper
- 1 tablespoon sesame seeds
- 4 green onions, sliced (white and green parts separated)

Nutritional Information (per serving):

- Calories: 400
- Protein: 30g
- Carbohydrates: 20g
- Fats: 22g
- Fiber: 2g

Instructions:

1. **Prepare the Marinade:** In a medium bowl, whisk together the soy sauce, brown sugar, sesame oil, minced garlic, grated ginger, rice vinegar, gochujang, black pepper, sesame seeds, and the white parts of the green onions.
2. **Marinate the Beef:** Place the thinly sliced beef in a resealable plastic bag or shallow dish. Pour the marinade over the beef, ensuring it is well coated. Seal the bag or cover the dish and refrigerate for at least 1 hour, or preferably overnight.
3. **Preheat the Griddle:** Preheat the gas griddle to medium-high heat. Allow it to heat up for about 5-10 minutes until it reaches a high temperature.
4. **Grease the Griddle:** Lightly spray or brush the griddle surface with vegetable oil to prevent sticking.
5. **Cook the Beef:**
    a. **Place Beef on Griddle:** Remove the beef from the marinade, allowing any excess marinade to drip off. Place the beef on the hot griddle.
    b. **Cook Until Done:** Grill the beef for about 3-4 minutes on each side, or until it is cooked through and has developed a nice caramelized exterior. Use a spatula to turn the beef strips for even cooking.
    c. **Add the Green Onions:** During the last minute of cooking, add the green parts of the sliced green onions to the griddle to lightly cook them alongside the beef.
6. **Serve Warm:** Transfer the grilled Korean BBQ beef to a serving platter.

Griddled Sausage and Peppers

Yield: 4 servings **Preparation Time:** 10 minutes **Cooking Time:** 20 minutes

Ingredients:

- 1 pound Italian sausage links (mild or hot, based on preference)
- 2 tablespoons olive oil
- 1 large red bell pepper, sliced into strips
- 1 large green bell pepper, sliced into strips
- 1 large yellow bell pepper, sliced into strips
- 1 large onion, sliced into strips
- 2 cloves garlic, minced
- 1 teaspoon dried oregano
- 1 teaspoon dried basil
- 1/2 teaspoon salt
- 1/4 teaspoon black pepper
- 1 tablespoon balsamic vinegar (optional)
- Olive oil spray or additional olive oil for greasing the griddle

Nutritional Information (per serving):

- Calories: 450
- Protein: 20g
- Carbohydrates: 20g
- Fats: 32g
- Fiber: 4g

Instructions:

1. **Prepare the Vegetables:**
   a. Slice the red, green, and yellow bell peppers into strips.
   b. Slice the onion into strips.
   c. Mince the garlic.
2. **Preheat the Griddle:** Preheat the gas griddle to medium-high heat. Allow it to heat up for about 5 minutes until evenly hot.
3. **Cook the Sausages:**
   a. **Place Sausages on the Griddle:** Lightly spray or brush the griddle surface with olive oil. Place the sausage links on the griddle.
   b. **Cook Until Browned:** Cook the sausages for about 10-12 minutes, turning occasionally, until they are browned and cooked through. Use a spatula to turn the sausages for even cooking. Once done, move them to a cooler zone or a separate plate to keep them warm.
4. **Cook the Vegetables:**
   a. **Add Vegetables to Griddle:** Add the sliced bell peppers and onions to the griddle. Drizzle with olive oil and sprinkle with minced garlic, dried oregano, dried basil, salt, and black pepper.
   b. **Cook Until Tender:** Stir-fry the vegetables for about 8-10 minutes, stirring occasionally, until they are tender and slightly charred. If desired, drizzle with balsamic vinegar during the last 2 minutes of cooking for added flavor.
5. **Combine and Heat Through:**
   a. **Mix Sausages and Vegetables:** Return the cooked sausages to the griddle, mixing them with the peppers and onions. Heat for an additional 2-3 minutes, allowing the flavors to meld together.
6. **Serve Warm:** Transfer the griddled sausage and peppers to a serving platter.

Grilled Beef Tacos with Fresh Salsa

Yield: 4 servings **Preparation Time:** 20 minutes **Cooking Time:** 20 minutes

Ingredients:

For the Beef:

- 1.5 pounds flank steak or skirt steak
- 2 tablespoons olive oil
- 1 teaspoon salt
- 1 teaspoon black pepper
- 1 teaspoon ground cumin
- 1 teaspoon chili powder
- 1 teaspoon garlic powder
- 1 teaspoon smoked paprika

For the Fresh Salsa:

- 2 large tomatoes, diced
- 1/2 red onion, finely chopped
- 1 jalapeño, seeded and finely chopped
- 1/4 cup fresh cilantro, chopped
- 1 lime, juiced
- 1/2 teaspoon salt
- 1/4 teaspoon black pepper

For the Tacos:

- 8 small corn or flour tortillas

- 1/2 cup crumbled cotija cheese
- 1/2 cup sour cream
- 1 avocado, sliced
- Fresh lime wedges (for serving)

Nutritional Information (per serving):

- Calories: 450
- Protein: 28g
- Carbohydrates: 30g
- Fats: 23g
- Fiber: 6g

Instructions:

1. **Marinate the Beef:**
   a. In a small bowl, mix together the olive oil, salt, black pepper, ground cumin, chili powder, garlic powder, and smoked paprika.
   b. Rub this mixture evenly over the flank steak. Let the steak marinate at room temperature for at least 15 minutes.
2. **Prepare the Fresh Salsa:** In a medium bowl, combine the diced tomatoes, chopped red onion, chopped jalapeño, chopped cilantro, lime juice, salt, and black pepper. Mix well and set aside.
3. **Preheat the Griddle:** Preheat the gas griddle to medium-high heat. Allow it to heat up for about 5-10 minutes until it reaches a high temperature.
4. **Grease the Griddle:** Lightly spray or brush the griddle surface with olive oil to prevent sticking.
5. **Cook the Steak:**
   a. **Place Steak on Griddle:** Place the marinated flank steak on the hot griddle.
   b. **Sear the Steak:** Sear the steak for about 4-5 minutes on each side, or until it reaches your desired level of doneness. Use a meat thermometer to ensure the internal temperature reaches 130-135°F (54-57°C) for medium-rare.
6. **Rest the Steak:** Remove the steak from the griddle and let it rest for 5 minutes to allow the juices to redistribute.
7. **Slice the Steak:** Slice the steak against the grain into thin strips.
8. **Warm the Tortillas:** Place the tortillas on the griddle for about 30 seconds on each side to warm them up.
9. **Assemble the Tacos:** Place a few slices of steak on each warm tortilla. Top with a spoonful of fresh salsa, crumbled cotija cheese, a dollop of sour cream, and a few slices of avocado.

Griddled Peppercorn Steak

Yield: 4 servings **Preparation Time:** 10 minutes **Cooking Time:** 15 minutes

Ingredients:

- 4 (8-ounce) ribeye or sirloin steaks, about 1-inch thick
- 2 tablespoons olive oil
- 2 tablespoons whole black peppercorns, crushed
- 1 teaspoon salt
- 2 cloves garlic, minced
- 1 tablespoon fresh thyme, chopped
- 1/4 cup unsalted butter

Nutritional Information (per serving):

- Calories: 600
- Protein: 50g
- Carbohydrates: 2g
- Fats: 44g
- Fiber: 0g

Instructions:

1. **Prepare the Steaks:**
   a. Pat the steaks dry with paper towels. Brush both sides with olive oil.
   b. Evenly coat each steak with crushed peppercorns and salt, pressing the seasoning into the meat.
2. **Preheat the Griddle:** Preheat the gas griddle to high heat. Allow it to heat up for about 5-10 minutes until it reaches a high temperature.
3. **Grease the Griddle:** Lightly spray or brush the griddle surface with olive oil to prevent sticking.
4. **Cook the Steaks:**
   a. **Place Steaks on Griddle:** Arrange the seasoned steaks on the hot griddle.

    b. **Sear the Steaks:** Sear the steaks for about 4-5 minutes on each side for medium-rare, or until they reach your desired level of doneness. Use a meat thermometer to ensure the internal temperature reaches 130-135°F (54-57°C) for medium-rare.
5. **Add Garlic and Thyme Butter:** During the last 2 minutes of cooking, add the minced garlic, chopped thyme, and butter to the griddle. Use a spoon to baste the steaks with the melted butter mixture, enhancing the flavor.
6. **Ensure Even Cooking:** If parts of the steaks are cooking faster than others, move them to a cooler zone on the griddle to ensure even cooking.
7. **Rest the Steaks:** Remove the steaks from the griddle and let them rest for 5 minutes to allow the juices to redistribute.
8. **Serve Warm:** Transfer the steaks to a serving platter and spoon any remaining garlic and thyme butter from the griddle over the top.

Griddled Pork Belly Bites

Yield: 4 servings **Preparation Time:** 15 minutes **Cooking Time:** 25 minutes

Ingredients:

- 1.5 pounds pork belly, skin removed and cut into 1-inch cubes
- 2 tablespoons olive oil
- 1 tablespoon soy sauce
- 1 tablespoon hoisin sauce
- 1 tablespoon honey
- 1 tablespoon rice vinegar
- 2 cloves garlic, minced
- 1 teaspoon fresh ginger, grated
- 1 teaspoon sesame oil
- 1/2 teaspoon black pepper
- 2 green onions, sliced (for garnish)
- 1 tablespoon sesame seeds (for garnish)

Nutritional Information (per serving):

- Calories: 450
- Protein: 18g
- Carbohydrates: 10g
- Fats: 36g
- Fiber: 1g

Instructions:

1. **Prepare the Pork Belly:** Cut the pork belly into 1-inch cubes, ensuring uniform size for even cooking.
2. **Make the Marinade:** In a large bowl, whisk together the soy sauce, hoisin sauce, honey, rice vinegar, minced garlic, grated ginger, sesame oil, and black pepper.
3. **Marinate the Pork Belly:** Add the pork belly cubes to the marinade, tossing to coat evenly. Let it marinate at room temperature for at least 15 minutes.
4. **Preheat the Griddle:** Preheat the gas griddle to medium-high heat. Allow it to heat up for about 5-10 minutes until it reaches a high temperature.
5. **Grease the Griddle:** Lightly spray or brush the griddle surface with olive oil to prevent sticking.
    a. **Cook the Pork Belly Bites:**
    b. **Place Pork Belly on Griddle:** Arrange the marinated pork belly cubes on the hot griddle.
    c. **Cook Until Crispy:** Cook the pork belly bites for about 20-25 minutes, turning occasionally, until they are crispy and caramelized on all sides. Use a spatula to turn the pork bites for even cooking.
6. **Ensure Even Cooking:** If parts of the pork belly bites are cooking faster than others, move them to a cooler zone on the griddle to ensure even cooking.
7. **Serve Warm:** Transfer the griddled pork belly bites to a serving platter.
8. **Garnish:** Sprinkle with sliced green onions and sesame seeds before serving.

Grilled Veal Chops with Herb Butter

Yield: 4 servings **Preparation Time:** 15 minutes **Cooking Time:** 20 minutes

Ingredients:

For the Veal Chops:

- 4 veal chops (about 1 inch thick, 8-10 ounces each)
- 2 tablespoons olive oil
- 1 teaspoon salt
- 1/2 teaspoon black pepper
- 1 teaspoon garlic powder
- 1 teaspoon fresh rosemary, chopped
- 1 teaspoon fresh thyme, chopped

For the Herb Butter:

- 1/2 cup unsalted butter, softened

- 2 cloves garlic, minced
- 1 tablespoon fresh parsley, chopped
- 1 tablespoon fresh thyme, chopped
- 1 tablespoon fresh rosemary, chopped
- 1 teaspoon lemon zest
- 1/2 teaspoon salt
- 1/4 teaspoon black pepper

Nutritional Information (per serving):

- Calories: 520
- Protein: 38g
- Carbohydrates: 2g
- Fats: 40g
- Fiber: 0g

Instructions:

1. **Prepare the Veal Chops:**
   a. Pat the veal chops dry with paper towels. Brush both sides with olive oil.
   b. Season the veal chops evenly with salt, black pepper, garlic powder, chopped rosemary, and thyme.
2. **Prepare the Herb Butter:** In a small bowl, mix together the softened butter, minced garlic, chopped parsley, thyme, rosemary, lemon zest, salt, and black pepper until well combined. Place the herb butter on a piece of plastic wrap and shape it into a log. Wrap tightly and refrigerate until firm, about 15-20 minutes.
3. **Preheat the Griddle:** Preheat the gas griddle to medium-high heat. Allow it to heat up for about 5-10 minutes until it reaches a high temperature.
4. **Grease the Griddle:** Lightly spray or brush the griddle surface with olive oil to prevent sticking.
5. **Cook the Veal Chops:**
   a. **Place Veal Chops on Griddle:** Arrange the seasoned veal chops on the hot griddle.
   b. **Sear the Veal Chops:** Sear the veal chops for about 4-5 minutes on each side, or until they reach your desired level of doneness. Use a meat thermometer to ensure the internal temperature reaches 145°F (63°C) for medium-rare.
   c. **Zone Cooking:** If parts of the veal chops are cooking faster than others, move them to a cooler zone on the griddle to ensure even cooking.
   d. **Add Herb Butter:** During the last minute of cooking, add a slice of the prepared herb butter on top of each veal chop. Allow the butter to melt and baste the veal chops, enhancing the flavor.
6. **Rest the Veal Chops:** Remove the veal chops from the griddle and let them rest for 5 minutes to allow the juices to redistribute.
7. **Serve Warm:** Transfer the veal chops to a serving platter and garnish with any remaining herb butter.

Grilled Short Ribs with BBQ Sauce

Yield: 4 servings **Preparation Time:** 15 minutes (plus marinating time) **Cooking Time:** 30 minutes

Ingredients:

For the Short Ribs:

- 2 pounds beef short ribs, flanken cut (about 1/2 inch thick)
- 2 tablespoons olive oil
- 1 teaspoon salt
- 1 teaspoon black pepper
- 1 teaspoon garlic powder
- 1 teaspoon onion powder
- 1 teaspoon smoked paprika

For the BBQ Sauce:

- 1 cup ketchup
- 1/4 cup apple cider vinegar
- 1/4 cup brown sugar
- 2 tablespoons Worcestershire sauce
- 1 tablespoon mustard
- 1 teaspoon smoked paprika
- 1 teaspoon garlic powder
- 1 teaspoon onion powder
- 1/2 teaspoon black pepper
- 1/2 teaspoon salt
- 1/4 teaspoon cayenne pepper (optional, for heat)

Nutritional Information (per serving):

- Calories: 550
- Protein: 30g
- Carbohydrates: 40g
- Fats: 30g
- Fiber: 2g

Instructions:

1. **Prepare the Short Ribs:**

    a. Pat the short ribs dry with paper towels. Brush both sides with olive oil.
    b. In a small bowl, mix together the salt, black pepper, garlic powder, onion powder, and smoked paprika.
    c. Rub this mixture evenly over the short ribs. Let them sit at room temperature for 15 minutes to marinate.
2. **Prepare the BBQ Sauce:**
    a. In a medium saucepan, combine the ketchup, apple cider vinegar, brown sugar, Worcestershire sauce, mustard, smoked paprika, garlic powder, onion powder, black pepper, salt, and cayenne pepper (if using).
    b. Bring the mixture to a simmer over medium heat, stirring occasionally. Reduce the heat to low and let it cook for 15 minutes, allowing the flavors to meld. Remove from heat and set aside.
3. **Preheat the Griddle:** Preheat the gas griddle to medium-high heat. Allow it to heat up for about 5-10 minutes until it reaches a high temperature.
4. **Grease the Griddle:** Lightly spray or brush the griddle surface with olive oil to prevent sticking.
5. **Cook the Short Ribs:**
    a. **Place Short Ribs on Griddle:** Arrange the short ribs on the hot griddle.
    b. **Sear the Short Ribs:** Sear the short ribs for about 5-7 minutes on each side, or until they are nicely browned and caramelized.
6. **Apply BBQ Sauce:**
    a. **Baste the Short Ribs:** During the last few minutes of cooking, brush the BBQ sauce generously over the short ribs. Turn and baste frequently to caramelize the sauce and form a sticky glaze.
    b. **Cook Until Done:** Continue cooking the short ribs until they are cooked through and the internal temperature reaches 160°F (71°C).
7. **Ensure Even Cooking:** If parts of the short ribs are cooking faster than others, move them to a cooler zone on the griddle to ensure even cooking.
8. **Serve Warm:** Transfer the grilled short ribs to a serving platter.

Griddled Sirloin Tips

Yield: 4 servings **Preparation Time:** 15 minutes (plus marinating time) **Cooking Time:** 20 minutes

Ingredients:

- 1.5 pounds sirloin tips, cut into 1-inch cubes
- 2 tablespoons olive oil
- 1 teaspoon salt
- 1 teaspoon black pepper
- 1 teaspoon garlic powder
- 1 teaspoon onion powder
- 1 teaspoon smoked paprika
- 1 teaspoon dried thyme

For the Marinade:

- 1/4 cup soy sauce
- 2 tablespoons Worcestershire sauce
- 2 tablespoons olive oil
- 2 cloves garlic, minced
- 1 tablespoon fresh rosemary, chopped
- 1 tablespoon fresh thyme, chopped

Nutritional Information (per serving):

- Calories: 350
- Protein: 30g
- Carbohydrates: 5g
- Fats: 22g
- Fiber: 1g

Instructions:

1. **Prepare the Marinade:** In a large bowl, whisk together the soy sauce, Worcestershire sauce, olive oil, minced garlic, chopped rosemary, and chopped thyme.
2. **Marinate the Sirloin Tips:** Add the sirloin tips to the marinade, tossing to coat evenly. Cover and refrigerate for at least 1 hour, or preferably overnight for more flavor.
3. **Season the Sirloin Tips:**
    a. In a small bowl, mix together the salt, black pepper, garlic powder, onion powder, smoked paprika, and dried thyme.
    b. After marinating, remove the sirloin tips from the marinade and pat them dry with paper towels. Sprinkle the seasoning mixture evenly over the sirloin tips.
4. **Preheat the Griddle:** Preheat the gas griddle to medium-high heat. Allow it to heat up for about 5-10 minutes until it reaches a high temperature.
5. **Grease the Griddle:** Lightly spray or brush the griddle surface with olive oil to prevent sticking.
6. **Cook the Sirloin Tips:**
    a. **Place Sirloin Tips on Griddle:** Arrange the seasoned sirloin tips on the hot griddle.

b. **Sear the Sirloin Tips:** Sear the sirloin tips for about 4-5 minutes on each side, or until they reach your desired level of doneness. Use a meat thermometer to ensure the internal temperature reaches 135°F (57°C) for medium-rare or adjust to your preferred doneness.

7. **Ensure Even Cooking:** If parts of the sirloin tips are cooking faster than others, move them to a cooler zone on the griddle to ensure even cooking.
8. **Serve Warm:** Transfer the griddled sirloin tips to a serving platter.

Grilled T-Bone Steaks

Yield: 4 servings **Preparation Time:** 10 minutes **Cooking Time:** 15-20 minutes

Ingredients:

- 4 T-bone steaks (about 1 inch thick, 12-16 ounces each)
- 2 tablespoons olive oil
- 2 teaspoons salt
- 2 teaspoons black pepper
- 2 teaspoons garlic powder
- 1 teaspoon smoked paprika
- 1 teaspoon fresh rosemary, chopped
- 1 teaspoon fresh thyme, chopped
- **For the Herb Butter:**
- 1/2 cup unsalted butter, softened
- 2 cloves garlic, minced
- 1 tablespoon fresh parsley, chopped
- 1 tablespoon fresh thyme, chopped
- 1 teaspoon lemon zest
- 1/2 teaspoon salt
- 1/4 teaspoon black pepper

Nutritional Information (per serving):

- Calories: 650
- Protein: 50g
- Carbohydrates: 2g
- Fats: 48g
- Fiber: 0g

Instructions:

1. **Prepare the Steaks:**
   a. Pat the T-bone steaks dry with paper towels. Brush both sides with olive oil.
   b. In a small bowl, mix together the salt, black pepper, garlic powder, smoked paprika, chopped rosemary, and chopped thyme.
   c. Evenly coat each steak with the seasoning mixture, pressing it into the meat.
2. **Prepare the Herb Butter:**
   a. In a small bowl, mix together the softened butter, minced garlic, chopped parsley, chopped thyme, lemon zest, salt, and black pepper until well combined.
   b. Place the herb butter on a piece of plastic wrap and shape it into a log. Wrap tightly and refrigerate until firm, about 15-20 minutes.
3. **Preheat the Griddle:** Preheat the gas griddle to high heat. Allow it to heat up for about 5-10 minutes until it reaches a high temperature.
4. **Grease the Griddle:** Lightly spray or brush the griddle surface with olive oil to prevent sticking.
5. **Cook the Steaks:**
   a. **Place Steaks on Griddle:** Arrange the seasoned T-bone steaks on the hot griddle.
   b. **Sear the Steaks:** Sear the steaks for about 4-5 minutes on each side for medium-rare, or until they reach your desired level of doneness. Use a meat thermometer to ensure the internal temperature reaches 130-135°F (54-57°C) for medium-rare.
   c. **Add Herb Butter:** During the last minute of cooking, add a slice of the prepared herb butter on top of each steak. Allow the butter to melt and baste the steaks, enhancing the flavor.
6. **Ensure Even Cooking:** If parts of the steaks are cooking faster than others, move them to a cooler zone on the griddle to ensure even cooking.
7. **Rest the Steaks:** Remove the steaks from the griddle and let them rest for 5 minutes to allow the juices to redistribute.
8. **Serve Warm:** Transfer the steaks to a serving platter and garnish with any remaining herb butter.

Griddled Beef Stroganoff

Yield: 4 servings **Preparation Time:** 15 minutes **Cooking Time:** 20 minutes

Ingredients:

- 1.5 pounds beef sirloin or tenderloin, thinly sliced into strips
- 2 tablespoons olive oil
- 1 teaspoon salt
- 1/2 teaspoon black pepper
- 1 teaspoon garlic powder
- 1 teaspoon smoked paprika
- 1 large onion, thinly sliced
- 8 ounces cremini or white mushrooms, sliced
- 2 cloves garlic, minced
- 1/4 cup beef broth
- 1 cup sour cream
- 2 tablespoons Dijon mustard
- 1 tablespoon Worcestershire sauce
- 2 tablespoons fresh parsley, chopped (for garnish)
- Olive oil spray or additional olive oil for greasing the griddle

Nutritional Information (per serving):

- Calories: 450
- Protein: 35g
- Carbohydrates: 10g
- Fats: 30g
- Fiber: 2g

Instructions:

1. **Prepare the Beef:**
   a. Thinly slice the beef sirloin or tenderloin into strips.
   b. Season the beef strips with salt, black pepper, garlic powder, and smoked paprika.
2. **Prepare the Sauce Ingredients:** In a small bowl, mix together the sour cream, Dijon mustard, and Worcestershire sauce. Set aside.
3. **Preheat the Griddle:** Preheat the gas griddle to medium-high heat. Allow it to heat up for about 5-10 minutes until it reaches a high temperature.
4. **Grease the Griddle:** Lightly spray or brush the griddle surface with olive oil to prevent sticking.
5. **Cook the Beef:**
   a. **Place Beef on Griddle:** Arrange the seasoned beef strips on the hot griddle.
   b. **Sear the Beef:** Sear the beef for about 2-3 minutes on each side until browned and cooked through. Use a spatula to turn the beef strips for even cooking. Once done, move the beef to a cooler zone or a separate plate to keep it warm.
6. **Cook the Vegetables:**
   a. **Add Onions and Mushrooms to Griddle:** Add the sliced onions and mushrooms to the griddle. Drizzle with olive oil if needed.
   b. **Cook Until Tender:** Cook the vegetables for about 5-7 minutes, stirring occasionally, until they are tender and caramelized.
   c. **Add Garlic:** Add the minced garlic and cook for an additional 1-2 minutes until fragrant.
7. **Combine and Finish:**
   a. **Return Beef to Griddle:** Return the cooked beef to the griddle with the onions and mushrooms.
   b. **Add Beef Broth:** Pour the beef broth over the mixture, stirring to combine and deglaze the griddle.
8. **Add Sauce:** Reduce the heat to medium. Stir in the prepared sour cream mixture, cooking until heated through and well combined, about 2-3 minutes.
9. **Serve Warm:** Transfer the griddled beef stroganoff to a serving platter. Garnish with chopped fresh parsley.

Grilled Meatball Skewers

Yield: 4 servings **Preparation Time:** 20 minutes **Cooking Time:** 15 minutes

Ingredients:

For the Meatballs:

- 1 pound ground beef (80% lean)
- 1/2 cup breadcrumbs
- 1/4 cup grated Parmesan cheese
- 1/4 cup milk
- 1 large egg
- 2 cloves garlic, minced
- 1 tablespoon fresh parsley, chopped
- 1 teaspoon salt
- 1/2 teaspoon black pepper
- 1/2 teaspoon dried oregano
- 1/2 teaspoon dried basil

For the Skewers:

- 1 large red bell pepper, cut into 1-inch pieces
- 1 large yellow bell pepper, cut into 1-inch pieces
- 1 large red onion, cut into 1-inch pieces
- Olive oil spray or additional olive oil for greasing the griddle

Nutritional Information (per serving):

- Calories: 400
- Protein: 28g
- Carbohydrates: 18g
- Fats: 24g
- Fiber: 2g

Instructions:

1. **Prepare the Meatballs:**
   a. In a large bowl, combine the ground beef, breadcrumbs, grated Parmesan cheese, milk, egg, minced garlic, chopped parsley, salt, black pepper, dried oregano, and dried basil.
   b. Mix until all ingredients are well combined.
   c. Shape the mixture into 1-inch meatballs (approximately 20 meatballs).
2. **Prepare the Skewers:**
   a. If using wooden skewers, soak them in water for at least 30 minutes to prevent burning.
   b. Thread the meatballs onto the skewers, alternating with pieces of red bell pepper, yellow bell pepper, and red onion.
3. **Preheat the Griddle:** Preheat the gas griddle to medium-high heat. Allow it to heat up for about 5-10 minutes until it reaches a high temperature.
4. **Grease the Griddle:** Lightly spray or brush the griddle surface with olive oil to prevent sticking.
5. **Cook the Meatball Skewers:**
6. **Place Skewers on Griddle:** Arrange the meatball skewers on the hot griddle.
7. **Cook Until Done:** Cook the skewers for about 12-15 minutes, turning occasionally, until the meatballs are cooked through and the vegetables are tender and slightly charred. Use a spatula to turn the skewers for even cooking.
8. **Ensure Even Cooking:** If parts of the skewers are cooking faster than others, move them to a cooler zone on the griddle to ensure even cooking.
9. **Serve Warm:** Transfer the grilled meatball skewers to a serving platter.

Griddled Ham Steaks with Pineapple

Yield: 4 servings **Preparation Time:** 10 minutes **Cooking Time:** 15 minutes

Ingredients:

- 4 ham steaks (about 6-8 ounces each, 1/2 inch thick)
- 8 pineapple rings (canned or fresh)
- 2 tablespoons brown sugar
- 2 tablespoons honey
- 2 tablespoons Dijon mustard
- 1 tablespoon olive oil
- 1/2 teaspoon ground cinnamon
- 1/4 teaspoon ground cloves
- Olive oil spray or additional olive oil for greasing the griddle

Nutritional Information (per serving):

- Calories: 350
- Protein: 25g
- Carbohydrates: 20g
- Fats: 15g
- Fiber: 2g

Instructions:

1. **Prepare the Glaze:** In a small bowl, mix together the brown sugar, honey, Dijon mustard, olive oil, ground cinnamon, and ground cloves until well combined.
2. **Prepare the Ham and Pineapple:**
   a. Pat the ham steaks dry with paper towels.
   b. Brush both sides of the ham steaks and pineapple rings with the prepared glaze.
3. **Preheat the Griddle:** Preheat the gas griddle to medium-high heat. Allow it to heat up for about 5-10 minutes until it reaches a high temperature.
4. **Grease the Griddle:** Lightly spray or brush the griddle surface with olive oil to prevent sticking.
5. **Cook the Ham Steaks:**
   a. **Place Ham Steaks on Griddle:** Arrange the ham steaks on the hot griddle.
   b. **Sear the Ham Steaks:** Cook the ham steaks for about 3-4 minutes on each side until they are nicely browned and heated through. Use a spatula to turn the ham steaks for even cooking.
6. **Cook the Pineapple Rings:**

    a. **Place Pineapple Rings on Griddle:** Add the pineapple rings to the griddle.
    b. **Cook Until Caramelized:** Cook the pineapple rings for about 2-3 minutes on each side until they are caramelized and heated through.
7. **Serve Warm:** Transfer the griddled ham steaks and pineapple rings to a serving platter.

Grilled Prime Rib with Garlic Crust

Yield: 6 servings **Preparation Time:** 20 minutes **Cooking Time:** 1 hour 30 minutes

Ingredients:

- 1 (4-pound) prime rib roast, bone-in
- 1/4 cup olive oil
- 6 cloves garlic, minced
- 2 tablespoons fresh rosemary, chopped
- 2 tablespoons fresh thyme, chopped
- 1 tablespoon kosher salt
- 1 tablespoon black pepper
- 1 tablespoon Dijon mustard
- Olive oil spray or additional olive oil for greasing the griddle

Nutritional Information (per serving):

- Calories: 600
- Protein: 45g
- Carbohydrates: 2g
- Fats: 45g
- Fiber: 1g

Instructions:

1. **Prepare the Prime Rib:**
    a. Pat the prime rib roast dry with paper towels.
    b. In a small bowl, mix together the olive oil, minced garlic, chopped rosemary, chopped thyme, kosher salt, black pepper, and Dijon mustard.
    c. Rub this mixture all over the prime rib roast, ensuring an even coat. Let the roast sit at room temperature for about 1 hour before cooking.
2. **Preheat the Griddle:** Preheat the gas griddle to medium-high heat. Allow it to heat up for about 5-10 minutes until it reaches a high temperature.
3. **Sear the Prime Rib:**
4. **Grease the Griddle:** Lightly spray or brush the griddle surface with olive oil to prevent sticking.
5. **Place Prime Rib on Griddle:** Place the prime rib roast on the hot griddle.
6. **Sear All Sides:** Sear the prime rib for about 3-4 minutes on each side, including the ends, until it is nicely browned all over.
7. **Cook the Prime Rib:**
    a. **Lower the Heat:** After searing, lower the heat to medium.
    b. **Use Zones:** Move the prime rib to a cooler zone of the griddle if possible, or reduce the heat to maintain a consistent medium heat.
    c. **Cover and Cook:** If your griddle has a lid, cover it. If not, tent the prime rib with aluminum foil to create an oven-like environment.
    d. **Cook Until Desired Doneness:** Cook the prime rib until it reaches your desired level of doneness, about 1 hour for medium-rare (130°F internal temperature). Use a meat thermometer to check the internal temperature.
8. **Rest the Prime Rib:** Remove the prime rib from the griddle and let it rest for 15-20 minutes. This allows the juices to redistribute and the roast to finish cooking.
9. **Slice and Serve:** Slice the prime rib against the grain into 1/2-inch thick slices.

Griddled Pork Schnitzel

Yield: 4 servings **Preparation Time:** 20 minutes **Cooking Time:** 15 minutes

Ingredients:

- 4 boneless pork chops (about 6 ounces each, 1/2 inch thick)
- 1 cup all-purpose flour
- 2 teaspoons salt, divided
- 1 teaspoon black pepper
- 2 large eggs
- 2 tablespoons milk
- 2 cups breadcrumbs (preferably panko)
- 1 teaspoon paprika
- 1 teaspoon garlic powder
- 1/2 teaspoon dried thyme

- Olive oil spray or additional olive oil for greasing the griddle
- Lemon wedges, for serving
- Fresh parsley, chopped, for garnish

Nutritional Information (per serving):

- Calories: 450
- Protein: 30g
- Carbohydrates: 40g
- Fats: 20g
- Fiber: 2g

Instructions:

1. **Prepare the Pork Chops:** Place the pork chops between two sheets of plastic wrap or parchment paper. Use a meat mallet or rolling pin to pound the pork chops to about 1/4 inch thickness.
2. **Set Up the Breading Station:**
   a. **Flour Mixture:** In a shallow dish, combine the flour, 1 teaspoon salt, and black pepper.
   b. **Egg Mixture:** In another shallow dish, beat the eggs with the milk.
   c. **Breadcrumb Mixture:** In a third shallow dish, combine the breadcrumbs, remaining 1 teaspoon salt, paprika, garlic powder, and dried thyme.
3. **Bread the Pork Chops:**
   a. Dredge each pork chop in the flour mixture, shaking off any excess.
   b. Dip the floured pork chop into the egg mixture, allowing any excess to drip off.
   c. Coat the pork chop in the breadcrumb mixture, pressing the breadcrumbs onto the meat to ensure an even coating.
4. **Preheat the Griddle:** Preheat the gas griddle to medium-high heat. Allow it to heat up for about 5-10 minutes until it reaches an even temperature.
5. **Grease the Griddle:** Lightly spray or brush the griddle surface with olive oil to prevent sticking.
6. **Cook the Pork Schnitzel:**
   a. **Place Pork Schnitzel on Griddle:** Arrange the breaded pork chops on the hot griddle.
   b. **Cook Until Golden and Crisp:** Cook the pork schnitzel for about 3-4 minutes on each side, or until they are golden brown and cooked through. Use a spatula to turn the schnitzel for even cooking.
7. **Serve Warm:** Transfer the griddled pork schnitzel to a serving platter.
8. **Garnish and Serve:** Garnish with fresh parsley and serve with lemon wedges.

Griddled Braised Beef Short Ribs

Yield: 4 servings **Preparation Time:** 30 minutes **Cooking Time:** 2 hours 30 minutes (including braising time)

Ingredients:

- 2 pounds of beef short ribs, bone-in
- 2 tablespoons olive oil
- 1 teaspoon salt
- 1/2 teaspoon black pepper
- 1 large onion, diced
- 2 carrots, diced
- 2 celery stalks, diced
- 4 cloves garlic, minced
- 1 cup beef broth
- 1 cup red wine
- 2 tablespoons tomato paste
- 1 teaspoon fresh thyme, chopped
- 1 teaspoon fresh rosemary, chopped
- 2 bay leaves
- Olive oil spray or additional olive oil for greasing the griddle

Nutritional Information (per serving):

- Calories: 600
- Protein: 40g
- Carbohydrates: 15g
- Fats: 40g
- Fiber: 3g

Instructions:

1. **Prepare the Short Ribs:**
   a. Season the short ribs with salt and black pepper on all sides.
   b. Heat the olive oil in a large, heavy-bottomed pot or Dutch oven over medium-high heat.

    c. Sear the short ribs on all sides until they are browned, about 3-4 minutes per side. Remove the short ribs from the pot and set them aside.
2. **Braise the Short Ribs:**
    a. In the same pot, add the diced onion, carrots, and celery. Cook for about 5-7 minutes until the vegetables are softened.
    b. Add the minced garlic and cook for an additional 1-2 minutes until fragrant.
    c. Stir in the tomato paste and cook for another 2 minutes.
    d. Add the beef broth, red wine, thyme, rosemary, and bay leaves. Bring the mixture to a simmer.
    e. Return the short ribs to the pot, ensuring they are submerged in the liquid. Cover the pot with a lid and let it simmer on low heat for about 2 hours, or until the short ribs are tender and falling off the bone.
3. **Preheat the Griddle:** Preheat the gas griddle to medium-high heat. Allow it to heat up for about 5-10 minutes until it reaches a high temperature.
4. **Prepare the Griddle:** Lightly spray or brush the griddle surface with olive oil to prevent sticking.
5. **Finish the Short Ribs on the Griddle:**
    a. Remove the short ribs from the braising liquid and let them rest for a few minutes.
    b. Place the short ribs on the hot griddle and sear for about 2-3 minutes on each side until they are caramelized and crispy on the outside.
6. **Reduce the Braising Liquid:** Strain the braising liquid into a saucepan and bring it to a boil. Reduce the liquid by half to create a rich sauce.
7. **Serve Warm:** Transfer the griddled short ribs to a serving platter and drizzle with the reduced braising sauce.

Griddled Marinated Flank Steak

Yield: 4 servings **Preparation Time:** 15 minutes (plus marinating time) **Cooking Time:** 15 minutes

Ingredients:

- 1.5 pounds flank steak
- 1/4 cup soy sauce
- 1/4 cup olive oil
- 2 tablespoons Worcestershire sauce
- 2 tablespoons honey
- 4 cloves garlic, minced
- 1 tablespoon fresh lime juice
- 1 tablespoon fresh parsley, chopped
- 1 teaspoon ground cumin
- 1 teaspoon smoked paprika
- 1/2 teaspoon black pepper
- Olive oil spray or additional olive oil for greasing the griddle

Nutritional Information (per serving):

- Calories: 400
- Protein: 35g
- Carbohydrates: 8g
- Fats: 24g
- Fiber: 1g

Instructions:

1. **Marinate the Flank Steak:**
    a. In a medium bowl, combine the soy sauce, olive oil, Worcestershire sauce, honey, minced garlic, lime juice, chopped parsley, ground cumin, smoked paprika, and black pepper.
    b. Place the flank steak in a resealable plastic bag or a shallow dish. Pour the marinade over the steak, ensuring it is well coated. Seal the bag or cover the dish and refrigerate for at least 2 hours, preferably overnight, to allow the flavors to infuse.
2. **Preheat the Griddle:** Preheat the gas griddle to medium-high heat. Allow it to heat up for about 5-10 minutes until it reaches a high temperature.
3. **Prepare the Griddle:** Lightly spray or brush the griddle surface with olive oil to prevent sticking.
4. **Cook the Flank Steak:**
    a. **Remove Steak from Marinade:** Take the marinated flank steak out of the refrigerator and let it sit at room temperature for about 15 minutes.
    b. **Place Steak on Griddle:** Place the flank steak on the hot griddle.
    c. **Sear the Steak:** Cook the steak for about 4-5 minutes on each side for medium-rare, or until it reaches your desired level of doneness. Use a meat thermometer to check the internal temperature, which should be 130-135°F (54-57°C) for medium-rare.
5. **Ensure Even Cooking:** If parts of the steak are cooking faster than others, move them to a cooler zone on the griddle to ensure even cooking.
6. **Rest the Steak:** Remove the steak from the griddle and let it rest for 5-10 minutes to allow the juices to redistribute.

7. **Slice and Serve:** Slice the steak thinly against the grain into strips. This ensures the meat is tender. Arrange the slices on a serving platter.

Grilled Pork Ribs with Honey Glaze

Yield: 4 servings **Preparation Time:** 20 minutes (plus marinating time) **Cooking Time:** 1 hour 15 minutes

Ingredients:

For the Ribs:

- 2 racks of baby back pork ribs (about 2 pounds each)
- 1/4 cup olive oil
- 2 tablespoons salt
- 2 tablespoons black pepper
- 2 tablespoons garlic powder
- 2 tablespoons smoked paprika
- 1 teaspoon ground cumin
- 1 teaspoon dried thyme

For the Honey Glaze:

- 1/2 cup honey
- 1/4 cup soy sauce
- 1/4 cup apple cider vinegar
- 2 tablespoons Dijon mustard
- 2 cloves garlic, minced
- 1 teaspoon ground black pepper

Nutritional Information (per serving):

- Calories: 700
- Protein: 45g
- Carbohydrates: 40g
- Fats: 40g
- Fiber: 1g

Instructions:

1. **Prepare the Ribs:**
    a. Remove the membrane from the back of the ribs for more tender results.
    b. In a small bowl, mix together the olive oil, salt, black pepper, garlic powder, smoked paprika, ground cumin, and dried thyme.
    c. Rub the mixture all over the ribs, ensuring they are well coated. Let the ribs marinate in the refrigerator for at least 2 hours, or overnight for best results.
2. **Prepare the Honey Glaze:** In a medium bowl, combine the honey, soy sauce, apple cider vinegar, Dijon mustard, minced garlic, and ground black pepper. Mix well until all ingredients are thoroughly combined.
3. **Preheat the Griddle:** Preheat the gas griddle to medium heat. Allow it to heat up for about 5-10 minutes until it reaches an even temperature.
4. **Cook the Ribs:**
    a. **Grease the Griddle:** Lightly spray or brush the griddle surface with olive oil to prevent sticking.
    b. **Sear the Ribs:** Place the ribs on the griddle, meaty side down, and sear for about 5 minutes on each side to develop a good crust.
    c. **Reduce the Heat:** Lower the heat to medium-low. Move the ribs to a cooler zone if your griddle allows for different heat zones, or use a griddle lid to create an oven-like environment.
    d. **Cook Until Tender:** Cover the ribs with a griddle lid or tent with aluminum foil and cook for about 1 hour, turning occasionally and basting with the honey glaze every 15 minutes. The internal temperature of the ribs should reach 190°F (88°C) for tender, fall-off-the-bone meat.
    e. **Final Sear and Glaze:** In the last 5-10 minutes of cooking, increase the heat to medium-high and give the ribs a final sear while applying a final coat of the honey glaze. This will caramelize the glaze and enhance the flavor.
5. **Rest and Serve:**
    a. Remove the ribs from the griddle and let them rest for 10 minutes before slicing.
    b. Slice the ribs between the bones and transfer them to a serving platter.

Grilled Rack of Lamb

Yield: 4 servings **Preparation Time:** 20 minutes **Cooking Time:** 25-30 minutes

Ingredients:

- 1 rack of lamb (8 ribs, about 2 pounds)
- 3 tablespoons olive oil
- 4 cloves garlic, minced
- 1 tablespoon fresh rosemary, chopped
- 1 tablespoon fresh thyme, chopped
- 1 teaspoon salt
- 1 teaspoon black pepper

- 1 teaspoon Dijon mustard
- 1 tablespoon lemon juice

Nutritional Information (per serving):

- Calories: 450
- Protein: 25g
- Carbohydrates: 2g
- Fats: 38g
- Fiber: 1g

Instructions:

1. **Prepare the Marinade:** In a small bowl, mix together the olive oil, minced garlic, chopped rosemary, chopped thyme, salt, black pepper, Dijon mustard, and lemon juice.
2. **Marinate the Lamb:** Rub the marinade all over the rack of lamb, ensuring it is well coated. Let the lamb sit at room temperature for about 30 minutes to marinate and come to room temperature.
3. **Preheat the Griddle:** Preheat the gas griddle to medium-high heat. Allow it to heat up for about 5-10 minutes until it reaches an even temperature.
4. **Grease the Griddle:** Lightly spray or brush the griddle surface with olive oil to prevent sticking.
5. **Place Lamb on Griddle:** Place the rack of lamb, fat side down, on the hot griddle.
6. **Sear Both Sides:** Sear the lamb for about 3-4 minutes on each side until it develops a nice brown crust.
7. **Reduce the Heat:** Lower the heat to medium.
8. **Use Zones:** If your griddle allows for different heat zones, move the lamb to a cooler zone to finish cooking. If not, continue cooking over medium heat.
9. **Cook to Desired Doneness:** Cook the lamb for about 15-20 minutes, turning occasionally, until the internal temperature reaches 125°F (51°C) for medium-rare or 135°F (57°C) for medium. Use a meat thermometer to check the internal temperature.
10. **Rest the Lamb:** Remove the lamb from the griddle and let it rest for 10 minutes to allow the juices to redistribute.
11. **Slice and Serve:** Slice the rack of lamb into individual chops and arrange them on a serving platter.

Griddled BBQ Pork Ribs

Yield: 4 servings **Preparation Time:** 20 minutes (plus marinating time) **Cooking Time:** 1 hour 30 minutes

Ingredients:

- 2 racks of baby back pork ribs (about 2 pounds each)
- 1/4 cup olive oil
- 2 tablespoons salt
- 2 tablespoons black pepper
- 2 tablespoons smoked paprika
- 1 tablespoon garlic powder
- 1 tablespoon onion powder
- 1 teaspoon ground cumin
- 1 teaspoon dried thyme

For the BBQ Sauce:

- 1 cup ketchup
- 1/4 cup apple cider vinegar
- 1/4 cup brown sugar
- 2 tablespoons Worcestershire sauce
- 2 tablespoons Dijon mustard
- 2 cloves garlic, minced
- 1 teaspoon smoked paprika
- 1/2 teaspoon cayenne pepper (optional, for heat)
- Salt and pepper to taste

Nutritional Information (per serving):

- Calories: 750
- Protein: 45g
- Carbohydrates: 40g
- Fats: 45g
- Fiber: 2g

Instructions:

1. **Prepare the Ribs:**
   a. Remove the membrane from the back of the ribs for more tender results.
   b. In a small bowl, mix together the olive oil, salt, black pepper, smoked paprika, garlic powder, onion powder, ground cumin, and dried thyme.
   c. Rub the mixture all over the ribs, ensuring they are well coated. Let the ribs marinate in the refrigerator for at least 2 hours, or overnight for best results.
2. **Prepare the BBQ Sauce:** In a medium saucepan, combine the ketchup, apple cider vinegar, brown sugar, Worcestershire sauce, Dijon mustard, minced garlic, smoked paprika, and cayenne pepper (if using). Bring the mixture

to a simmer over medium heat, stirring occasionally, until the sauce thickens, about 10-15 minutes. Season with salt and pepper to taste. Set aside.

3. **Preheat the Griddle:** Preheat the gas griddle to medium heat. Allow it to heat up for about 5-10 minutes until it reaches an even temperature.
4. **Cook the Ribs:**
    a. **Grease the Griddle:** Lightly spray or brush the griddle surface with olive oil to prevent sticking.
    b. **Sear the Ribs:** Place the ribs on the griddle, meaty side down, and sear for about 5 minutes on each side to develop a good crust.
    c. **Reduce the Heat:** Lower the heat to medium-low. Move the ribs to a cooler zone if your griddle allows for different heat zones, or use a griddle lid to create an oven-like environment.
    d. **Cook Until Tender:** Cover the ribs with a griddle lid or tent with aluminum foil and cook for about 1 hour, turning occasionally and basting with the BBQ sauce every 15 minutes. The internal temperature of the ribs should reach 190°F (88°C) for tender, fall-off-the-bone meat.
    e. **Final Sear and Glaze:** In the last 5-10 minutes of cooking, increase the heat to medium-high and give the ribs a final sear while applying a final coat of the BBQ sauce. This will caramelize the glaze and enhance the flavor.
5. **Rest and Serve:** Remove the ribs from the griddle and let them rest for 10 minutes before slicing. Slice the ribs between the bones and transfer them to a serving platter.

Grilled Beef Tenderloin with Mushroom Sauce

Yield: 4 servings **Preparation Time:** 20 minutes **Cooking Time:** 25 minutes

Ingredients:

For the Beef Tenderloin:

- 2 pounds beef tenderloin, trimmed and cut into 4 equal portions
- 2 tablespoons olive oil
- 1 teaspoon salt
- 1 teaspoon black pepper
- 2 cloves garlic, minced
- 1 teaspoon fresh rosemary, chopped
- 1 teaspoon fresh thyme, chopped

For the Mushroom Sauce:

- 2 tablespoons butter
- 1 tablespoon olive oil
- 1 shallot, finely chopped
- 2 cloves garlic, minced
- 8 ounces cremini mushrooms, sliced
- 1/2 cup beef broth
- 1/2 cup heavy cream
- 1 teaspoon Worcestershire sauce
- 1 teaspoon fresh thyme, chopped
- Salt and pepper to taste

Nutritional Information (per serving):

- Calories: 650
- Protein: 45g
- Carbohydrates: 10g
- Fats: 48g
- Fiber: 2g

Instructions:

1. **Prepare the Beef Tenderloin:**
    a. In a small bowl, combine the olive oil, salt, black pepper, minced garlic, rosemary, and thyme.
        i. Rub the mixture all over the beef tenderloin portions. Let them sit at room temperature for about 20 minutes to marinate and come to room temperature.
2. **Prepare the Mushroom Sauce:**
    a. In a saucepan over medium heat, melt the butter with the olive oil.
    b. Add the chopped shallot and minced garlic, and sauté until the shallot is translucent, about 2-3 minutes.
    c. Add the sliced mushrooms and cook until they are browned and tender, about 5-7 minutes.
    d. Stir in the beef broth, heavy cream, Worcestershire sauce, and chopped thyme. Simmer for about 5 minutes until the sauce thickens slightly.
    e. Season with salt and pepper to taste. Keep the sauce warm.
3. **Preheat the Griddle:** Preheat the gas griddle to medium-high heat. Allow it to heat up for about 5-10 minutes until it reaches an even temperature.
4. **Cook the Beef Tenderloin:**
    a. **Grease the Griddle:** Lightly spray or brush the griddle surface with olive oil to prevent sticking.
    b. **Sear the Beef:** Place the beef tenderloin portions on the hot griddle.

c. **Cook Until Desired Doneness:** Cook the beef for about 4-5 minutes on each side for medium-rare, or until it reaches your desired level of doneness. Use a meat thermometer to check the internal temperature, which should be 130-135°F (54-57°C) for medium-rare.
d. **Rest the Beef:** Remove the beef from the griddle and let it rest for 5-10 minutes to allow the juices to redistribute.

5. **Serve Warm:** Place each beef tenderloin portion on a serving plate. Spoon the warm mushroom sauce over the beef tenderloin.

Griddled Sausage Patties

Yield: 4 servings (8 patties) **Preparation Time:** 15 minutes **Cooking Time:** 10 minutes

Ingredients:

- 1 pound ground pork
- 1 teaspoon salt
- 1/2 teaspoon black pepper
- 1 teaspoon garlic powder
- 1 teaspoon onion powder
- 1 teaspoon smoked paprika
- 1/2 teaspoon dried thyme
- 1/2 teaspoon dried sage
- 1/4 teaspoon red pepper flakes (optional, for heat)
- 1 tablespoon maple syrup (optional, for a touch of sweetness)
- Olive oil spray or additional olive oil for greasing the griddle

Nutritional Information (per serving):

- Calories: 250
- Protein: 20g
- Carbohydrates: 2g
- Fats: 18g
- Fiber: 0g

Instructions:

1. **Prepare the Sausage Mixture:**
   a. In a large bowl, combine the ground pork, salt, black pepper, garlic powder, onion powder, smoked paprika, dried thyme, dried sage, red pepper flakes (if using), and maple syrup (if using).
   b. Mix the ingredients thoroughly until well combined.
2. **Shape the Patties:** Divide the sausage mixture into 8 equal portions. Shape each portion into a patty, about 3 inches in diameter and 1/2 inch thick. Make sure the patties are even in thickness to ensure even cooking.
3. **Preheat the Griddle:** Preheat the gas griddle to medium-high heat. Allow it to heat up for about 5-10 minutes until it reaches an even temperature. Lightly spray or brush the griddle surface with olive oil to prevent sticking.
4. **Cook the Sausage Patties:**
   a. **Place Patties on Griddle:** Arrange the sausage patties on the hot griddle.
   b. **Cook Until Golden and Cooked Through:** Cook the patties for about 4-5 minutes on each side, or until they are golden brown and cooked through. The internal temperature should reach 160°F (71°C).
5. **Use Zones:** If your griddle allows for different heat zones, move the patties to a cooler zone if they are browning too quickly before cooking through.
6. **Serve Warm:** Transfer the cooked sausage patties to a serving plate.

Grilled Beef Brisket Tacos

Yield: 4 servings (8 tacos) **Preparation Time:** 30 minutes (plus marinating and braising time) **Cooking Time:** 1 hour 30 minutes

Ingredients:

For the Brisket:

- 2 pounds of beef brisket
- 2 tablespoons olive oil
- 1 tablespoon salt
- 1 tablespoon black pepper
- 2 teaspoons smoked paprika
- 1 teaspoon garlic powder
- 1 teaspoon onion powder
- 1 teaspoon ground cumin
- 1/2 teaspoon dried oregano
- 1/2 teaspoon chili powder
- 1 cup beef broth
- 1/2 cup apple cider vinegar
- 1/4 cup soy sauce
- 1/4 cup Worcestershire sauce

For the Tacos:

- 8 small corn or flour tortillas
- 1 cup shredded lettuce
- 1/2 cup diced tomatoes
- 1/2 cup diced red onion
- 1/4 cup chopped fresh cilantro
- Lime wedges, for serving

Nutritional Information (per serving):

- Calories: 500
- Protein: 35g
- Carbohydrates: 35g
- Fats: 25g
- Fiber: 5g

Instructions:

1. **Prepare the Brisket:**
    a. In a small bowl, mix together the salt, black pepper, smoked paprika, garlic powder, onion powder, ground cumin, dried oregano, and chili powder.
    b. Rub the spice mixture all over the brisket, ensuring it is well coated. Let the brisket sit at room temperature for about 30 minutes.
2. **Preheat the Griddle:** Preheat the gas griddle to medium-high heat. Allow it to heat up for about 5-10 minutes until it reaches an even temperature.
3. **Sear the Brisket:** Lightly spray or brush the griddle surface with olive oil to prevent sticking. Place the brisket on the hot griddle and sear for about 3-4 minutes on each side until it develops a nice brown crust.
4. **Braise the Brisket:**
    a. **Prepare the Braising Liquid:** In a medium bowl, combine the beef broth, apple cider vinegar, soy sauce, and Worcestershire sauce.
    b. **Braise on the Griddle:** Pour the braising liquid into a disposable aluminum pan or a griddle-safe baking dish. Place the seared brisket into the pan and cover tightly with aluminum foil.
    c. **Reduce Heat:** Lower the griddle heat to medium-low.
    d. **Cook Until Tender:** Cook the brisket for about 1 hour, or until it is tender and can be easily shredded with a fork. Check occasionally and add more liquid if needed to keep the brisket moist.
    e. **Shred the Brisket:** Remove the brisket from the griddle and let it rest for about 10 minutes. Then, using two forks, shred the brisket into bite-sized pieces.
5. **Warm the Tortillas:** On the griddle, warm the tortillas for about 1 minute on each side until they are soft and pliable.
6. **Assemble the Tacos:**
    a. Place a generous portion of shredded brisket onto each tortilla.
    b. Top with shredded lettuce, diced tomatoes, diced red onion, and chopped cilantro.
    c. Serve with lime wedges on the side.

Griddled Maple Glazed Pork Chops

Yield: 4 servings **Preparation Time:** 15 minutes **Cooking Time:** 15 minutes

Ingredients:

- 4 bone-in pork chops (about 1 inch thick)
- 2 tablespoons olive oil
- 1 teaspoon salt
- 1/2 teaspoon black pepper
- 1/2 teaspoon garlic powder
- 1/2 teaspoon onion powder
- 1/4 teaspoon smoked paprika

For the Maple Glaze:

- 1/2 cup pure maple syrup
- 2 tablespoons Dijon mustard
- 1 tablespoon soy sauce
- 1 tablespoon apple cider vinegar
- 1/2 teaspoon ground ginger
- 1/2 teaspoon red pepper flakes (optional, for heat)

Nutritional Information (per serving):

- Calories: 350
- Protein: 30g
- Carbohydrates: 25g
- Fats: 15g
- Fiber: 0g

Instructions:

1. **Prepare the Pork Chops:** Pat the pork chops dry with paper towels. In a small bowl, mix together the salt, black pepper, garlic powder, onion powder, and smoked paprika. Rub the spice mixture all over the pork chops, ensuring they are well coated. Let the pork chops sit at room temperature for about 10 minutes.

2. **Prepare the Maple Glaze:** In a small saucepan, combine the maple syrup, Dijon mustard, soy sauce, apple cider vinegar, ground ginger, and red pepper flakes (if using). Bring the mixture to a simmer over medium heat, stirring occasionally, until the glaze thickens slightly, about 5 minutes. Remove from heat and set aside.
3. **Preheat the Griddle:** Preheat the gas griddle to medium-high heat. Allow it to heat up for about 5-10 minutes until it reaches an even temperature. Lightly spray or brush the griddle surface with olive oil to prevent sticking.
4. **Cook the Pork Chops:**
   a. **Place Pork Chops on Griddle:** Arrange the pork chops on the hot griddle.
   b. **Sear the Pork Chops:** Cook the pork chops for about 4-5 minutes on each side until they develop a nice golden brown crust.
   c. **Reduce Heat:** Lower the heat to medium. Brush the pork chops with the maple glaze on both sides.
   d. **Cook Until Done:** Continue to cook the pork chops, flipping and brushing with more glaze as needed, until they reach an internal temperature of 145°F (63°C), about 3-5 more minutes.
   e. **Rest the Pork Chops:** Remove the pork chops from the griddle and let them rest for about 5 minutes to allow the juices to redistribute.
5. **Serve Warm:** Serve the griddled maple glazed pork chops on a platter, drizzling any remaining glaze over the top.

Grilled Garlic Herb Lamb Chops

Yield: 4 servings **Preparation Time:** 20 minutes **Cooking Time:** 15 minutes

Ingredients:

- 8 lamb chops (about 1 inch thick)
- 3 tablespoons olive oil
- 4 cloves garlic, minced
- 1 tablespoon fresh rosemary, chopped
- 1 tablespoon fresh thyme, chopped
- 1 teaspoon salt
- 1 teaspoon black pepper
- 1 tablespoon lemon juice

Nutritional Information (per serving):

- Calories: 350
- Protein: 30g
- Carbohydrates: 2g
- Fats: 25g
- Fiber: 1g

Instructions:

1. **Prepare the Lamb Chops:**
   a. In a small bowl, combine the olive oil, minced garlic, chopped rosemary, chopped thyme, salt, black pepper, and lemon juice.
   b. Rub the mixture all over the lamb chops, ensuring they are well coated. Let the lamb chops sit at room temperature for about 15-20 minutes to marinate and come to room temperature.
2. **Preheat the Griddle:** Preheat the gas griddle to medium-high heat. Allow it to heat up for about 5-10 minutes until it reaches an even temperature. Lightly spray or brush the griddle surface with olive oil to prevent sticking.
3. **Cook the Lamb Chops:**
   a. **Place Lamb Chops on Griddle:** Arrange the lamb chops on the hot griddle.
   b. **Sear the Lamb Chops:** Cook the lamb chops for about 4-5 minutes on each side until they develop a nice golden brown crust.
   c. **Use Zones:** If your griddle allows for different heat zones, move the lamb chops to a cooler zone if they are browning too quickly before cooking through.
   d. **Cook Until Desired Doneness:** Cook the lamb chops until they reach an internal temperature of 135°F (57°C) for medium-rare or your desired level of doneness. Use a meat thermometer to check the internal temperature.
   e. **Rest the Lamb Chops:** Remove the lamb chops from the griddle and let them rest for 5-10 minutes to allow the juices to redistribute.
4. **Serve Warm:** Arrange the lamb chops on a serving platter.

Griddled Teriyaki Beef

Yield: 4 servings **Preparation Time:** 15 minutes (plus 30 minutes marinating time) **Cooking Time:** 15 minutes

Ingredients:

For the Teriyaki Marinade:

- 1/2 cup soy sauce
- 1/4 cup mirin
- 1/4 cup sake (or substitute with additional mirin)
- 2 tablespoons brown sugar
- 2 cloves garlic, minced
- 1 tablespoon fresh ginger, grated
- 1 tablespoon sesame oil
- 1 teaspoon cornstarch mixed with 1 tablespoon water (slurry)

For the Beef:

- 1 pound beef sirloin or flank steak, thinly sliced against the grain
- 2 tablespoons vegetable oil
- 1/2 cup sliced green onions
- 1 tablespoon sesame seeds (optional, for garnish)

Nutritional Information (per serving):

- Calories: 350
- Protein: 30g
- Carbohydrates: 15g
- Fats: 18g
- Fiber: 1g

Instructions:

1. **Prepare the Marinade:**
   a. In a small saucepan, combine the soy sauce, mirin, sake, brown sugar, minced garlic, grated ginger, and sesame oil.
   b. Bring the mixture to a simmer over medium heat, stirring until the sugar dissolves.
   c. Add the cornstarch slurry to the marinade and cook until it thickens slightly about 1-2 minutes.
   d. Remove from heat and let it cool to room temperature.
2. **Marinate the Beef:**
   a. Place the thinly sliced beef in a large resealable plastic bag or a shallow dish.
   b. Pour the cooled teriyaki marinade over the beef, ensuring all pieces are well coated.
   c. Seal the bag or cover the dish and marinate in the refrigerator for at least 30 minutes, up to overnight for best results.
3. **Preheat the Griddle:** Preheat the gas griddle to medium-high heat. Allow it to heat up for about 5-10 minutes until it reaches an even temperature. Lightly spray or brush the griddle surface with vegetable oil to prevent sticking.
4. **Cook the Beef:**
   a. **Place Beef on Griddle:** Remove the beef from the marinade, letting any excess marinade drip off, and place the slices on the hot griddle.
   b. **Sear the Beef:** Cook the beef for about 2-3 minutes on each side, or until it is nicely seared and cooked through.
   c. **Use Zones:** If your griddle allows for different heat zones, move the beef to a cooler zone if it is cooking too quickly to ensure even cooking.
   d. **Add Green Onions:** During the last minute of cooking, add the sliced green onions to the griddle and cook until slightly wilted and aromatic.
5. **Serve Warm:** Transfer the cooked beef to a serving platter. Garnish with sesame seeds, if using.

Griddled Herb Crusted Pork Loin

Yield: 4 servings **Preparation Time:** 20 minutes **Cooking Time:** 25 minutes

Ingredients:

- 1.5 pounds of pork loin
- 3 tablespoons olive oil
- 1 tablespoon fresh rosemary, chopped
- 1 tablespoon fresh thyme, chopped
- 1 tablespoon fresh parsley, chopped
- 3 cloves garlic, minced
- 1 teaspoon salt
- 1 teaspoon black pepper
- 1 teaspoon Dijon mustard
- 1 lemon, zested and juiced

Nutritional Information (per serving):

- Calories: 350
- Protein: 30g
- Carbohydrates: 3g
- Fats: 22g
- Fiber: 1g

Instructions:

1. **Prepare the Herb Crust:** In a small bowl, combine the olive oil, chopped rosemary, thyme, parsley, minced garlic, salt, black pepper, Dijon mustard, lemon zest, and lemon juice. Mix well to form a herb paste.

2. **Prepare the Pork Loin:**
    a. Pat the pork loin dry with paper towels.
    b. Rub the herb paste all over the pork loin, ensuring it is well coated. Let the pork loin sit at room temperature for about 15-20 minutes to marinate and come to room temperature.
3. **Preheat the Griddle:** Preheat the gas griddle to medium-high heat. Allow it to heat up for about 5-10 minutes until it reaches an even temperature. Lightly spray or brush the griddle surface with olive oil to prevent sticking.
4. **Sear the Pork Loin:** Place the pork loin on the hot griddle.
5. **Sear the Pork Loin:** Cook the pork loin for about 4-5 minutes on each side until it develops a nice golden brown crust.
6. **Cook Through:**
    a. **Reduce Heat:** Lower the heat to medium.
    b. **Use Zones:** If your griddle allows for different heat zones, move the pork loin to a cooler zone to finish cooking without burning the crust.
    c. **Cover and Cook:** Cover the pork loin with a griddle lid or tent with aluminum foil. Continue to cook for about 15-20 minutes, turning occasionally, until the internal temperature reaches 145°F (63°C).
7. **Rest the Pork Loin:** Remove the pork loin from the griddle and let it rest for about 10 minutes before slicing. This allows the juices to be redistributed.
8. **Slice and Serve:** Slice the pork loin into medallions and arrange on a serving platter.

Grilled Pork Tenderloin with Apple Chutney

Yield: 4 servings **Preparation Time:** 20 minutes **Cooking Time:** 25 minutes

Ingredients:

For the Pork Tenderloin:

- 1.5 pounds pork tenderloin
- 3 tablespoons olive oil
- 1 teaspoon salt
- 1 teaspoon black pepper
- 1 teaspoon garlic powder
- 1 teaspoon onion powder
- 1 teaspoon smoked paprika
- 1 tablespoon fresh rosemary, chopped

For the Apple Chutney:

- 2 large apples, peeled, cored, and diced
- 1/2 cup onion, finely chopped
- 1/4 cup apple cider vinegar
- 1/4 cup brown sugar
- 1/4 cup raisins
- 1 tablespoon fresh ginger, grated
- 1/2 teaspoon ground cinnamon
- 1/4 teaspoon ground cloves
- 1/4 teaspoon ground nutmeg
- 1/4 teaspoon salt

Nutritional Information (per serving):

- Calories: 450
- Protein: 30g
- Carbohydrates: 40g
- Fats: 20g
- Fiber: 5g

Instructions:

1. **Prepare the Pork Tenderloin:**
    a. In a small bowl, mix together the olive oil, salt, black pepper, garlic powder, onion powder, smoked paprika, and chopped rosemary.
    b. Rub the mixture all over the pork tenderloin, ensuring it is well coated. Let the pork tenderloin sit at room temperature for about 15-20 minutes to marinate and come to room temperature.
2. **Prepare the Apple Chutney:**
    a. In a medium saucepan, combine the diced apples, chopped onion, apple cider vinegar, brown sugar, raisins, grated ginger, ground cinnamon, ground cloves, ground nutmeg, and salt.
    b. Bring the mixture to a simmer over medium heat. Cook, stirring occasionally, until the apples are tender and the chutney has thickened, about 15-20 minutes. Remove from heat and set aside.
3. **Preheat the Griddle:** Preheat the gas griddle to medium-high heat. Allow it to heat up for about 5-10 minutes until it reaches an even temperature.
4. **Grease the Griddle:** Lightly spray or brush the griddle surface with olive oil to prevent sticking.
5. **Cook the Pork Tenderloin:**
    a. **Place Pork Tenderloin on Griddle:** Place the pork tenderloin on the hot griddle.
    b. **Sear the Pork Tenderloin:** Cook the pork tenderloin for about 4-5 minutes on each side until it develops a nice golden brown crust.

c. **Reduce Heat:** Lower the heat to medium. If your griddle allows for different heat zones, move the pork tenderloin to a cooler zone to finish cooking without burning the crust.
d. **Cook Until Done:** Continue to cook, turning occasionally, until the internal temperature reaches 145°F (63°C), about 15-20 minutes.
e. **Rest the Pork Tenderloin:** Remove the pork tenderloin from the griddle and let it rest for about 10 minutes before slicing. This allows the juices to be redistributed.

6. **Slice and Serve:** Slice the pork tenderloin into medallions and arrange on a serving platter. Spoon the apple chutney over the pork medallions or serve on the side.

Griddled Chili Lime Beef Skewers

Yield: 4 servings **Preparation Time:** 20 minutes (plus 30 minutes marinating time) **Cooking Time:** 15 minutes

Ingredients:

For the Marinade:

- 1/4 cup lime juice (about 2 limes)
- 2 tablespoons olive oil
- 2 tablespoons soy sauce
- 2 tablespoons honey
- 1 teaspoon chili powder
- 1/2 teaspoon ground cumin
- 1/2 teaspoon smoked paprika
- 1/2 teaspoon garlic powder
- 1/2 teaspoon onion powder
- 1/2 teaspoon salt
- 1/2 teaspoon black pepper
- 1/4 teaspoon cayenne pepper (optional, for extra heat)
- Zest of 1 lime

For the Skewers:

- 1.5 pounds beef sirloin or flank steak, cut into 1-inch cubes
- 1 red bell pepper, cut into 1-inch pieces
- 1 green bell pepper, cut into 1-inch pieces
- 1 red onion, cut into 1-inch pieces
- Wooden or metal skewers (if using wooden skewers, soak them in water for 30 minutes to prevent burning)

Nutritional Information (per serving):

- Calories: 400
- Protein: 30g
- Carbohydrates: 20g
- Fats: 25g
- Fiber: 3g

Instructions:

1. **Prepare the Marinade:** In a large bowl, whisk together the lime juice, olive oil, soy sauce, honey, chili powder, ground cumin, smoked paprika, garlic powder, onion powder, salt, black pepper, cayenne pepper (if using), and lime zest.
2. **Marinate the Beef:** Add the beef cubes to the marinade, ensuring they are well coated. Cover and refrigerate for at least 30 minutes, up to 2 hours for best results.
3. **Prepare the Skewers:** Thread the marinated beef cubes, red bell pepper pieces, green bell pepper pieces, and red onion pieces onto the skewers, alternating between beef and vegetables.
4. **Preheat the Griddle:** Preheat the gas griddle to medium-high heat. Allow it to heat up for about 5-10 minutes until it reaches an even temperature.
5. **Grease the Griddle:** Lightly spray or brush the griddle surface with olive oil to prevent sticking.
6. **Cook the Skewers:**
   a. **Place Skewers on Griddle:** Arrange the beef skewers on the hot griddle.
   b. **Sear the Skewers:** Cook the skewers for about 4-5 minutes on each side until the beef is cooked to your desired level of doneness and the vegetables are tender and slightly charred.
   c. **Use Zones:** If your griddle allows for different heat zones, move the skewers to a cooler zone if they are cooking too quickly to ensure even cooking.
7. **Serve Warm:** Transfer the cooked skewers to a serving platter.

Griddled Filet Mignon with Garlic Butter

Yield: 4 servings **Preparation Time:** 15 minutes **Cooking Time:** 10-15 minutes

Ingredients:

For the Filet Mignon:

- 4 (6-ounce) filet mignon steaks
- 2 tablespoons olive oil
- 1 teaspoon salt
- 1 teaspoon black pepper

- 1 teaspoon garlic powder
- 1 teaspoon fresh rosemary, finely chopped

For the Garlic Butter:

- 1/2 cup unsalted butter, softened
- 4 cloves garlic, minced
- 1 tablespoon fresh parsley, chopped
- 1 teaspoon fresh thyme, chopped
- 1 teaspoon lemon juice
- 1/4 teaspoon salt
- 1/4 teaspoon black pepper

Nutritional Information (per serving):

- Calories: 500
- Protein: 35g
- Carbohydrates: 2g
- Fats: 40g
- Fiber: 0g

Instructions:

1. **Prepare the Steaks:**
    a. Pat the filet mignon steaks dry with paper towels.
    b. In a small bowl, mix together the salt, black pepper, garlic powder, and chopped rosemary.
    c. Rub the olive oil and the seasoning mixture all over the steaks. Let the steaks sit at room temperature for about 15 minutes to marinate and come to room temperature.
2. **Prepare the Garlic Butter:** In a small bowl, combine the softened butter, minced garlic, chopped parsley, chopped thyme, lemon juice, salt, and black pepper. Mix well until all ingredients are evenly incorporated. Set aside.
3. **Preheat the Griddle:** Preheat the gas griddle to high heat. Allow it to heat up for about 5-10 minutes until it reaches an even temperature. Lightly spray or brush the griddle surface with olive oil to prevent sticking.
4. **Cook the Filet Mignon:**
    a. **Place Steaks on Griddle:** Place the filet mignon steaks on the hot griddle.
    b. **Sear the Steaks:** Cook the steaks for about 3-4 minutes on each side for medium-rare, 4-5 minutes for medium, or until they reach your desired level of doneness. Use a meat thermometer to check the internal temperature (125°F for medium-rare, 135°F for medium).
    c. **Use Zones:** If your griddle allows for different heat zones, move the steaks to a cooler zone if they are browning too quickly to ensure even cooking.
    d. **Rest the Steaks:** Remove the steaks from the griddle and let them rest for about 5 minutes to allow the juices to redistribute.
5. **Serve Warm:** Place a generous dollop of garlic butter on top of each steak while they rest. The butter will melt and create a flavorful sauce.

Grilled Lamb Kofta with Tzatziki

Yield: 4 servings **Preparation Time:** 20 minutes (plus 30 minutes chilling time) **Cooking Time:** 15 minutes

Ingredients:

For the Lamb Kofta:

- 1 pound ground lamb
- 1 small onion, finely grated
- 3 cloves garlic, minced
- 1/4 cup fresh parsley, finely chopped
- 1 tablespoon fresh mint, finely chopped
- 1 teaspoon ground cumin
- 1 teaspoon ground coriander
- 1 teaspoon ground cinnamon
- 1/2 teaspoon ground allspice
- 1 teaspoon salt
- 1/2 teaspoon black pepper
- 1 tablespoon olive oil (for greasing the griddle)
- Wooden or metal skewers (if using wooden skewers, soak them in water for 30 minutes to prevent burning)

For the Tzatziki:

- 1 cup Greek yogurt
- 1/2 cucumber, grated, and excess water squeezed out
- 2 cloves garlic, minced
- 1 tablespoon fresh dill, finely chopped
- 1 tablespoon fresh lemon juice
- 1 tablespoon olive oil
- 1/2 teaspoon salt
- 1/4 teaspoon black pepper

Nutritional Information (per serving):

- Calories: 450
- Protein: 30g
- Carbohydrates: 10g
- Fats: 32g
- Fiber: 2g

Instructions:

1. **Prepare the Tzatziki:** In a medium bowl, combine the Greek yogurt, grated cucumber, minced garlic, fresh dill, lemon juice, olive oil, salt, and black pepper. Mix well and refrigerate for at least 30 minutes to allow the flavors to meld.
2. **Prepare the Lamb Kofta Mixture:**
    a. In a large bowl, combine the ground lamb, grated onion, minced garlic, chopped parsley, chopped mint, ground cumin, ground coriander, ground cinnamon, ground allspice, salt, and black pepper.
    b. Mix until all ingredients are well incorporated.
    c. Divide the mixture into 8 equal portions and shape each portion around a skewer, forming long, thin cylinders.
    d. Refrigerate the kofta skewers for at least 30 minutes to help them firm up.
3. **Preheat the Griddle:** Preheat the gas griddle to medium-high heat. Allow it to heat up for about 5-10 minutes until it reaches an even temperature. Lightly spray or brush the griddle surface with olive oil to prevent sticking.
4. **Cook the Lamb Kofta:**
    a. **Place Kofta on Griddle:** Arrange the kofta skewers on the hot griddle.
    b. **Sear the Kofta:** Cook the kofta skewers for about 4-5 minutes on each side, turning occasionally, until they are well browned and cooked through.
    c. **Use Zones:** If your griddle allows for different heat zones, move the kofta skewers to a cooler zone if they are cooking too quickly to ensure even cooking.
5. **Serve Warm:** Remove the kofta skewers from the griddle and let them rest for a few minutes. Serve the lamb kofta with a side of tzatziki sauce.

Poultry Recipes

Griddled BBQ Chicken Thighs

Yield: 4 servings **Preparation Time:** 15 minutes **Marinating Time:** 30 minutes to 2 hours **Cooking Time:** 20 minutes

Ingredients:

- 8 boneless, skinless chicken thighs
- 1/4 cup olive oil
- 1/4 cup BBQ sauce (plus extra for basting)
- 2 tablespoons apple cider vinegar
- 1 tablespoon Worcestershire sauce
- 1 tablespoon soy sauce
- 2 cloves garlic, minced
- 1 teaspoon smoked paprika
- 1 teaspoon onion powder
- 1/2 teaspoon salt
- 1/2 teaspoon black pepper

Nutritional Information (per serving):

- Calories: 450
- Protein: 30g
- Carbohydrates: 10g
- Fats: 30g
- Fiber: 1g

Instructions:

1. **Marinate the Chicken:**
    a. In a large bowl, combine the olive oil, 1/4 cup BBQ sauce, apple cider vinegar, Worcestershire sauce, soy sauce, minced garlic, smoked paprika, onion powder, salt, and black pepper. Mix well.
    b. Add the chicken thighs to the bowl, ensuring they are well coated with the marinade. Cover and refrigerate for at least 30 minutes, up to 2 hours for best results.
2. **Preheat the Griddle:** Preheat the gas griddle to medium-high heat. Allow it to heat up for about 5-10 minutes until it reaches an even temperature. Lightly spray or brush the griddle surface with olive oil to prevent sticking.
3. **Cook the Chicken Thighs:**
    a. **Place Chicken on Griddle:** Remove the chicken thighs from the marinade and place them on the hot griddle.
    b. **Sear the Chicken:** Cook the chicken thighs for about 5-7 minutes on each side, pressing gently with a spatula to ensure even contact with the griddle surface.
4. **Baste with BBQ Sauce:** In the last few minutes of cooking, baste the chicken thighs with additional BBQ sauce, turning them to ensure they are well coated and caramelized. The internal temperature should reach 165°F (74°C).
5. **Use Zones:** If your griddle allows for different heat zones, you can move the chicken thighs to a cooler zone if they are cooking too quickly, to ensure even cooking and prevent burning.
6. **Serve Warm:** Transfer the cooked chicken thighs to a serving platter.

Grilled Chicken Wings with Honey Mustard

Yield: 4 servings **Preparation Time:** 15 minutes **Marinating Time:** 30 minutes to 2 hours **Cooking Time:** 20-25 minutes

Ingredients:

For the Chicken Wings:

- 2 pounds chicken wings, separated into flats and drumettes
- 2 tablespoons olive oil
- 1 teaspoon salt
- 1 teaspoon black pepper
- 1 teaspoon garlic powder
- 1 teaspoon smoked paprika

For the Honey Mustard Sauce:

- 1/4 cup honey
- 1/4 cup Dijon mustard
- 2 tablespoons yellow mustard
- 1 tablespoon apple cider vinegar
- 1 teaspoon soy sauce
- 1/2 teaspoon garlic powder
- 1/2 teaspoon onion powder

Nutritional Information (per serving):

- Calories: 400
- Protein: 25g
- Carbohydrates: 25g
- Fats: 25g
- Fiber: 1g

Instructions:

1. **Marinate the Chicken Wings:**
   a. In a large bowl, combine the chicken wings with olive oil, salt, black pepper, garlic powder, and smoked paprika. Toss well to coat evenly.
   b. Cover and refrigerate for at least 30 minutes, up to 2 hours for best results.
2. **Prepare the Honey Mustard Sauce:** In a medium bowl, whisk together the honey, Dijon mustard, yellow mustard, apple cider vinegar, soy sauce, garlic powder, and onion powder until smooth. Set aside.
3. **Preheat the Griddle:** Preheat the gas griddle to medium-high heat. Allow it to heat up for about 5-10 minutes until it reaches an even temperature.
4. **Grease the Griddle:** Lightly spray or brush the griddle surface with olive oil to prevent sticking.
5. **Cook the Chicken Wings:**
   a. **Place Wings on Griddle:** Arrange the chicken wings on the hot griddle.
   b. **Sear the Wings:** Cook the wings for about 8-10 minutes on each side, turning occasionally, until they are golden brown and cooked through. The internal temperature should reach 165°F (74°C).
   c. **Use Zones:** If your griddle allows for different heat zones, you can move the wings to a cooler zone if they are cooking too quickly, to ensure even cooking and prevent burning.
6. **Glaze the Wings:** During the last few minutes of cooking, brush the honey mustard sauce over the chicken wings, turning them to coat evenly. Let them cook for another 2-3 minutes to caramelize the glaze.
7. **Serve Warm:** Transfer the glazed chicken wings to a serving platter.

Grilled Spicy Chicken Drumsticks

Yield: 4 servings **Preparation Time:** 15 minutes **Marinating Time:** 1 hour (optional, for better flavor) **Cooking Time:** 25-30 minutes

Ingredients:

For the Chicken Drumsticks:

- 8 chicken drumsticks
- 2 tablespoons olive oil
- 1 teaspoon salt
- 1 teaspoon black pepper
- 2 teaspoons smoked paprika
- 1 teaspoon cayenne pepper
- 1 teaspoon garlic powder
- 1 teaspoon onion powder
- 1 teaspoon dried oregano
- 1 teaspoon dried thyme
- 1 teaspoon ground cumin
- 1/2 teaspoon chili powder
- Juice of 1 lime

Nutritional Information (per serving):

- Calories: 350
- Protein: 30g
- Carbohydrates: 4g

- Fats: 24g
- Fiber: 1g

Instructions:

1. **Marinate the Chicken Drumsticks:** In a large bowl, combine the olive oil, salt, black pepper, smoked paprika, cayenne pepper, garlic powder, onion powder, dried oregano, dried thyme, ground cumin, chili powder, and lime juice. Mix well to create a marinade. Add the chicken drumsticks to the bowl and toss to coat evenly. Cover and refrigerate for at least 1 hour, up to overnight, to allow the flavors to penetrate the meat.
2. **Preheat the Griddle:** Preheat the gas griddle to medium-high heat. Allow it to heat up for about 5-10 minutes until it reaches an even temperature. Lightly spray or brush the griddle surface with olive oil to prevent sticking.
3. **Cook the Chicken Drumsticks:**
4. **Place Drumsticks on Griddle:** Arrange the chicken drumsticks on the hot griddle.
5. **Sear the Drumsticks:** Cook the drumsticks for about 10 minutes on each side, turning occasionally, until they are golden brown and cooked through. The internal temperature should reach 165°F (74°C).
6. **Use Zones:** If your griddle allows for different heat zones, you can move the drumsticks to a cooler zone if they are cooking too quickly, to ensure even cooking and prevent burning.
7. **Baste the Drumsticks:** During the last few minutes of cooking, baste the chicken drumsticks with any remaining marinade, turning them to coat evenly. Let them cook for another 2-3 minutes to caramelize the glaze.
8. **Serve Warm:** Transfer the cooked chicken drumsticks to a serving platter.

Grilled Chicken and Pineapple Skewers

Yield: 4 servings **Preparation Time:** 20 minutes **Marinating Time:** 30 minutes (optional, for better flavor) **Cooking Time:** 15-20 minutes

Ingredients:

For the Chicken and Pineapple Skewers:

- 1.5 pounds boneless, skinless chicken breasts, cut into 1-inch cubes
- 2 cups fresh pineapple chunks (1-inch pieces)
- 1 red bell pepper, cut into 1-inch pieces
- 1 yellow bell pepper, cut into 1-inch pieces
- 1 red onion, cut into 1-inch pieces
- 2 tablespoons olive oil
- 1/4 cup soy sauce
- 1/4 cup pineapple juice
- 2 tablespoons honey
- 2 cloves garlic, minced
- 1 teaspoon ground ginger
- 1/2 teaspoon black pepper
- 1/2 teaspoon salt
- Wooden or metal skewers (if using wooden skewers, soak them in water for 30 minutes to prevent burning)

Nutritional Information (per serving):

- Calories: 380
- Protein: 35g
- Carbohydrates: 35g
- Fats: 12g
- Fiber: 3g

Instructions:

1. **Marinate the Chicken:**
   a. In a large bowl, whisk together the olive oil, soy sauce, pineapple juice, honey, minced garlic, ground ginger, black pepper, and salt.
   b. Add the chicken cubes to the bowl, tossing to coat evenly with the marinade.
   c. Cover and refrigerate for at least 30 minutes, up to 2 hours for best results.
2. **Prepare the Skewers:** Thread the marinated chicken, pineapple chunks, red bell pepper pieces, yellow bell pepper pieces, and red onion pieces onto the skewers, alternating between chicken and vegetables.
3. **Preheat the Griddle:** Preheat the gas griddle to medium-high heat. Allow it to heat up for about 5-10 minutes until it reaches an even temperature.
4. **Grease the Griddle:** Lightly spray or brush the griddle surface with olive oil to prevent sticking.
5. **Cook the Skewers:**
   a. **Place Skewers on Griddle:** Arrange the chicken and pineapple skewers on the hot griddle.
   b. **Sear the Skewers:** Cook the skewers for about 10-12 minutes, turning every 2-3 minutes to ensure even cooking and caramelization on all sides. The chicken should be cooked through and have an internal temperature of 165°F (74°C).

6. **Use Zones:** If your griddle allows for different heat zones, move the skewers to a cooler zone if they are cooking too quickly, to ensure even cooking and prevent burning.
7. **Serve Warm:** Transfer the cooked chicken and pineapple skewers to a serving platter.

Grilled Mediterranean Chicken Kebabs

Yield: 4 servings **Preparation Time:** 20 minutes **Marinating Time:** 1 hour (optional, for better flavor) **Cooking Time:** 15-20 minutes

Ingredients:

For the Chicken Kebabs:

- 1.5 pounds boneless, skinless chicken breasts, cut into 1-inch cubes
- 1 red bell pepper, cut into 1-inch pieces
- 1 yellow bell pepper, cut into 1-inch pieces
- 1 red onion, cut into 1-inch pieces
- 1 zucchini, cut into 1-inch rounds
- Wooden or metal skewers (if using wooden skewers, soak them in water for 30 minutes to prevent burning)

For the Marinade:

- 1/4 cup olive oil
- 3 tablespoons lemon juice
- 3 cloves garlic, minced
- 2 teaspoons dried oregano
- 1 teaspoon dried thyme
- 1 teaspoon smoked paprika
- 1 teaspoon salt
- 1/2 teaspoon black pepper

Nutritional Information (per serving):

- Calories: 350
- Protein: 35g
- Carbohydrates: 20g
- Fats: 15g
- Fiber: 4g

Instructions:

1. **Marinate the Chicken:**
   a. In a large bowl, whisk together the olive oil, lemon juice, minced garlic, dried oregano, dried thyme, smoked paprika, salt, and black pepper.
   b. Add the chicken cubes to the bowl, tossing to coat evenly with the marinade.
   c. Cover and refrigerate for at least 1 hour, up to 4 hours for best results.
2. **Prepare the Skewers:** Thread the marinated chicken, red bell pepper pieces, yellow bell pepper pieces, red onion pieces, and zucchini rounds onto the skewers, alternating between chicken and vegetables.
3. **Preheat the Griddle:** Preheat the gas griddle to medium-high heat. Allow it to heat up for about 5-10 minutes until it reaches an even temperature. Lightly spray or brush the griddle surface with olive oil to prevent sticking.
4. **Cook the Kebabs:**
   a. **Place Kebabs on the Griddle:** Arrange the chicken and vegetable skewers on the hot griddle.
   b. **Sear the Kebabs:** Cook the kebabs for about 10-12 minutes, turning every 2-3 minutes to ensure even cooking and caramelization on all sides. The chicken should be cooked through and have an internal temperature of 165°F (74°C).
5. **Use Zones:** If your griddle allows for different heat zones, move the kebabs to a cooler zone if they are cooking too quickly, to ensure even cooking and prevent burning.
6. **Serve Warm:** Transfer the cooked chicken kebabs to a serving platter.

Herbed Turkey Breast Steaks

Yield: 4 servings **Preparation Time:** 15 minutes **Marinating Time:** 30 minutes (optional, for better flavor) **Cooking Time:** 20 minutes

Ingredients:

For the Turkey Breast Steaks:

- 4 turkey breast steaks (approximately 6 ounces each)
- 3 tablespoons olive oil
- 2 tablespoons fresh lemon juice
- 3 cloves garlic, minced
- 1 tablespoon fresh rosemary, finely chopped
- 1 tablespoon fresh thyme, finely chopped
- 1 tablespoon fresh parsley, finely chopped
- 1 teaspoon salt
- 1/2 teaspoon black pepper

Nutritional Information (per serving):

- Calories: 300
- Protein: 40g
- Carbohydrates: 2g
- Fats: 15g
- Fiber: 0g

Instructions:

1. **Marinate the Turkey Breast Steaks:**
    a. In a large bowl, combine the olive oil, lemon juice, minced garlic, chopped rosemary, thyme, parsley, salt, and black pepper. Mix well.
    b. Add the turkey breast steaks to the bowl, tossing to coat evenly with the marinade.
    c. Cover and refrigerate for at least 30 minutes, up to 2 hours for best results.
2. **Preheat the Griddle:** Preheat the gas griddle to medium-high heat. Allow it to heat up for about 5-10 minutes until it reaches an even temperature.
3. **Grease the Griddle:** Lightly spray or brush the griddle surface with olive oil to prevent sticking.
4. **Cook the Turkey Breast Steaks:** Arrange the turkey breast steaks on the hot griddle.
5. **Sear the Steaks:** Cook the steaks for about 5-6 minutes on each side, turning once, until they are golden brown and cooked through. The internal temperature should reach 165°F (74°C).
6. **Use Zones:** If your griddle allows for different heat zones, move the steaks to a cooler zone if they are cooking too quickly, to ensure even cooking and prevent burning.
7. **Serve Warm:** Transfer the cooked turkey breast steaks to a serving platter.

Griddled Chicken and Veggie Stir-Fry

Yield: 4 servings **Preparation Time:** 20 minutes **Marinating Time:** 30 minutes (optional, for better flavor) **Cooking Time:** 15-20 minutes

Ingredients:

For the Chicken and Veggie Stir-Fry:

- 1.5 pounds boneless, skinless chicken breasts, thinly sliced
- 1 red bell pepper, sliced into strips
- 1 yellow bell pepper, sliced into strips
- 1 green bell pepper, sliced into strips
- 1 red onion, thinly sliced
- 2 cups broccoli florets
- 2 medium carrots, julienned
- 1 zucchini, sliced into rounds
- 2 tablespoons vegetable oil

For the Marinade:

- 1/4 cup soy sauce
- 2 tablespoons hoisin sauce
- 2 tablespoons rice vinegar
- 2 tablespoons honey
- 2 cloves garlic, minced
- 1 tablespoon fresh ginger, minced
- 1 teaspoon sesame oil
- 1/2 teaspoon red pepper flakes (optional)

Nutritional Information (per serving):

- Calories: 350
- Protein: 35g
- Carbohydrates: 30g
- Fats: 12g
- Fiber: 5g

Instructions:

1. **Marinate the Chicken:**
    a. In a large bowl, whisk together the soy sauce, hoisin sauce, rice vinegar, honey, minced garlic, minced ginger, sesame oil, and red pepper flakes (if using).
    b. Add the thinly sliced chicken breasts to the bowl, tossing to coat evenly with the marinade.
    c. Cover and refrigerate for at least 30 minutes, up to 2 hours for best results.
2. **Prepare the Vegetables:** Slice and prepare all the vegetables as described in the ingredients list.
3. **Preheat the Griddle:** Preheat the gas griddle to medium-high heat. Allow it to heat up for about 5-10 minutes until it reaches an even temperature.
4. **Grease the Griddle:** Lightly spray or brush the griddle surface with vegetable oil to prevent sticking.
5. **Cook the Chicken:**
    a. **Place Chicken on Griddle:** Arrange the marinated chicken slices on one side of the hot griddle.
    b. **Sear the Chicken:** Cook the chicken for about 5-7 minutes, turning occasionally, until it is fully cooked and golden brown. Use a spatula to turn the chicken slices for even cooking.
6. **Cook the Vegetables:**

   a. **Place Vegetables on Griddle:** On the other side of the griddle, add the sliced bell peppers, red onion, broccoli florets, carrots, and zucchini rounds.
   b. **Sauté the Vegetables:** Cook the vegetables for about 8-10 minutes, stirring occasionally, until they are tender-crisp and slightly charred. Adjust the heat to medium if needed to prevent burning.
7. **Combine Chicken and Vegetables:** Once the chicken and vegetables are cooked, combine them on the griddle. Toss everything together to mix well and heat through for another 2-3 minutes.
8. **Serve Warm:** Transfer the griddled chicken and veggie stir-fry to a serving platter.

Grilled Turkey and Veggie Kebabs

Yield: 4 servings **Preparation Time:** 20 minutes **Marinating Time:** 30 minutes (optional, for better flavor) **Cooking Time:** 15-20 minutes

Ingredients:

For the Turkey and Veggie Kebabs:

- 1.5 pounds turkey breast, cut into 1-inch cubes
- 1 red bell pepper, cut into 1-inch pieces
- 1 yellow bell pepper, cut into 1-inch pieces
- 1 zucchini, sliced into rounds
- 1 red onion, cut into 1-inch pieces
- 8 cherry tomatoes
- Wooden or metal skewers (if using wooden skewers, soak them in water for 30 minutes to prevent burning)

For the Marinade:

- 1/4 cup olive oil
- 3 tablespoons lemon juice
- 2 cloves garlic, minced
- 1 tablespoon fresh rosemary, finely chopped
- 1 tablespoon fresh thyme, finely chopped
- 1 tablespoon fresh parsley, finely chopped
- 1 teaspoon salt
- 1/2 teaspoon black pepper

Nutritional Information (per serving):

- Calories: 350
- Protein: 35g
- Carbohydrates: 15g
- Fats: 18g
- Fiber: 5g

Instructions:

1. **Marinate the turkey:**
   a. In a large bowl, whisk together the olive oil, lemon juice, minced garlic, chopped rosemary, thyme, parsley, salt, and black pepper.
   b. Add the turkey cubes to the bowl, tossing to coat evenly with the marinade.
   c. Cover and refrigerate for at least 30 minutes, up to 2 hours for best results.
2. **Prepare the Skewers:** Thread the marinated turkey, red bell pepper pieces, yellow bell pepper pieces, zucchini rounds, red onion pieces, and cherry tomatoes onto the skewers, alternating between turkey and vegetables.
3. **Preheat the Griddle:** Preheat the gas griddle to medium-high heat. Allow it to heat up for about 5-10 minutes until it reaches an even temperature. Lightly spray or brush the griddle surface with olive oil to prevent sticking.
4. **Cook the Kebabs:**
   a. **Place Kebabs on the Griddle:** Arrange the turkey and vegetable skewers on the hot griddle.
   b. **Sear the Kebabs:** Cook the kebabs for about 12-15 minutes, turning every 2-3 minutes to ensure even cooking and caramelization on all sides. The turkey should be cooked through and have an internal temperature of 165°F (74°C).
5. **Use Zones:** If your griddle allows for different heat zones, move the kebabs to a cooler zone if they are cooking too quickly, to ensure even cooking and prevent burning.
6. **Serve Warm:** Transfer the cooked turkey and veggie kebabs to a serving platter.

Griddled Turkey Tacos

Yield: 4 servings **Preparation Time:** 20 minutes **Cooking Time:** 15 minutes

Ingredients:

For the Turkey Filling:

- 1 pound ground turkey
- 1 tablespoon olive oil
- 1 small onion, finely chopped
- 2 cloves garlic, minced
- 1 red bell pepper, finely chopped
- 1 teaspoon ground cumin

- 1 teaspoon smoked paprika
- 1/2 teaspoon chili powder
- 1/2 teaspoon salt
- 1/4 teaspoon black pepper
- 1/4 cup fresh cilantro, chopped

For the Tacos:

- 8 small corn or flour tortillas
- 1 cup shredded lettuce
- 1/2 cup diced tomatoes
- 1/2 cup shredded cheddar cheese
- 1/4 cup sour cream
- 1/4 cup salsa
- Lime wedges, for serving

Nutritional Information (per serving):

- Calories: 350
- Protein: 28g
- Carbohydrates: 30g
- Fats: 15g
- Fiber: 4g

Instructions:

1. **Prepare the Turkey Filling:** Heat the olive oil on the gas griddle over medium-high heat. Add the chopped onion and red bell pepper to the griddle. Sauté for 2-3 minutes until they begin to soften. Add the minced garlic and sauté for another 1 minute until fragrant.
2. **Cook the turkey:**
   a. Move the vegetables to the side of the griddle to create space for the ground turkey.
   b. Add the ground turkey to the griddle and cook for about 5-7 minutes, breaking it up with a spatula, until it is browned and cooked through.
   c. Mix the cooked turkey with the sautéed vegetables.
   d. Sprinkle the ground cumin, smoked paprika, chili powder, salt, and black pepper over the turkey mixture. Stir to combine and cook for an additional 2-3 minutes.
3. **Heat the Tortillas:** On a clean section of the griddle, place the tortillas in a single layer. Heat each tortilla for about 1-2 minutes per side until warmed and slightly charred. Use a spatula to flip them over.
4. **Assemble the Tacos:** Remove the warmed tortillas from the griddle and place them on a serving platter. Spoon the turkey filling onto each tortilla.
5. **Add Toppings:** Top each taco with shredded lettuce, diced tomatoes, shredded cheddar cheese, sour cream, and salsa. Garnish with fresh cilantro and serve with lime wedges.

Grilled Duck Breast with Orange Glaze

Yield: 4 servings **Preparation Time:** 20 minutes **Cooking Time:** 25-30 minutes

Ingredients:

For the Duck Breast:

- 4 duck breasts, skin-on
- 1 teaspoon salt
- 1/2 teaspoon black pepper
- 1 tablespoon olive oil

For the Orange Glaze:

- 1 cup fresh orange juice (about 3-4 oranges)
- 2 tablespoons honey
- 2 tablespoons soy sauce
- 1 tablespoon balsamic vinegar
- 1 teaspoon orange zest
- 1 clove garlic, minced
- 1 teaspoon fresh ginger, minced
- 1/4 teaspoon red pepper flakes (optional)

Nutritional Information (per serving):

- Calories: 450
- Protein: 35g
- Carbohydrates: 15g
- Fats: 28g
- Fiber: 1g

Instructions:

1. **Prepare the Duck Breast:** Score the skin of each duck breast in a crosshatch pattern, being careful not to cut into the meat. Season both sides of the duck breasts with salt and black pepper.
2. **Prepare the Orange Glaze:**
   a. In a small saucepan, combine the orange juice, honey, soy sauce, balsamic vinegar, orange zest, minced garlic, minced ginger, and red pepper flakes (if using).
   b. Bring the mixture to a boil over medium-high heat, then reduce the heat to medium-low and simmer for 10-15 minutes, or until the glaze has reduced by half and has a syrupy consistency. Stir occasionally.

3. **Preheat the Griddle:** Preheat the gas griddle to medium-high heat. Allow it to heat up for about 5-10 minutes until it reaches an even temperature.
4. **Cook the Duck Breast:**
    a. Lightly brush the griddle surface with olive oil to prevent sticking.
    b. Place the duck breasts skin-side down on the hot griddle. Cook for about 6-8 minutes until the skin is crispy and golden brown. Reduce the heat to medium if the skin begins to burn.
    c. Flip the duck breasts over and cook for an additional 4-6 minutes, or until the internal temperature reaches 135°F (57°C) for medium-rare, or longer if you prefer well-done.
5. **Glaze the Duck:** In the last few minutes of cooking, brush the orange glaze over the duck breasts, allowing it to caramelize slightly on the griddle. Remove the duck breasts from the griddle and let them rest for 5 minutes before slicing.
6. **Serve Warm:** Slice the duck breasts thinly and arrange them on a serving platter. Drizzle with any remaining orange glaze.

Griddled Herb Roasted Chicken Legs

Yield: 4 servings **Preparation Time:** 15 minutes **Marinating Time:** 30 minutes (optional, for better flavor) **Cooking Time:** 25-30 minutes

Ingredients:

For the Chicken Legs:

- 8 chicken legs (drumsticks)
- 2 tablespoons olive oil
- 1 tablespoon fresh rosemary, finely chopped
- 1 tablespoon fresh thyme, finely chopped
- 1 tablespoon fresh parsley, finely chopped
- 2 cloves garlic, minced
- 1 teaspoon salt
- 1/2 teaspoon black pepper
- Juice of 1 lemon

Nutritional Information (per serving):

- Calories: 350
- Protein: 30g
- Carbohydrates: 2g
- Fats: 23g
- Fiber: 0g

Instructions:

1. **Prepare the Marinade:**
    a. In a large bowl, combine the olive oil, chopped rosemary, thyme, parsley, minced garlic, salt, black pepper, and lemon juice.
    b. Add the chicken legs to the bowl, tossing to coat evenly with the herb mixture.
    c. Cover and refrigerate for at least 30 minutes, up to 2 hours for best results.
2. **Preheat the Griddle:** Preheat the gas griddle to medium-high heat. Allow it to heat up for about 5-10 minutes until it reaches an even temperature.
3. **Grease the Griddle:** Lightly brush the griddle surface with olive oil to prevent sticking.
4. **Cook the Chicken Legs:**
    a. **Initial Sear:** Place the marinated chicken legs on the hot griddle. Sear each side for about 3-4 minutes until they develop a golden-brown crust.
    b. **Reduce Heat:** Lower the heat to medium and cover the chicken legs with a griddle dome or use an aluminum foil tent to help cook them through without burning.
    c. **Cook Through:** Continue cooking the chicken legs for an additional 15-20 minutes, turning occasionally, until they reach an internal temperature of 165°F (74°C).
5. **Rest and Serve:** Remove the chicken legs from the griddle and let them rest for 5 minutes to allow the juices to redistribute. Arrange the chicken legs on a serving platter.

Duck and Sweet Potato Hash

Yield: 4 servings **Preparation Time:** 15 minutes **Cooking Time:** 30 minutes

Ingredients:

- 2 duck breasts, skin-on
- 2 large sweet potatoes, peeled and diced into 1/2-inch cubes
- 1 red bell pepper, diced
- 1 yellow bell pepper, diced
- 1 small red onion, finely chopped
- 2 cloves garlic, minced

- 2 tablespoons olive oil
- 1 teaspoon fresh thyme, chopped
- 1 teaspoon fresh rosemary, chopped
- Salt and black pepper to taste
- 2 tablespoons fresh parsley, chopped (for garnish)

Nutritional Information (per serving):

- Calories: 450
- Protein: 28g
- Carbohydrates: 35g
- Fats: 22g
- Fiber: 6g

Instructions:

1. **Prepare the Duck Breasts:** Score the skin of each duck breast in a crosshatch pattern, being careful not to cut into the meat. Season both sides of the duck breasts with salt and black pepper.
2. **Prepare the Sweet Potatoes:** Dice the sweet potatoes into 1/2-inch cubes and place them in a bowl. Toss the sweet potatoes with 1 tablespoon of olive oil, salt, and black pepper.
3. **Preheat the Griddle:** Preheat the gas griddle to medium-high heat. Allow it to heat up for about 5-10 minutes until it reaches an even temperature.
4. **Cook the Duck Breasts:**
   a. Place the duck breasts skin-side down on the hot griddle. Cook for about 6-8 minutes until the skin is crispy and golden brown.
   b. Flip the duck breasts over and cook for an additional 4-6 minutes, or until the internal temperature reaches 135°F (57°C) for medium-rare, or longer if you prefer well-done.
   c. Remove the duck breasts from the griddle and let them rest for 5 minutes before slicing.
5. **Cook the Sweet Potatoes:** Add the diced sweet potatoes to the griddle. Spread them out in a single layer and cook for about 10-12 minutes, turning occasionally, until they are tender and slightly crispy.
6. **Cook the Vegetables:** Move the sweet potatoes to one side of the griddle and add the remaining 1 tablespoon of olive oil. Add the diced red bell pepper, yellow bell pepper, red onion, and minced garlic to the griddle. Sauté for 5-7 minutes until the vegetables are tender.
7. **Combine the Ingredients:** Mix the sweet potatoes with the sautéed vegetables. Add the chopped thyme and rosemary, stirring to combine.
8. **Slice the Duck Breasts:** Slice the cooked duck breasts thinly and mix the slices into the sweet potato and vegetable mixture on the griddle. Cook for an additional 2-3 minutes to heat everything through.
9. **Serve Warm:** Transfer the duck and sweet potato hash to a serving platter. Garnish with fresh parsley.

Grilled Duck Salad with Raspberry Vinaigrette

Yield: 4 servings **Preparation Time:** 20 minutes **Cooking Time:** 20-25 minutes

Ingredients:

For the Duck:

- 2 duck breasts, skin-on
- 1 teaspoon salt
- 1/2 teaspoon black pepper

For the Salad:

- 4 cups mixed salad greens (arugula, spinach, and lettuce)
- 1/2 cup crumbled goat cheese
- 1/2 cup sliced almonds, toasted
- 1/2 red onion, thinly sliced
- 1 cup fresh raspberries
- 1 avocado, sliced

For the Raspberry Vinaigrette:

- 1/4 cup fresh raspberries
- 1/4 cup olive oil
- 2 tablespoons raspberry vinegar or red wine vinegar
- 1 tablespoon honey
- 1 teaspoon Dijon mustard
- Salt and black pepper to taste

Nutritional Information (per serving):

- Calories: 450
- Protein: 28g
- Carbohydrates: 20g
- Fats: 30g
- Fiber: 6g

Instructions:

1. **Prepare the Duck Breasts:** Score the skin of each duck breast in a crosshatch pattern, being careful not to cut into the meat. Season both sides of the duck breasts with salt and black pepper.

2. **Prepare the Vinaigrette:**
    a. In a small bowl, mash the fresh raspberries with a fork.
    b. Add the olive oil, raspberry vinegar, honey, Dijon mustard, salt, and black pepper.
    c. Whisk until well combined. Set aside.
3. **Preheat the Griddle:** Preheat the gas griddle to medium-high heat. Allow it to heat up for about 5-10 minutes until it reaches an even temperature.
4. **Cook the Duck Breasts:**
    a. Place the duck breasts skin-side down on the hot griddle. Cook for about 6-8 minutes until the skin is crispy and golden brown.
    b. Flip the duck breasts over and cook for an additional 4-6 minutes, or until the internal temperature reaches 135°F (57°C) for medium-rare, or longer if you prefer well-done.
    c. Remove the duck breasts from the griddle and let them rest for 5 minutes before slicing.
5. **Prepare the Salad:** In a large bowl, combine the mixed salad greens, crumbled goat cheese, toasted sliced almonds, thinly sliced red onion, fresh raspberries, and avocado slices.
6. **Slice the Duck Breasts:** Thinly slice the rested duck breasts and arrange the slices on top of the salad.
7. **Dress the Salad:** Drizzle the raspberry vinaigrette over the salad and gently toss to combine.

Duck and Brie Panini

Yield: 4 servings **Preparation Time:** 15 minutes **Cooking Time:** 20-25 minutes

Ingredients:

- 2 duck breasts, skin-on
- Salt and black pepper to taste
- 8 slices ciabatta or sourdough bread
- 4 tablespoons butter, softened
- 8 ounces Brie cheese, thinly sliced
- 1/2 cup caramelized onions
- 1 cup arugula or baby spinach
- 4 tablespoons cranberry sauce or fig jam

Nutritional Information (per serving):

- Calories: 550
- Protein: 32g
- Carbohydrates: 40g
- Fats: 28g
- Fiber: 3g

Instructions:

1. **Prepare the Duck Breasts:** Score the skin of each duck breast in a crosshatch pattern, being careful not to cut into the meat. Season both sides of the duck breasts with salt and black pepper.
2. **Prepare the Bread:** Butter one side of each slice of bread.
3. **Preheat the Griddle:** Preheat the gas griddle to medium-high heat. Allow it to heat up for about 5-10 minutes until it reaches an even temperature.
4. **Cook the Duck Breasts:**
    a. Place the duck breasts skin-side down on the hot griddle. Cook for about 6-8 minutes until the skin is crispy and golden brown.
    b. Flip the duck breasts over and cook for an additional 4-6 minutes, or until the internal temperature reaches 135°F (57°C) for medium-rare, or longer if you prefer well-done.
    c. Remove the duck breasts from the griddle and let them rest for 5 minutes before slicing thinly.
5. **Assemble the Panini:**
    a. Place the buttered side of a bread slice down on the griddle.
    b. Layer with sliced duck breast, Brie cheese, caramelized onions, and arugula or baby spinach.
    c. Spread a tablespoon of cranberry sauce or fig jam on the inside of the top bread slice, then place it on top, buttered side up.
6. **Cook the Panini:** Use a spatula or press lid to press down on the panini. Cook for 3-4 minutes on each side until the bread is golden brown and crispy and the cheese is melted. If necessary, lower the heat to medium to prevent burning.
7. **Serve Warm:** Remove the panini from the griddle and let it cool for a minute. Cut each panini in half and serve warm.

Fish and Seafood

Grilled Salmon with Dill Sauce

Yield: 4 servings **Preparation Time:** 15 minutes **Cooking Time:** 15 minutes

Ingredients:
For the Salmon:

- 4 salmon fillets (6 oz each)
- 2 tablespoons olive oil
- Salt and pepper to taste
- 1 lemon, sliced

For the Dill Sauce:

- 1/2 cup plain Greek yogurt
- 2 tablespoons mayonnaise
- 1 tablespoon lemon juice
- 1 tablespoon fresh dill, finely chopped
- 1 teaspoon garlic powder
- Salt and pepper to taste

For the Griddle:

- 2 tablespoons vegetable oil or non-stick cooking spray

Nutritional Information (per serving):

- Calories: 320
- Protein: 35g
- Carbohydrates: 3g
- Fats: 19g
- Fiber: 0g

Instructions:

1. **Prepare the Dill Sauce:** In a small bowl, combine the Greek yogurt, mayonnaise, lemon juice, dill, garlic powder, salt, and pepper. Mix well and refrigerate until ready to use.
2. **Preheat the Gas Griddle:** Set your gas griddle to medium-high heat (approximately 375°F). Allow it to preheat for about 5 minutes.
3. **Prepare the Salmon:** Pat the salmon fillets dry with a paper towel. Rub each fillet with olive oil and season with salt and pepper on both sides.
4. **Griddle Preparation:** Once the griddle is hot, apply a thin layer of vegetable oil or non-stick cooking spray to prevent sticking.
5. **Cooking the Salmon:**
   a. Place the salmon fillets skin-side down on the griddle. Cook for about 4-5 minutes on the first side. Do not move the fillets around; let them cook undisturbed to develop a nice sear.
   b. Using a wide spatula, carefully flip the fillets. Place lemon slices on top of each fillet.
   c. Cook for another 4-5 minutes or until the salmon is opaque and flakes easily with a fork.
6. **Zone Cooking Tip:** If your griddle has zones, you can use a medium zone for searing and a lower heat zone to finish cooking the salmon if needed. This technique ensures the salmon is cooked through without burning.
7. **Serving:** Remove the salmon from the griddle and let it rest for a minute. Serve each fillet with a generous dollop of dill sauce on top.

Griddled Shrimp Scampi

Yield: 4 servings **Preparation Time:** 15 minutes **Cooking Time:** 10 minutes

Ingredients:
For the Shrimp:

- 1 1/2 pounds large shrimp, peeled and deveined
- 4 tablespoons olive oil, divided
- 4 cloves garlic, minced
- 1/2 teaspoon crushed red pepper flakes (optional)
- Salt and pepper to taste
- 1/4 cup white wine or chicken broth
- 2 tablespoons lemon juice
- 2 tablespoons unsalted butter
- 1/4 cup fresh parsley, chopped

For the Griddle:

- 1 tablespoon vegetable oil or non-stick cooking spray

Nutritional Information (per serving):

- Calories: 290
- Protein: 24g
- Carbohydrates: 4g
- Fats: 19g
- Fiber: 0g

Instructions:

1. **Marinate the Shrimp:** In a bowl, combine the shrimp, 2 tablespoons of olive oil, minced garlic, crushed red pepper flakes (if using), salt, and pepper. Toss to coat and let it marinate for 10 minutes.
2. **Preheat the Gas Griddle:** Set your gas griddle to medium-high heat (approximately 375°F). Allow it to preheat for about 5 minutes. Once the griddle is hot, apply a thin layer of vegetable oil or non-stick cooking spray to prevent sticking.
3. **Cook the Shrimp:**
    a. Place the marinated shrimp on the hot griddle in a single layer. Cook for about 2-3 minutes on each side until the shrimp are pink and opaque. Use a spatula to turn the shrimp halfway through the cooking time.
    b. Once cooked, move the shrimp to a cooler zone of the griddle to keep warm.
4. **Make the Sauce:**
    a. On the hot zone of the griddle, add the remaining 2 tablespoons of olive oil. Add the white wine (or chicken broth) and lemon juice to deglaze the griddle, scraping up any browned bits with a spatula. Let the liquid reduce for about 1-2 minutes.
    b. Add the butter to the griddle and stir until melted and combined with the sauce.
5. **Combine and Finish:** Move the shrimp back to the hot zone and toss to coat in the sauce. Sprinkle with fresh parsley and give it a final toss to combine all flavors.

Grilled Tuna Steaks with Sesame Crust

Yield: 4 servings **Preparation Time:** 15 minutes **Cooking Time:** 10 minutes

Ingredients:

For the Tuna Steaks:

- 4 tuna steaks (6 oz each, about 1 inch thick)
- 2 tablespoons soy sauce
- 1 tablespoon sesame oil
- 1 tablespoon rice vinegar
- 2 tablespoons black sesame seeds
- 2 tablespoons white sesame seeds
- Salt and pepper to taste

For the Griddle:

- 2 tablespoons vegetable oil or non-stick cooking spray

Nutritional Information (per serving):

- Calories: 310
- Protein: 38g
- Carbohydrates: 2g
- Fats: 16g
- Fiber: 1g

Instructions:

1. **Marinate the Tuna:** In a shallow dish, combine the soy sauce, sesame oil, and rice vinegar. Add the tuna steaks, turning to coat evenly. Marinate for about 10 minutes.
2. **Prepare the Sesame Crust:** On a plate, mix the black and white sesame seeds. Remove the tuna steaks from the marinade and press each steak into the sesame seeds, coating both sides evenly. Season lightly with salt and pepper.
3. **Preheat the Gas Griddle:** Set your gas griddle to high heat (approximately 450°F). Allow it to preheat for about 5 minutes. Once the griddle is hot, apply a thin layer of vegetable oil or non-stick cooking spray to prevent sticking.
4. **Cook the Tuna Steaks:**
    a. Place the sesame-crusted tuna steaks on the hot griddle. Cook for about 2-3 minutes on the first side. Do not move the steaks around; let them cook undisturbed to develop a nice sear.
    b. Using a wide spatula, carefully flip the steaks and cook for another 2-3 minutes on the other side. For medium-rare tuna, the center should remain pink.
5. **Zone Cooking Tip:** If your griddle has zones, use the high heat zone for searing the tuna and a medium heat zone to finish cooking if needed. This technique ensures the tuna is seared on the outside but remains tender on the inside.
6. **Serving:** Remove the tuna steaks from the griddle and let them rest for a minute before serving.

Grilled Lobster Tails with Garlic Butter

Yield: 4 servings **Preparation Time:** 15 minutes **Cooking Time:** 10 minutes

Ingredients:

For the Lobster Tails:

- 4 lobster tails (6-8 oz each)
- 1/4 cup olive oil
- Salt and pepper to taste

For the Garlic Butter:

- 1/2 cup unsalted butter
- 4 cloves garlic, minced

- 1 tablespoon fresh lemon juice
- 1 tablespoon fresh parsley, chopped
- 1/4 teaspoon salt
- 1/4 teaspoon black pepper

For the Griddle:

- 2 tablespoons vegetable oil or non-stick cooking spray

Nutritional Information (per serving):

- Calories: 350
- Protein: 25g
- Carbohydrates: 2g
- Fats: 27g
- Fiber: 0g

Instructions:

1. **Prepare the Lobster Tails:** Using kitchen shears, cut through the top shell of each lobster tail, stopping at the base of the tail. Carefully pull the shell apart to expose the meat. Lift the meat slightly, leaving it attached at the base, and place it on top of the shell for easy grilling. Brush the meat with olive oil and season with salt and pepper.
2. **Prepare the Garlic Butter:** In a small saucepan, melt the butter over medium heat. Add the minced garlic and cook for 1-2 minutes until fragrant. Remove from heat and stir in the lemon juice, parsley, salt, and pepper. Keep warm.
3. **Preheat the Gas Griddle:** Set your gas griddle to medium-high heat (approximately 375-400°F). Allow it to preheat for about 5 minutes. Once the griddle is hot, apply a thin layer of vegetable oil or non-stick cooking spray to prevent sticking.
4. **Cook the Lobster Tails:**
    a. Place the lobster tails on the hot griddle, meat-side down. Cook for 4-5 minutes until the meat is opaque and has a slight char.
    b. Using tongs, carefully flip the lobster tails shell-side down. Brush the meat with the garlic butter and cook for another 4-5 minutes, basting occasionally with more garlic butter, until the lobster meat is fully cooked and reaches an internal temperature of 135°F.
5. **Zone Cooking Tip:** If your griddle has zones, use a medium-high heat zone for cooking the lobster tails and a lower heat zone to keep the garlic butter warm. This technique ensures even cooking and prevents the butter from burning.
6. **Serving:** Remove the lobster tails from the griddle and brush with any remaining garlic butter. Let them rest for a minute before serving.

Griddled Scallops with Lemon Butter

Yield: 4 servings **Preparation Time:** 10 minutes **Cooking Time:** 10 minutes

Ingredients:

For the Scallops:

- 1 1/2 pounds large sea scallops (about 16-20 scallops)
- 2 tablespoons olive oil
- Salt and pepper to taste
- 1 tablespoon vegetable oil or non-stick cooking spray for the griddle

For the Lemon Butter:

- 1/4 cup unsalted butter
- 2 tablespoons fresh lemon juice
- 1 tablespoon fresh parsley, chopped
- 1 teaspoon lemon zest
- Salt and pepper to taste

Nutritional Information (per serving):

- Calories: 250
- Protein: 25g
- Carbohydrates: 3g
- Fats: 16g
- Fiber: 0g

Instructions:

1. **Prepare the Scallops:** Pat the scallops dry with paper towels to remove excess moisture. Season both sides with salt and pepper. Brush the scallops with olive oil to coat evenly.
2. **Prepare the Lemon Butter:** In a small saucepan, melt the butter over medium heat. Add the lemon juice, parsley, lemon zest, salt, and pepper. Stir to combine and keep warm.
3. **Preheat the Gas Griddle:** Set your gas griddle to medium-high heat (approximately 375-400°F). Allow it to preheat for about 5 minutes. Once the griddle is hot, apply a thin layer of vegetable oil or non-stick cooking spray to prevent sticking.
4. **Cook the Scallops:**
    a. Place the scallops on the hot griddle in a single layer, ensuring they do not touch. Cook for 2-3 minutes without moving them to achieve a nice sear.
    b. Using tongs or a spatula, carefully flip each scallop and cook for an additional 2-3 minutes until the scallops are opaque and firm to the touch. The internal temperature should reach 115-120°F.
5. **Zone Cooking Tip:** If your griddle has zones, use the high heat zone for searing the scallops and a medium heat zone to finish cooking them if needed. This technique ensures a perfect sear without overcooking.

6. **Finish with Lemon Butter:** Once the scallops are cooked, remove them from the griddle and transfer them to a serving plate. Drizzle the warm lemon butter over the scallops.

Grilled Swordfish with Mango Salsa

Yield: 4 servings **Preparation Time:** 20 minutes **Cooking Time:** 10 minutes

Ingredients:

For the Swordfish:

- 4 swordfish steaks (6 oz each, about 1 inch thick)
- 2 tablespoons olive oil
- Salt and pepper to taste
- 1 teaspoon paprika
- 1 tablespoon vegetable oil or non-stick cooking spray for the griddle

For the Mango Salsa:

- 1 ripe mango, peeled, pitted, and diced
- 1/2 red bell pepper, diced
- 1/4 red onion, finely chopped
- 1 small jalapeño, seeded and finely chopped
- 2 tablespoons fresh cilantro, chopped
- 1 tablespoon fresh lime juice
- Salt and pepper to taste

Nutritional Information (per serving):

- Calories: 320
- Protein: 32g
- Carbohydrates: 12g
- Fats: 16g
- Fiber: 2g

Instructions:

1. **Prepare the Mango Salsa:** In a medium bowl, combine the diced mango, red bell pepper, red onion, jalapeño, cilantro, and lime juice. Season with salt and pepper to taste. Mix well and set aside to let the flavors meld.
2. **Prepare the Swordfish:** Pat the swordfish steaks dry with paper towels. Brush both sides of each steak with olive oil. Season with salt, pepper, and paprika.
3. **Preheat the Gas Griddle:** Set your gas griddle to medium-high heat (approximately 375-400°F). Allow it to preheat for about 5 minutes. Once the griddle is hot, apply a thin layer of vegetable oil or non-stick cooking spray to prevent sticking.
4. **Cook the Swordfish Steaks:**
    a. Place the swordfish steaks on the hot griddle. Cook for about 4-5 minutes on the first side without moving them to develop a nice sear.
    b. Using a spatula, carefully flip the steaks and cook for an additional 4-5 minutes on the other side until the fish is opaque and flakes easily with a fork. The internal temperature should reach 145°F.
5. **Zone Cooking Tip:** If your griddle has zones, use the high heat zone for searing the swordfish and a medium heat zone to finish cooking them if needed. This technique ensures a perfect sear without overcooking.
6. **Serving:** Remove the swordfish steaks from the griddle and let them rest for a minute before serving. Top each steak with a generous spoonful of mango salsa.

Griddled Shrimp Fajitas

Yield: 4 servings **Preparation Time:** 20 minutes **Cooking Time:** 15 minutes

Ingredients:

For the Shrimp:

- 1 1/2 pounds large shrimp, peeled and deveined
- 2 tablespoons olive oil
- 2 tablespoons lime juice
- 1 teaspoon chili powder
- 1 teaspoon paprika
- 1/2 teaspoon cumin
- 1/2 teaspoon garlic powder
- Salt and pepper to taste

For the Vegetables:

- 1 red bell pepper, sliced into strips
- 1 yellow bell pepper, sliced into strips
- 1 green bell pepper, sliced into strips
- 1 large onion, sliced into strips
- 2 tablespoons olive oil
- Salt and pepper to taste

For the Griddle:

- 1 tablespoon vegetable oil or non-stick cooking spray

For Serving:

- 8 small flour tortillas
- 1/2 cup sour cream
- 1/2 cup salsa
- 1/4 cup fresh cilantro, chopped
- 1 lime, cut into wedges

Nutritional Information (per serving):

- Calories: 370
- Protein: 28g
- Carbohydrates: 38g
- Fats: 12g
- Fiber: 4g

Instructions:

1. **Prepare the Shrimp Marinade:** In a bowl, combine the shrimp, olive oil, lime juice, chili powder, paprika, cumin, garlic powder, salt, and pepper. Toss to coat the shrimp evenly and let it marinate for 10-15 minutes.
2. **Prepare the Vegetables:** In a separate bowl, toss the sliced bell peppers and onion with olive oil, salt, and pepper.
3. **Preheat the Gas Griddle:** Set your gas griddle to medium-high heat (approximately 375-400°F). Allow it to preheat for about 5 minutes. Once the griddle is hot, apply a thin layer of vegetable oil or non-stick cooking spray to prevent sticking.
4. **Cook the Vegetables:** Place the bell peppers and onion on the hot griddle. Cook for about 6-8 minutes, stirring occasionally, until the vegetables are tender and slightly charred. Move the cooked vegetables to a cooler zone of the griddle to keep warm.
5. **Cook the Shrimp:** Place the marinated shrimp on the hot griddle. Cook for about 2-3 minutes on each side until the shrimp are pink and opaque. Use a spatula to turn the shrimp halfway through the cooking time. Combine the shrimp with the cooked vegetables on the cooler zone of the griddle.
6. **Zone Cooking Tip:** Utilize different heat zones on your griddle: a high heat zone for searing the shrimp and a medium heat zone for cooking the vegetables. This technique ensures everything is cooked perfectly and prevents overcooking.
7. **Warm the Tortillas:** Place the flour tortillas on the griddle for about 30 seconds on each side to warm them up.
8. **Serving:** Remove the shrimp, vegetables, and tortillas from the griddle. Serve the shrimp and vegetables in the warmed tortillas. Top with sour cream, salsa, fresh cilantro, and a squeeze of lime juice.

Grilled Clams with White Wine Sauce

Yield: 4 servings **Preparation Time:** 15 minutes **Cooking Time:** 15 minutes

Ingredients:

For the Clams:

- 4 pounds littleneck or Manila clams, scrubbed and rinsed
- 2 tablespoons olive oil
- 1/2 teaspoon salt
- 1/2 teaspoon black pepper

For the White Wine Sauce:

- 1/2 cup dry white wine
- 2 tablespoons unsalted butter
- 4 cloves garlic, minced
- 1/4 teaspoon red pepper flakes (optional)
- 1 lemon, juiced
- 2 tablespoons fresh parsley, chopped
- Salt and pepper to taste

For the Griddle:

- 1 tablespoon vegetable oil or non-stick cooking spray

Nutritional Information (per serving):

- Calories: 280
- Protein: 25g
- Carbohydrates: 10g
- Fats: 12g
- Fiber: 0g

Instructions:

1. **Prepare the Clams:** Ensure all clams are scrubbed and rinsed thoroughly. Discard any clams that are cracked or do not close when tapped.
2. **Preheat the Gas Griddle:** Set your gas griddle to medium-high heat (approximately 375-400°F). Allow it to preheat for about 5 minutes. Once the griddle is hot, apply a thin layer of vegetable oil or non-stick cooking spray to prevent sticking.
3. **Cook the Clams:** Place the clams on the hot griddle. Cook for about 6-8 minutes, turning occasionally, until the clams open. Discard any clams that do not open after cooking.
4. **Make the White Wine Sauce:**
   a. On a cooler zone of the griddle, place a small, heat-resistant pan. Add the olive oil and butter, allowing the butter to melt.
   b. Add the minced garlic and red pepper flakes (if using). Cook for 1-2 minutes until fragrant.
   c. Pour in the white wine and lemon juice, stirring to combine. Let the sauce simmer for 3-4 minutes until slightly reduced. Season with salt and pepper to taste.
   d. Stir in the chopped parsley and remove from heat.
5. **Combine and Serve:** Once the clams are cooked, transfer them to a serving bowl. Pour the white wine sauce over the clams, ensuring they are well-coated.

Griddled Teriyaki Salmon

Yield: 4 servings **Preparation Time:** 15 minutes (plus 30 minutes for marinating) **Cooking Time:** 15 minutes

Ingredients:

For the Salmon:

- 4 salmon fillets (6 oz each, skin on)
- 2 tablespoons vegetable oil or non-stick cooking spray

For the Teriyaki Marinade:

- 1/2 cup soy sauce
- 1/4 cup mirin (Japanese sweet rice wine)
- 1/4 cup sake (or substitute with dry white wine)
- 1/4 cup brown sugar
- 2 tablespoons honey
- 1 tablespoon fresh ginger, grated
- 2 cloves garlic, minced
- 1 tablespoon cornstarch (optional, for thicker sauce)
- 2 tablespoons water (optional, for thickening sauce)

For Garnish:

- 2 tablespoons sesame seeds
- 2 green onions, finely sliced

Nutritional Information (per serving):

- Calories: 380
- Protein: 32g
- Carbohydrates: 25g
- Fats: 18g
- Fiber: 1g

Instructions:

1. **Prepare the Teriyaki Marinade:** In a small saucepan, combine soy sauce, mirin, sake, brown sugar, honey, ginger, and garlic. Bring to a boil over medium heat, then reduce the heat and simmer for 5-7 minutes until slightly reduced. For a thicker sauce, dissolve cornstarch in water and add to the simmering sauce. Cook for an additional 1-2 minutes until thickened. Let the sauce cool to room temperature.
2. **Marinate the Salmon:** Place the salmon fillets in a shallow dish or resealable plastic bag. Pour half of the cooled teriyaki sauce over the salmon, reserving the other half for basting and serving. Marinate the salmon in the refrigerator for at least 30 minutes.
3. **Preheat the Gas Griddle:** Set your gas griddle to medium-high heat (approximately 375-400°F). Allow it to preheat for about 5 minutes. Once the griddle is hot, apply a thin layer of vegetable oil or non-stick cooking spray to prevent sticking.
4. **Cook the Salmon:**
   a. Remove the salmon from the marinade, letting any excess drip off. Place the salmon fillets on the hot griddle, skin side down. Cook for about 4-5 minutes without moving them to develop a nice sear.
   b. Carefully flip the salmon fillets using a spatula. Baste the salmon with some of the reserved teriyaki sauce. Cook for an additional 3-4 minutes until the salmon is opaque and flakes easily with a fork.
   c. **Zone Cooking Tip:** If your griddle has zones, use the medium-high heat zone for searing the salmon and a lower heat zone to finish cooking them if needed. This technique ensures the salmon is seared on the outside but remains tender and juicy on the inside.
5. **Garnish and Serve:** Transfer the cooked salmon to a serving plate. Drizzle with the remaining teriyaki sauce and sprinkle with sesame seeds and sliced green onions.

Grilled Octopus with Garlic and Olive Oil

Yield: 4 servings **Preparation Time:** 20 minutes (plus 1 hour for boiling octopus) **Cooking Time:** 10 minutes

Ingredients:

For the Octopus:

- 2 pounds octopus, cleaned
- 1 lemon, halved
- 1 bay leaf
- 4 garlic cloves, smashed
- 1 tablespoon black peppercorns
- 1/4 cup olive oil
- Salt and pepper to taste

For the Garlic and Olive Oil Sauce:

- 1/4 cup olive oil
- 4 cloves garlic, minced
- 2 tablespoons fresh parsley, chopped
- 1 tablespoon lemon juice
- Salt and pepper to taste

For the Griddle:

- 1 tablespoon vegetable oil or non-stick cooking spray

Nutritional Information (per serving):

- Calories: 350
- Protein: 35g
- Carbohydrates: 4g
- Fats: 20g
- Fiber: 1g

Instructions:

1. **Boil the Octopus:** In a large pot, bring water to a boil. Add the lemon halves, bay leaf, smashed garlic cloves, and black peppercorns. Submerge the octopus in the boiling water and cook for about 45 minutes to 1 hour, until the octopus is tender. Remove from water, drain, and let cool slightly. Cut the octopus into manageable pieces, such as tentacles and body sections.
2. **Prepare the Garlic and Olive Oil Sauce:** In a small saucepan, heat the olive oil over medium heat. Add the minced garlic and cook until fragrant, about 1-2 minutes. Remove from heat, stir in the chopped parsley and lemon juice, and season with salt and pepper. Set aside.
3. **Preheat the Gas Griddle:** Set your gas griddle to high heat (approximately 450°F). Allow it to preheat for about 5 minutes.
4. **Prepare the Octopus:** Toss the boiled octopus pieces in olive oil and season with salt and pepper. Once the griddle is hot, apply a thin layer of vegetable oil or non-stick cooking spray to prevent sticking.
5. **Grill the Octopus:** Place the octopus pieces on the hot griddle. Cook for about 3-4 minutes on each side until the octopus is charred and crispy on the edges. Use a spatula to turn the octopus halfway through the cooking time.
6. **Zone Cooking Tip:** If your griddle has zones, use the high heat zone for searing the octopus and a medium heat zone to keep the octopus warm while finishing the rest. This technique ensures the octopus is seared on the outside but remains tender inside.
7. **Serving:** Remove the octopus from the griddle and transfer it to a serving plate. Drizzle the garlic and olive oil sauce over the top.

Grilled Shrimp and Avocado Salad

Yield: 4 servings **Preparation Time:** 20 minutes **Cooking Time:** 10 minutes

Ingredients:

For the Shrimp:

- 1 1/2 pounds large shrimp, peeled and deveined
- 2 tablespoons olive oil
- 1 tablespoon lime juice
- 2 cloves garlic, minced
- 1 teaspoon paprika
- 1/2 teaspoon cumin
- Salt and pepper to taste

For the Salad:

- 2 avocados, diced
- 1 cup cherry tomatoes, halved
- 1/4 red onion, thinly sliced
- 1/4 cup fresh cilantro, chopped
- 4 cups mixed greens (arugula, spinach, or spring mix)

For the Dressing:

- 3 tablespoons olive oil
- 2 tablespoons lime juice
- 1 tablespoon honey
- 1 teaspoon Dijon mustard
- Salt and pepper to taste

For the Griddle:

- 1 tablespoon vegetable oil or non-stick cooking spray

Nutritional Information (per serving):

- Calories: 380
- Protein: 30g
- Carbohydrates: 15g
- Fats: 25g
- Fiber: 7g

Instructions:

1. **Marinate the Shrimp:** In a bowl, combine the shrimp, olive oil, lime juice, minced garlic, paprika, cumin, salt, and pepper. Toss to coat evenly and let it marinate for 10-15 minutes.
2. **Prepare the Dressing:** In a small bowl, whisk together the olive oil, lime juice, honey, Dijon mustard, salt, and pepper. Set aside.
3. **Preheat the Gas Griddle:** Set your gas griddle to medium-high heat (approximately 375-400°F). Allow it to preheat for about 5 minutes.Once the griddle is hot, apply a thin layer of vegetable oil or non-stick cooking spray to prevent sticking.
4. **Cook the Shrimp:** Place the marinated shrimp on the hot griddle. Cook for about 2-3 minutes on each side until the shrimp are pink and opaque. Use a spatula to turn the shrimp halfway through the cooking time.
5. **Zone Cooking Tip:** If your griddle has zones, use the medium-high heat zone for cooking the shrimp and a lower heat zone to keep them warm while you assemble the salad.

6. **Assemble the Salad:** In a large salad bowl, combine the mixed greens, diced avocado, cherry tomatoes, red onion, and cilantro. Add the cooked shrimp on top of the salad ingredients.
7. **Dress the Salad:** Drizzle the prepared dressing over the salad and toss gently to combine.

Grilled Sea Bass with Lemon Butter

Yield: 4 servings **Preparation Time:** 15 minutes **Cooking Time:** 15 minutes

Ingredients:

For the Sea Bass:

- 4 sea bass fillets (6 oz each)
- 2 tablespoons olive oil
- Salt and pepper to taste

For the Lemon Butter:

- 1/4 cup unsalted butter
- 2 tablespoons fresh lemon juice
- 1 teaspoon lemon zest
- 2 cloves garlic, minced
- 1 tablespoon fresh parsley, chopped
- Salt and pepper to taste

For the Griddle:

- 1 tablespoon vegetable oil or non-stick cooking spray

Nutritional Information (per serving):

- Calories: 320
- Protein: 30g
- Carbohydrates: 2g
- Fats: 20g
- Fiber: 1g

Instructions:

1. **Prepare the Lemon Butter:** In a small saucepan, melt the butter over medium heat. Add the minced garlic and cook until fragrant, about 1-2 minutes. Stir in the lemon juice, lemon zest, and parsley. Season with salt and pepper to taste. Keep warm.
2. **Prepare the Sea Bass:** Pat the sea bass fillets dry with paper towels. Brush both sides of each fillet with olive oil and season with salt and pepper.
3. **Preheat the Gas Griddle:** Set your gas griddle to medium-high heat (approximately 375-400°F). Allow it to preheat for about 5 minutes. Once the griddle is hot, apply a thin layer of vegetable oil or non-stick cooking spray to prevent sticking.
4. **Cook the Sea Bass:** Place the sea bass fillets on the hot griddle, skin side down. Cook for about 4-5 minutes without moving them to develop a nice sear. Carefully flip the fillets using a spatula. Cook for an additional 3-4 minutes until the fish is opaque and flakes easily with a fork. The internal temperature should reach 145°F.
5. **Zone Cooking Tip:** If your griddle has zones, use the medium-high heat zone for searing the sea bass and a lower heat zone to keep the fillets warm while finishing the rest. This technique ensures the sea bass is seared on the outside but remains tender and juicy on the inside.
6. **Final Touch:** Just before removing the sea bass from the griddle, brush with a little of the lemon butter sauce for extra flavor.
7. **Serving:** Remove the sea bass fillets from the griddle and transfer them to a serving plate. Drizzle the warm lemon butter sauce over the top.

Griddled Seafood Paella

Yield: 6 servings **Preparation Time:** 20 minutes **Cooking Time:** 30 minutes

Ingredients:

For the Paella:

- 1 1/2 cups Arborio rice
- 4 cups chicken or seafood broth
- 1/2 teaspoon saffron threads
- 1/4 cup olive oil
- 1 onion, finely chopped
- 4 cloves garlic, minced
- 1 red bell pepper, diced
- 1 green bell pepper, diced
- 1 cup diced tomatoes
- 1 teaspoon smoked paprika
- 1 teaspoon salt
- 1/2 teaspoon black pepper
- 1/2 cup frozen peas, thawed
- 12 large shrimp, peeled and deveined
- 12 mussels, scrubbed
- 12 clams, scrubbed
- 1/2 pound calamari rings
- Lemon wedges, for serving
- Fresh parsley, chopped, for garnish

For the Griddle:

- 2 tablespoons vegetable oil or non-stick cooking spray

Nutritional Information (per serving):

- Calories: 420
- Protein: 30g
- Carbohydrates: 40g
- Fats: 15g
- Fiber: 4g

Instructions:

1. **Prepare the Broth:** Heat the chicken or seafood broth in a saucepan until warm. Add the saffron threads and let it steep for a few minutes.
2. **Preheat the Gas Griddle:** Set your gas griddle to medium-high heat (approximately 375-400°F). Allow it to preheat for about 5 minutes.
3. **Cook the Vegetables:** Once the griddle is hot, apply a thin layer of vegetable oil or non-stick cooking spray. Add the olive oil, chopped onion, garlic, and diced bell peppers to the griddle. Cook for about 5 minutes until the vegetables are softened and fragrant.
4. **Add the Rice and Spices:** Add the Arborio rice to the vegetable mixture and stir to coat the rice in the oil. Cook for 2-3 minutes until the rice is slightly toasted. Stir in the diced tomatoes, smoked paprika, salt, and black pepper.
5. **Add the Broth:** Slowly add the warm broth with saffron to the rice mixture, stirring to combine. Spread the rice mixture evenly across the griddle surface.
6. **Cook the Paella:** Reduce the heat to medium and cook the rice mixture for about 15-20 minutes, stirring occasionally, until the rice is tender and has absorbed most of the liquid. If necessary, add more broth or water to keep the rice from drying out.
7. **Add the Seafood:** Arrange the shrimp, mussels, clams, and calamari rings on top of the rice mixture. Cover with a large, heatproof lid or aluminum foil to create an oven-like environment. Cook for about 5-7 minutes until the seafood is cooked through and the mussels and clams have opened. Discard any mussels or clams that do not open.
8. **Finish the Paella:** Sprinkle the thawed peas over the top and cook for an additional 2 minutes until the peas are heated through.
9. **Serve:** Remove the paella from the griddle and transfer it to a serving platter. Garnish with fresh parsley and lemon wedges.

Burgers and Skewers

Classic Griddled Cheeseburgers

Yield: 4 servings **Preparation Time:** 15 minutes **Cooking Time:** 10 minutes

Ingredients:

For the Cheeseburgers:

- 1 1/2 pounds ground beef (80% lean)
- Salt and pepper to taste
- 4 slices cheddar cheese
- 4 burger buns
- 1 tablespoon olive oil

For the Toppings:

- 1 large tomato, sliced
- 4 leaves of lettuce
- 4 slices of red onion
- Pickles, as desired
- Ketchup, mustard, and mayonnaise, as desired

For the Griddle:

- 2 tablespoons vegetable oil or non-stick cooking spray

Nutritional Information (per serving):

- Calories: 550
- Protein: 35g
- Carbohydrates: 30g
- Fats: 30g
- Fiber: 2g

Instructions:

1. **Form the Patties:** Divide the ground beef into 4 equal portions and shape each portion into a patty, about 3/4 inch thick. Make a slight indentation in the center of each patty to prevent them from puffing up during cooking. Season both sides with salt and pepper.
2. **Preheat the Gas Griddle:** Set your gas griddle to high heat (approximately 450°F). Allow it to preheat for about 5 minutes. Once the griddle is hot, apply a thin layer of vegetable oil or non-stick cooking spray to prevent sticking.
3. **Cook the Patties:** Place the burger patties on the hot griddle. Cook for about 3-4 minutes on the first side without pressing them down, to develop a nice sear. Flip the patties using a spatula and cook for another 3-4 minutes on the

other side, or until they reach the desired doneness. During the last minute of cooking, place a slice of cheddar cheese on each patty and cover with a lid or dome to melt the cheese.

4. **Warm the Buns:** While the patties are cooking, lightly brush the cut sides of the burger buns with olive oil. Place them on the griddle for about 1-2 minutes until they are toasted and golden brown.
5. **Assemble the Burgers:** Place a lettuce leaf on the bottom half of each toasted bun, followed by a tomato slice and a slice of red onion. Place the cooked patties with melted cheese on top of the vegetables. Add pickles and any desired condiments (ketchup, mustard, mayonnaise). Top with the other half of the bun.
6. **Serve:** Serve the cheeseburgers immediately with your favorite side dishes.

Griddled BBQ Bacon Burgers

Yield: 4 servings **Preparation Time:** 20 minutes **Cooking Time:** 20 minutes

Ingredients:

For the Burgers:

- 1 1/2 pounds ground beef (80% lean)
- 8 slices bacon
- 1/2 cup barbecue sauce
- 4 slices cheddar cheese
- 4 burger buns
- 1 tablespoon olive oil
- Salt and pepper to taste

For the Toppings:

- 1 large tomato, sliced
- 4 leaves of lettuce
- 1/2 red onion, thinly sliced
- Pickles, as desired
- Additional barbecue sauce, for serving

For the Griddle:

- 2 tablespoons vegetable oil or non-stick cooking spray

Nutritional Information (per serving):

- Calories: 700
- Protein: 40g
- Carbohydrates: 45g
- Fats: 40g
- Fiber: 3g

Instructions:

1. **Prepare the Bacon:** Preheat the gas griddle to medium-high heat (approximately 375-400°F). Allow it to preheat for about 5 minutes. Once the griddle is hot, cook the bacon slices until crispy, about 3-4 minutes per side. Remove the bacon from the griddle and place on paper towels to drain excess grease. Set aside.
2. **Form the Patties:** Divide the ground beef into 4 equal portions and shape each portion into a patty, about 3/4 inch thick. Make a slight indentation in the center of each patty to prevent them from puffing up during cooking. Season both sides with salt and pepper.
3. **Cook the Patties:** Apply a thin layer of vegetable oil or non-stick cooking spray to the griddle to prevent sticking. Place the burger patties on the hot griddle. Cook for about 3-4 minutes on the first side without pressing them down, to develop a nice sear. Flip the patties using a spatula and cook for another 3-4 minutes on the other side, or until they reach the desired doneness. During the last minute of cooking, brush each patty with barbecue sauce and place a slice of cheddar cheese on top. Cover with a lid or dome to melt the cheese.
4. **Warm the Buns:** While the patties are cooking, lightly brush the cut sides of the burger buns with olive oil. Place them on the griddle for about 1-2 minutes until they are toasted and golden brown.
5. **Assemble the Burgers:** Place a lettuce leaf on the bottom half of each toasted bun, followed by a tomato slice and a slice of red onion. Place the cooked patties with melted cheese on top of the vegetables. Add two slices of crispy bacon on each patty. Add pickles and additional barbecue sauce if desired. Place the top half of the bun on the assembled burger.
6. **Serve:** Serve the BBQ bacon burgers immediately with your favorite side dishes.

Grilled Turkey Burgers with Avocado

Yield: 4 servings **Preparation Time:** 15 minutes **Cooking Time:** 10 minutes

Ingredients:

For the Turkey Burgers:

- 1 1/2 pounds ground turkey
- 1/4 cup breadcrumbs
- 1/4 cup finely chopped red onion
- 2 cloves garlic, minced
- 1 tablespoon Worcestershire sauce
- 1 tablespoon Dijon mustard
- 1 egg, beaten
- 1 teaspoon salt

- 1/2 teaspoon black pepper

For the Toppings:

- 1 large avocado, sliced
- 4 leaves of lettuce
- 1 large tomato, sliced
- 1/2 red onion, thinly sliced
- 4 whole wheat burger buns
- 1 tablespoon olive oil

For the Griddle:

- 2 tablespoons vegetable oil or non-stick cooking spray

Nutritional Information (per serving):

- Calories: 450
- Protein: 35g
- Carbohydrates: 30g
- Fats: 20g
- Fiber: 6g

Instructions:

1. **Prepare the Turkey Burger Mixture:** In a large bowl, combine the ground turkey, breadcrumbs, red onion, minced garlic, Worcestershire sauce, Dijon mustard, beaten egg, salt, and pepper. Mix well until all ingredients are thoroughly combined.
2. **Form the Patties:** Divide the mixture into 4 equal portions and shape each portion into a patty, about 3/4 inch thick. Place the patties on a plate and refrigerate for at least 15 minutes to help them firm up.
3. **Preheat the Gas Griddle:** Set your gas griddle to medium-high heat (approximately 375-400°F). Allow it to preheat for about 5 minutes. Once the griddle is hot, apply a thin layer of vegetable oil or non-stick cooking spray to prevent sticking.
4. **Cook the Turkey Patties:** Place the turkey patties on the hot griddle. Cook for about 4-5 minutes on the first side without moving them, to develop a nice sear. Using a spatula, carefully flip the patties and cook for an additional 4-5 minutes until the patties are golden brown and cooked through. The internal temperature should reach 165°F.
5. **Warm the Buns:** While the patties are cooking, lightly brush the cut sides of the burger buns with olive oil. Place them on the griddle for about 1-2 minutes until they are toasted and golden brown.
6. **Assemble the Burgers:** Place a lettuce leaf on the bottom half of each toasted bun, followed by a turkey patty, a slice of tomato, a slice of red onion, and avocado slices. Place the top half of the bun on the assembled burger.
7. **Serve:** Serve the turkey burgers immediately with your favorite side dishes.

Griddled Lamb Burgers with Tzatziki

Yield: 4 servings **Preparation Time:** 20 minutes **Cooking Time:** 10 minutes

Ingredients:

For the Lamb Burgers:

- 1 1/2 pounds ground lamb
- 1/4 cup finely chopped red onion
- 2 cloves garlic, minced
- 1 tablespoon fresh mint, chopped
- 1 tablespoon fresh parsley, chopped
- 1 teaspoon ground cumin
- 1 teaspoon ground coriander
- 1 teaspoon salt
- 1/2 teaspoon black pepper

For the Tzatziki Sauce:

- 1 cup Greek yogurt
- 1/2 cucumber, grated, and excess water squeezed out
- 1 tablespoon lemon juice
- 1 tablespoon olive oil
- 1 clove garlic, minced
- 1 tablespoon fresh dill, chopped
- Salt and pepper to taste

For the Toppings:

- 4 whole wheat burger buns
- 1 large tomato, sliced
- 4 leaves of lettuce
- 1/2 red onion, thinly sliced
- 1/2 cup crumbled feta cheese

For the Griddle:

- 2 tablespoons vegetable oil or non-stick cooking spray

Nutritional Information (per serving):

- Calories: 550
- Protein: 35g
- Carbohydrates: 40g
- Fats: 28g
- Fiber: 4g

Instructions:

1. **Prepare the Tzatziki Sauce:** In a medium bowl, combine the Greek yogurt, grated cucumber, lemon juice, olive oil, minced garlic, fresh dill, salt, and pepper. Mix well and refrigerate until ready to use.

2. **Prepare the Lamb Burger Mixture:** In a large bowl, combine the ground lamb, chopped red onion, minced garlic, fresh mint, fresh parsley, ground cumin, ground coriander, salt, and pepper. Mix until all ingredients are thoroughly combined.
3. **Form the Patties:** Divide the mixture into 4 equal portions and shape each portion into a patty, about 3/4 inch thick. Make a slight indentation in the center of each patty to prevent them from puffing up during cooking.
4. **Preheat the Gas Griddle:** Set your gas griddle to medium-high heat (approximately 375-400°F). Allow it to preheat for about 5 minutes. Once the griddle is hot, apply a thin layer of vegetable oil or non-stick cooking spray to prevent sticking.
5. **Cook the Lamb Patties:** Place the lamb patties on the hot griddle. Cook for about 4-5 minutes on the first side without pressing them down, to develop a nice sear. Using a spatula, carefully flip the patties and cook for an additional 4-5 minutes until the patties are cooked through and reach an internal temperature of 160°F.
6. **Warm the Buns:** While the patties are cooking, place the burger buns, cut side down, on the griddle for about 1-2 minutes until they are toasted and golden brown.
7. **Assemble the Burgers:** Place a lettuce leaf on the bottom half of each toasted bun, followed by a slice of tomato and a slice of red onion. Place the cooked lamb patties on top of the vegetables. Top each patty with a generous spoonful of tzatziki sauce and some crumbled feta cheese. Place the top half of the bun on the assembled burger.
8. **Serve:** Serve the lamb burgers immediately with your favorite side dishes.

Grilled BBQ Pork Burgers

Yield: 4 servings **Preparation Time:** 15 minutes **Cooking Time:** 10 minutes

Ingredients:

For the Pork Burgers:

- 1 1/2 pounds ground pork
- 1/4 cup finely chopped red onion
- 2 cloves garlic, minced
- 2 tablespoons barbecue sauce
- 1 tablespoon Worcestershire sauce
- 1 teaspoon smoked paprika
- 1 teaspoon salt
- 1/2 teaspoon black pepper

For the Toppings:

- 4 whole wheat burger buns
- 4 slices cheddar cheese
- 4 slices crispy bacon (optional)
- 1 large tomato, sliced
- 4 leaves of lettuce
- 1/2 red onion, thinly sliced
- Additional barbecue sauce, for serving

For the Griddle:

- 2 tablespoons vegetable oil or non-stick cooking spray

Nutritional Information (per serving):

- Calories: 650
- Protein: 35g
- Carbohydrates: 40g
- Fats: 38g
- Fiber: 3g

Instructions:

1. **Prepare the Pork Burger Mixture:** In a large bowl, combine the ground pork, chopped red onion, minced garlic, barbecue sauce, Worcestershire sauce, smoked paprika, salt, and black pepper. Mix until all ingredients are thoroughly combined.
2. **Form the Patties:** Divide the mixture into 4 equal portions and shape each portion into a patty, about 3/4 inch thick. Make a slight indentation in the center of each patty to prevent them from puffing up during cooking.
3. **Preheat the Gas Griddle:** Set your gas griddle to medium-high heat (approximately 375-400°F). Allow it to preheat for about 5 minutes.
4. **Prepare the Griddle:** Once the griddle is hot, apply a thin layer of vegetable oil or non-stick cooking spray to prevent sticking.
5. **Cook the Pork Patties:** Place the pork patties on the hot griddle. Cook for about 4-5 minutes on the first side without pressing them down, to develop a nice sear. Using a spatula, carefully flip the patties and cook for an additional 4-5 minutes until the patties are cooked through and reach an internal temperature of 160°F. During the last minute of cooking, place a slice of cheddar cheese on each patty and cover with a lid or dome to melt the cheese.
6. **Warm the Buns:** While the patties are cooking, place the burger buns, cut side down, on the griddle for about 1-2 minutes until they are toasted and golden brown.
7. **Assemble the Burgers:** Place a lettuce leaf on the bottom half of each toasted bun, followed by a slice of tomato and a slice of red onion. Place the cooked pork patties with melted cheese on top of the vegetables. Add a slice of crispy bacon if desired. Drizzle additional barbecue sauce on the top half of each bun and place it on the assembled burger.
8. **Serve:** Serve the BBQ pork burgers immediately with your favorite side dishes.

Grilled Jalapeño Cheddar Burgers

Yield: 4 servings **Preparation Time:** 20 minutes **Cooking Time:** 10 minutes

Ingredients:

For the Burgers:

- 1 1/2 pounds ground beef (80% lean)
- 1/2 cup shredded sharp cheddar cheese
- 1/4 cup finely chopped jalapeños (seeds removed for less heat)
- 1/4 cup finely chopped red onion
- 2 cloves garlic, minced
- 1 tablespoon Worcestershire sauce
- 1 teaspoon salt
- 1/2 teaspoon black pepper

For the Toppings:

- 4 burger buns
- 4 slices cheddar cheese
- 1 large tomato, sliced
- 4 leaves of lettuce
- 1/2 red onion, thinly sliced
- Pickled jalapeño slices (optional)
- Mayonnaise, ketchup, and mustard as desired

For the Griddle:

- 2 tablespoons vegetable oil or non-stick cooking spray

Nutritional Information (per serving):

- Calories: 600
- Protein: 40g
- Carbohydrates: 35g
- Fats: 35g
- Fiber: 3g

Instructions:

1. **Prepare the Burger Mixture:** In a large bowl, combine the ground beef, shredded cheddar cheese, chopped jalapeños, chopped red onion, minced garlic, Worcestershire sauce, salt, and black pepper. Mix until all ingredients are thoroughly combined.
2. **Form the Patties:** Divide the mixture into 4 equal portions and shape each portion into a patty, about 3/4 inch thick. Make a slight indentation in the center of each patty to prevent them from puffing up during cooking.
3. **Preheat the Gas Griddle:** Set your gas griddle to medium-high heat (approximately 375-400°F). Allow it to preheat for about 5 minutes.
4. **Prepare the Griddle:** Once the griddle is hot, apply a thin layer of vegetable oil or non-stick cooking spray to prevent sticking.
5. **Cook the Patties:** Place the burger patties on the hot griddle. Cook for about 4-5 minutes on the first side without pressing them down, to develop a nice sear. Using a spatula, carefully flip the patties and cook for an additional 4-5 minutes until the patties are cooked through. During the last minute of cooking, place a slice of cheddar cheese on each patty and cover with a lid or dome to melt the cheese.
6. **Warm the Buns:** While the patties are cooking, place the burger buns, cut side down, on the griddle for about 1-2 minutes until they are toasted and golden brown.
7. **Assemble the Burgers:** Place a lettuce leaf on the bottom half of each toasted bun, followed by a slice of tomato and a slice of red onion. Place the cooked patties with melted cheese on top of the vegetables. Add pickled jalapeño slices if desired. Spread mayonnaise, ketchup, and mustard on the top half of each bun and place it on the assembled burger.
8. **Serve:** Serve the jalapeño cheddar burgers immediately with your favorite side dishes.

Sweet Treats and Desserts

Grilled Pineapple with Brown Sugar

Yield: 4 servings **Preparation Time:** 10 minutes **Cooking Time:** 10 minutes

Ingredients:

- 1 whole pineapple, peeled, cored, and cut into 1/2-inch thick rings
- 1/4 cup brown sugar
- 2 tablespoons melted unsalted butter
- 1 teaspoon ground cinnamon
- 1/2 teaspoon vanilla extract
- Pinch of salt

Nutritional Information (per serving):

- Calories: 150
- Protein: 1g

- Carbohydrates: 30g
- Fats: 4g
- Fiber: 2g

Instructions:

1. **Prepare the Pineapple:** In a large bowl, combine the brown sugar, melted butter, ground cinnamon, vanilla extract, and a pinch of salt. Mix well to create a smooth mixture. Add the pineapple rings to the bowl and toss until they are evenly coated with the sugar mixture.
2. Preheat **the Gas Griddle:** Set your gas griddle to medium-high heat (approximately 375-400°F). Allow it to preheat for about 5 minutes.
3. **Prepare the Griddle:** Once the griddle is hot, apply a thin layer of vegetable oil or non-stick cooking spray to prevent sticking.
4. **Cook the Pineapple:** Place the pineapple rings on the hot griddle in a single layer. Cook for about 3-4 minutes on the first side, until they start to caramelize and have nice grill marks. Using a spatula, carefully flip the pineapple rings and cook for an additional 3-4 minutes on the other side, until they are tender and caramelized.
5. **Serve:** Remove the grilled pineapple from the griddle and transfer it to a serving plate. Serve immediately.

Grilled Peaches with Honey and Yogurt

Yield: 4 servings **Preparation Time:** 10 minutes **Cooking Time:** 8 minutes

Ingredients:

- 4 ripe peaches, halved and pitted
- 2 tablespoons vegetable oil
- 1/4 cup honey
- 1 teaspoon ground cinnamon
- 1 cup Greek yogurt
- 1 teaspoon vanilla extract
- Fresh mint leaves for garnish (optional)

Nutritional Information (per serving):

- Calories: 180
- Protein: 6g
- Carbohydrates: 30g
- Fats: 5g
- Fiber: 2g

Instructions:

1. **Prepare the Peaches:** In a small bowl, mix the honey and ground cinnamon until well combined. Brush the cut sides of the peach halves with vegetable oil to prevent sticking.
2. **Preheat the Gas Griddle:** Set your gas griddle to medium heat (approximately 350°F). Allow it to preheat for about 5 minutes.
3. **Prepare the Griddle:** Once the griddle is hot, apply a thin layer of vegetable oil or non-stick cooking spray to prevent sticking.
4. **Cook the Peaches:** Place the peach halves, cut side down, on the hot griddle. Cook for about 4 minutes until the peaches are softened and have nice grill marks. Flip the peaches and cook for an additional 4 minutes on the other side until the peaches are tender and caramelized.
5. **Prepare the Yogurt:** While the peaches are cooking, in a medium bowl, mix the Greek yogurt with the vanilla extract until smooth and creamy.
6. **Serve:** Remove the grilled peaches from the griddle and place them on a serving platter. Drizzle the honey and cinnamon mixture over the grilled peaches. Serve each peach half with a dollop of vanilla Greek yogurt. Garnish with fresh mint leaves if desired. Griddle cooking for these honey-drizzled grilled peaches provides a quick, even sear that enhances the natural sweetness of the peaches while offering a delicious and beautifully caramelized dish. The open surface of the griddle makes it easy to cook multiple peach halves at once, making this dish both efficient and enjoyable to prepare. Enjoy the flavorful grilled peaches with your favorite meals for a delightful dining experience.

Grilled Pound Cake with Berries

Yield: 4 servings **Preparation Time:** 10 minutes **Cooking Time:** 10 minutes

Ingredients:

- 1 pound cake (store-bought or homemade), cut into 8 slices (about 1 inch thick each)
- 2 cups mixed berries (such as strawberries, blueberries, raspberries)
- 1/4 cup honey
- 1 tablespoon lemon juice

- 1 teaspoon lemon zest
- 1/2 teaspoon vanilla extract
- 2 tablespoons unsalted butter, melted

Nutritional Information (per serving):

- Calories: 400
- Protein: 5g
- Carbohydrates: 60g
- Fats: 15g
- Fiber: 4g

Instructions:

1. **Prepare the Berry Mixture:** In a medium bowl, combine the mixed berries, honey, lemon juice, lemon zest, and vanilla extract. Toss gently to coat the berries evenly. Set aside.
2. **Preheat the Gas Griddle:** Set your gas griddle to medium heat (approximately 350°F). Allow it to preheat for about 5 minutes.
3. **Prepare the Pound Cake Slices:** Brush both sides of each pound cake slice with the melted butter to prevent sticking and to promote even browning.
4. **Grill the Pound Cake:** Once the griddle is hot, place the pound cake slices on the griddle. Cook for about 2-3 minutes on the first side, until they are golden brown and have nice grill marks. Using a spatula, carefully flip the slices and cook for an additional 2-3 minutes on the other side, until they are evenly browned and heated through.
5. **Serve:** Remove the grilled pound cake slices from the griddle and place them on serving plates. Spoon the berry mixture over the top of each slice of grilled pound cake.

Grilled Pears with Caramel Sauce

Yield: 4 servings **Preparation Time:** 10 minutes **Cooking Time:** 10 minutes

Ingredients:

For the Grilled Pears:

- 4 ripe but firm pears, halved and cored
- 2 tablespoons unsalted butter, melted
- 2 tablespoons brown sugar
- 1 teaspoon ground cinnamon

For the Caramel Sauce:

- 1 cup granulated sugar
- 1/4 cup water
- 1/2 cup heavy cream
- 2 tablespoons unsalted butter
- 1/2 teaspoon vanilla extract
- Pinch of salt

Nutritional Information (per serving):

- Calories: 350
- Protein: 1g
- Carbohydrates: 55g
- Fats: 15g
- Fiber: 5g

Instructions:

1. **Prepare the Pears:** In a small bowl, combine the melted butter, brown sugar, and ground cinnamon. Brush the cut sides of the pear halves with the butter mixture.
2. **Preheat the Gas Griddle:** Set your gas griddle to medium heat (approximately 350°F). Allow it to preheat for about 5 minutes.
3. **Grill the Pears:** Once the griddle is hot, place the pear halves cut side down on the griddle. Cook for about 4-5 minutes until the pears are softened and have nice grill marks. Flip the pears and cook for an additional 4-5 minutes on the other side until they are tender.
4. **Prepare the Caramel Sauce:** In a medium saucepan, combine the granulated sugar and water. Cook over medium-high heat, stirring until the sugar dissolves. Stop stirring and let the mixture boil until it turns a deep amber color. Remove from heat and carefully whisk in the heavy cream, butter, vanilla extract, and a pinch of salt. The mixture will bubble up, so be cautious. Return the saucepan to low heat and stir until the sauce is smooth. Keep warm.
5. **Serve:** Remove the grilled pears from the griddle and place them on serving plates. Drizzle the warm caramel sauce over the grilled pears.

Grilled Chocolate Stuffed Marshmallows

Yield: 8 servings **Preparation Time:** 10 minutes **Cooking Time:** 5 minutes

Ingredients:

- 16 large marshmallows
- 8 squares of milk or dark chocolate (about 1 ounce each)

- 16 graham crackers (optional, for serving)
- 2 tablespoons unsalted butter, melted

Nutritional Information (per serving):

- Calories: 150
- Protein: 2g
- Carbohydrates: 28g
- Fats: 5g
- Fiber: 1g

Instructions:

1. **Prepare the Marshmallows:** Using a small knife or kitchen scissors, make a slit in each marshmallow from top to bottom, creating a pocket but not cutting all the way through. Insert a square of chocolate into the slit of each marshmallow, ensuring the chocolate is completely enclosed within the marshmallow.
2. **Preheat the Gas Griddle:** Set your gas griddle to low-medium heat (approximately 300°F). Allow it to preheat for about 5 minutes.
3. **Prepare the Griddle:** Once the griddle is hot, brush it with melted butter to prevent sticking and add flavor.
4. **Grill the Marshmallows:** Place the stuffed marshmallows on the griddle, ensuring the slit side is facing up to prevent the chocolate from melting out. Cook the marshmallows for about 2-3 minutes, until the bottoms are golden brown and slightly crispy. Carefully turn the marshmallows using a spatula or tongs, and cook for an additional 2-3 minutes until they are evenly browned and the chocolate inside is melted.
5. **Serve:** Remove the grilled marshmallows from the griddle and place them on a serving plate. If desired, serve with graham crackers to create a s'mores-like dessert.

Griddled Chocolate Lava Cakes

Yield: 4 servings **Preparation Time:** 15 minutes **Cooking Time:** 10 minutes

Ingredients:

- 4 ounces semi-sweet chocolate, chopped
- 1/2 cup unsalted butter
- 1 cup powdered sugar
- 2 large eggs
- 2 large egg yolks
- 1 teaspoon vanilla extract
- 1/4 cup all-purpose flour
- 1 tablespoon cocoa powder (for dusting)
- Non-stick cooking spray or additional butter for greasing

Nutritional Information (per serving):

- Calories: 450
- Protein: 6g
- Carbohydrates: 45g
- Fats: 28g
- Fiber: 3g

Instructions:

1. **Prepare the Chocolate Mixture:** In a microwave-safe bowl, combine the chopped chocolate and unsalted butter. Microwave in 30-second intervals, stirring between each, until fully melted and smooth. Whisk in the powdered sugar until well combined. Add the eggs, egg yolks, and vanilla extract. Whisk until smooth. Gently fold in the flour until just combined. Do not overmix.
2. **Prepare the Ramekins:** Spray four 6-ounce ramekins with non-stick cooking spray or grease them with butter. Dust the insides with cocoa powder, tapping out any excess. This helps the cakes release easily after cooking.
3. **Preheat the Gas Griddle:** Set your gas griddle to medium-low heat (approximately 300-325°F). Allow it to preheat for about 5 minutes.
4. **Cook the Lava Cakes:** Place the prepared ramekins on the griddle. Carefully pour the chocolate batter into each ramekin, filling them about 3/4 full. Cover the ramekins with a lid or a large baking pan to create an oven-like environment. This traps heat and allows the cakes to cook evenly.
5. **Cook and Check for Doneness:** Cook for about 8-10 minutes, or until the edges of the cakes are set but the centers are still soft. The tops should be slightly puffed and just beginning to crack. Carefully remove the lid or baking pan. Test for doneness by gently pressing the center of one cake—it should be soft but not liquid.
6. **Serve:** Let the ramekins cool for about 1-2 minutes. Run a knife around the edges of each cake to loosen them. Invert the ramekins onto serving plates and gently lift them to release the cakes. Serve immediately, optionally dusted with powdered sugar or with a scoop of vanilla ice cream.

Grilled Pound Cake with Berries

Yield: 4 servings **Preparation Time:** 10 minutes **Cooking Time:** 10 minutes

Ingredients:

- 1 pound cake (store-bought or homemade), cut into 8 slices (about 1 inch thick each)
- 2 cups mixed berries (such as strawberries, blueberries, raspberries)
- 1/4 cup honey
- 1 tablespoon lemon juice
- 1 teaspoon lemon zest
- 1/2 teaspoon vanilla extract
- 2 tablespoons unsalted butter, melted

Nutritional Information (per serving):

- Calories: 400
- Protein: 5g
- Carbohydrates: 60g
- Fats: 15g
- Fiber: 4g

Instructions:

1. **Prepare the Berry Mixture:** In a medium bowl, combine the mixed berries, honey, lemon juice, lemon zest, and vanilla extract. Toss gently to coat the berries evenly. Set aside.
2. **Preheat the Gas Griddle:** Set your gas griddle to medium heat (approximately 350°F). Allow it to preheat for about 5 minutes.
3. **Prepare the Pound Cake Slices:** Brush both sides of each pound cake slice with the melted butter to prevent sticking and to promote even browning.
4. **Grill the Pound Cake:** Once the griddle is hot, place the pound cake slices on the griddle. Cook for about 2-3 minutes on the first side, until they are golden brown and have nice grill marks.
   Using a spatula, carefully flip the slices and cook for an additional 2-3 minutes on the other side, until they are evenly browned and heated through.
5. **Serve:** Remove the grilled pound cake slices from the griddle and place them on serving plates.
   Spoon the berry mixture over the top of each slice of grilled pound cake.

Griddled Blueberry Cobbler

Yield: 6 servings **Preparation Time:** 15 minutes **Cooking Time:** 20 minutes

Ingredients:

For the Blueberry Filling:

- 4 cups fresh blueberries
- 1/2 cup granulated sugar
- 2 tablespoons lemon juice
- 1 tablespoon cornstarch
- 1 teaspoon vanilla extract

For the Cobbler Topping:

- 1 cup all-purpose flour
- 1/4 cup granulated sugar
- 1 teaspoon baking powder
- 1/4 teaspoon baking soda
- 1/4 teaspoon salt
- 1/2 cup buttermilk
- 1/4 cup unsalted butter, melted
- 1 teaspoon vanilla extract

For the Griddle:

- 2 tablespoons vegetable oil or non-stick cooking spray

Nutritional Information (per serving):

- Calories: 250
- Protein: 4g
- Carbohydrates: 45g
- Fats: 8g
- Fiber: 3g

Instructions:

1. **Prepare the Blueberry Filling:** In a large bowl, combine the blueberries, granulated sugar, lemon juice, cornstarch, and vanilla extract. Mix until the blueberries are well coated. Set aside.
2. **Prepare the Cobbler Topping:** In a medium bowl, whisk together the flour, granulated sugar, baking powder, baking soda, and salt. Add the buttermilk, melted butter, and vanilla extract to the dry ingredients. Stir until just combined.
3. **Preheat the Gas Griddle:** Set your gas griddle to medium heat (approximately 350°F). Allow it to preheat for about 5 minutes.
4. **Prepare the Griddle:** Once the griddle is hot, apply a thin layer of vegetable oil or non-stick cooking spray to prevent sticking.
5. **Cook the Blueberry Filling:** Place a large, heatproof skillet or cast-iron pan on the griddle. Add the blueberry mixture to the skillet. Cook the blueberries for about 5-7 minutes, stirring occasionally, until they begin to release their juices and thicken slightly.
6. **Add the Cobbler Topping:** Drop spoonfuls of the cobbler topping over the blueberry filling in the skillet. Spread the topping evenly, but do not cover completely. This allows some of the blueberry filling to bubble through. Cover the skillet with a lid or aluminum foil to create an oven-like environment.

7. **Cook the Cobbler:** Cook for about 12-15 minutes, or until the cobbler topping is golden brown and cooked through. Check occasionally to ensure even cooking.
8. **Serve:** Remove the skillet from the griddle. Allow the cobbler to cool slightly before serving. Serve warm with a scoop of vanilla ice cream or a dollop of whipped cream.

Kid-Approved Dishes

Grilled Mini Hot Dogs

Yield: 4 servings **Preparation Time:** 10 minutes **Cooking Time:** 10 minutes

Ingredients:

- 16 mini hot dog buns or dinner rolls
- 16 mini hot dogs or cocktail sausages
- 2 tablespoons olive oil
- 1/2 cup ketchup
- 1/2 cup mustard
- 1/2 cup relish
- 1/4 cup finely chopped onions (optional)
- 1/4 cup shredded cheese (optional)
- 1/4 cup sauerkraut (optional)
- Butter or non-stick cooking spray for greasing

Nutritional Information (per serving):

- Calories: 350
- Protein: 12g
- Carbohydrates: 30g
- Fats: 20g
- Fiber: 2g

Instructions:

1. **Prepare the Ingredients:** Slice the mini hot dog buns or dinner rolls if they are not pre-sliced.
   Preheat the Gas Griddle: Set your gas griddle to medium heat (approximately 350-375°F). Allow it to preheat for about 5 minutes.
2. **Prepare the Griddle:** Once the griddle is hot, apply a thin layer of butter or non-stick cooking spray to prevent sticking.
3. **Cook the Mini Hot Dogs:** Place the mini hot dogs or cocktail sausages on the hot griddle. Cook for about 4-5 minutes, turning frequently, until they are evenly browned and heated through.
4. **Toast the Buns:** While the hot dogs are cooking, place the mini buns cut side down on the griddle. Toast for about 1-2 minutes until they are golden brown and crisp.
5. **Assemble the Mini Hot Dogs:** Place a cooked mini hot dog in each toasted bun. Top with your favorite condiments: ketchup, mustard, relish, chopped onions, shredded cheese, or sauerkraut.
6. **Serve:** Remove the assembled mini hot dogs from the griddle and arrange them on a serving platter.

Griddled Pizza Pockets

Yield: 4 servings **Preparation Time:** 20 minutes **Cooking Time:** 10 minutes

Ingredients:

- 1 pound pizza dough (store-bought or homemade)
- 1 cup pizza sauce
- 1 1/2 cups shredded mozzarella cheese
- 1/2 cup pepperoni slices (optional)
- 1/2 cup finely chopped bell peppers
- 1/4 cup finely chopped onions
- 1/4 cup sliced black olives (optional)
- 2 tablespoons olive oil
- 1 teaspoon dried oregano
- 1 teaspoon dried basil
- 1/2 teaspoon garlic powder
- 1/4 teaspoon salt

Nutritional Information (per serving):

- Calories: 400
- Protein: 15g
- Carbohydrates: 45g
- Fats: 18g
- Fiber: 3g

Instructions:

1. **Prepare the Dough:** Divide the pizza dough into 8 equal portions. Roll each portion into a ball and then flatten it into a small circle, about 6 inches in diameter.
2. **Prepare the Filling:** In a medium bowl, mix the pizza sauce, shredded mozzarella cheese, pepperoni slices, bell peppers, onions, and black olives (if using).

3. **Fill the Pizza Pockets:** Place a generous spoonful of the filling mixture onto one half of each dough circle, leaving a small border around the edge. Fold the dough over the filling to form a pocket, pressing the edges together to seal. Use a fork to crimp the edges for a secure seal.
4. **Preheat the Gas Griddle:** Set your gas griddle to medium heat (approximately 350°F). Allow it to preheat for about 5 minutes. Once the griddle is hot, apply a thin layer of olive oil to prevent sticking.
5. **Cook the Pizza Pockets:** Place the pizza pockets on the hot griddle. Brush the tops with olive oil and sprinkle with dried oregano, basil, garlic powder, and salt. Cook for about 4-5 minutes on the first side, until golden brown and crispy. Carefully flip the pockets using a spatula, and cook for an additional 4-5 minutes on the other side until the dough is fully cooked and the cheese is melted inside.
6. **Serve:** Remove the pizza pockets from the griddle and let them cool for a few minutes before serving.

Grilled Fish Sticks

Yield: 4 servings **Preparation Time:** 15 minutes **Cooking Time:** 10 minutes

Ingredients:

- 1 pound white fish fillets (such as cod, tilapia, or haddock), cut into 1-inch wide strips
- 1 cup all-purpose flour
- 2 large eggs, beaten
- 1 cup panko breadcrumbs
- 1/2 cup grated Parmesan cheese
- 1 teaspoon garlic powder
- 1 teaspoon paprika
- 1/2 teaspoon salt
- 1/4 teaspoon black pepper
- 1/4 cup vegetable oil, for greasing
- Lemon wedges, for serving
- Tartar sauce or your favorite dipping sauce, for serving

Nutritional Information (per serving):

- Calories: 350
- Protein: 25g
- Carbohydrates: 30g
- Fats: 15g
- Fiber: 2g

Instructions:

1. **Prepare the Breading Stations:** Place the flour in a shallow bowl. Place the beaten eggs in another shallow bowl. In a third shallow bowl, combine the panko breadcrumbs, grated Parmesan cheese, garlic powder, paprika, salt, and black pepper.
2. **Bread the Fish Sticks:** Dredge each fish strip in the flour, shaking off any excess. Dip the floured fish strip into the beaten eggs, allowing any excess to drip off. Coat the fish strip in the panko mixture, pressing gently to adhere to the breadcrumbs.
3. **Preheat the Gas Griddle:** Set your gas griddle to medium-high heat (approximately 375-400°F). Allow it to preheat for about 5 minutes.
4. **Prepare the Griddle:** Once the griddle is hot, pour the vegetable oil onto the surface and spread it evenly with a spatula to ensure the entire cooking area is well-greased.
5. **Cook the Fish Sticks:** Place the breaded fish sticks on the hot griddle. Cook for about 3-4 minutes on the first side, until golden brown and crispy. Carefully flip the fish sticks using a spatula, and cook for an additional 3-4 minutes on the other side, until the fish is cooked through and the coating is golden and crispy.
6. **Serve:** Remove the fish sticks from the griddle and place them on a serving platter. Serve immediately with lemon wedges and your favorite dipping sauce, such as tartar sauce.

Griddled Mini Burgers

Yield: 4 servings (12 mini burgers) **Preparation Time:** 15 minutes **Cooking Time:** 10 minutes

Ingredients:

- 1 pound ground beef (80/20 blend for best flavor and juiciness)
- 1 small onion, finely grated
- 1 clove garlic, minced
- 1 tablespoon Worcestershire sauce
- 1 teaspoon salt
- 1/2 teaspoon black pepper
- 12 mini burger buns or dinner rolls
- 2 tablespoons vegetable oil
- 12 small slices of cheddar cheese (optional)
- Lettuce, tomato slices, pickles, ketchup, mustard, and mayonnaise for serving

Nutritional Information (per serving):

- Calories: 450

- Protein: 25g
- Carbohydrates: 30g
- Fats: 25g
- Fiber: 2g

Instructions:

1. **Prepare the Burger Mixture:** In a large bowl, combine the ground beef, grated onion, minced garlic, Worcestershire sauce, salt, and black pepper. Mix gently until just combined, being careful not to overwork the meat. Divide the mixture into 12 equal portions and shape each portion into a small patty, about 2 inches in diameter.
2. **Preheat the Gas Griddle:** Set your gas griddle to medium-high heat (approximately 375-400°F). Allow it to preheat for about 5 minutes. Once the griddle is hot, spread the vegetable oil evenly over the surface with a spatula to ensure the entire cooking area is well-greased.
3. **Cook the Mini Burgers:** Place the mini burger patties on the hot griddle. Cook for about 2-3 minutes on the first side, until the bottom is nicely seared and browned. Carefully flip the patties using a spatula, and cook for an additional 2-3 minutes on the other side until they reach your desired level of doneness. If using cheese, place a slice on each patty during the last minute of cooking to melt.
4. **Toast the Buns:** While the burgers are cooking, place the mini buns cut side down on the griddle to toast for about 1-2 minutes until golden brown and crispy.
5. **Assemble the Mini Burgers:** Place each cooked patty on the bottom half of a toasted bun. Add your favorite toppings such as lettuce, tomato slices, pickles, ketchup, mustard, and mayonnaise. Top with the remaining half of the bun.
6. **Serve:** Arrange the mini burgers on a serving platter and serve immediately.

Grilled Sausage and Cheese Breakfast Muffins

Yield: 4 servings (makes 8 muffins) **Preparation Time:** 15 minutes **Cooking Time:** 15 minutes

Ingredients:

- 1 pound breakfast sausage
- 1 cup shredded cheddar cheese
- 1 cup all-purpose flour
- 1/2 cup cornmeal
- 1 tablespoon baking powder
- 1/2 teaspoon salt
- 1 cup milk
- 1 large egg
- 2 tablespoons melted butter
- Additional butter or non-stick cooking spray for greasing the griddle

Nutritional Information (per serving):

- Calories: 400
- Protein: 18g
- Carbohydrates: 25g
- Fats: 25g
- Fiber: 2g

Instructions:

1. **Cook the Sausage:** Preheat your gas griddle to medium-high heat (approximately 375°F). Crumble the sausage onto the hot griddle and cook, stirring occasionally, until browned and fully cooked, about 5-7 minutes. Remove the cooked sausage from the griddle and set aside to cool slightly.
2. **Prepare the Muffin Batter:** In a large bowl, whisk together the flour, cornmeal, baking powder, and salt. In another bowl, whisk together the milk, egg, and melted butter. Pour the wet ingredients into the dry ingredients and stir until just combined. Fold in the cooked sausage and shredded cheddar cheese.
3. **Preheat the Griddle:** Clean the griddle and reheat it to medium heat (approximately 350°F). Apply a thin layer of butter or non-stick cooking spray to prevent sticking.
4. **Cook the Muffins:** Using a large spoon or a small ice cream scoop, drop dollops of the batter onto the hot griddle, spacing them out to allow for spreading. Each dollop should be about 1/4 cup of batter. Cook for about 3-4 minutes on the first side, until bubbles form on the surface and the edges look set. Carefully flip the muffins using a spatula, and cook for an additional 3-4 minutes on the other side until golden brown and cooked through.
5. **Serve:** Remove the muffins from the griddle and let them cool for a minute before serving.

Griddled Peanut Butter Banana Roll-Ups

Yield: 4 servings **Preparation Time:** 10 minutes **Cooking Time:** 5 minutes

Ingredients:

- 4 large flour tortillas
- 1/2 cup creamy peanut butter
- 2 bananas, sliced lengthwise

- 2 tablespoons honey
- 1 teaspoon ground cinnamon
- 2 tablespoons butter, melted
- Additional butter or non-stick cooking spray for greasing the griddle

Nutritional Information (per serving):

- Calories: 350
- Protein: 10g
- Carbohydrates: 45g
- Fats: 15g
- Fiber: 5g

Instructions:

1. **Prepare the Roll-Ups:** Lay out the flour tortillas on a clean surface. Spread a thin layer of peanut butter evenly over each tortilla. Place banana slices lengthwise in the center of each tortilla. Drizzle honey over the bananas and sprinkle with ground cinnamon. Roll up each tortilla tightly, tucking in the sides as you go to create a secure roll-up. Set your gas griddle to medium heat (approximately 350°F). Allow it to preheat for about 5 minutes.
2. **Prepare the Griddle:** Once the griddle is hot, apply a thin layer of butter or non-stick cooking spray to prevent sticking.
3. **Cook the Roll-Ups:** Brush the outside of each roll-up with melted butter. Place the roll-ups seam side down on the hot griddle. Cook for about 2-3 minutes on the first side, until golden brown and crispy. Carefully flip the roll-ups using a spatula, and cook for an additional 2-3 minutes on the other side until they are golden brown and the filling is heated through.
4. **Serve:** Remove the roll-ups from the griddle and let them cool for a minute before slicing each roll-up in half.

Grilled Chicken Nuggets

Yield: 4 servings **Preparation Time:** 15 minutes **Cooking Time:** 10 minutes

Ingredients:

- 1 1/2 pounds boneless, skinless chicken breasts, cut into 1-inch pieces
- 1 cup buttermilk
- 1 cup all-purpose flour
- 1 cup panko breadcrumbs
- 1/2 cup grated Parmesan cheese
- 1 teaspoon garlic powder
- 1 teaspoon onion powder
- 1 teaspoon paprika
- 1 teaspoon salt
- 1/2 teaspoon black pepper
- 1/4 cup vegetable oil, for greasing
- Dipping sauces (such as honey mustard, BBQ sauce, or ranch), for serving

Nutritional Information (per serving):

- Calories: 350
- Protein: 30g
- Carbohydrates: 25g
- Fats: 15g
- Fiber: 2g

Instructions:

1. **Marinate the Chicken:** In a large bowl, combine the chicken pieces with the buttermilk. Cover and refrigerate for at least 30 minutes or up to 2 hours.
2. **Prepare the Breading Stations:** Place the flour in a shallow bowl.
   In another shallow bowl, mix the panko breadcrumbs, grated Parmesan cheese, garlic powder, onion powder, paprika, salt, and black pepper.
3. **Bread the Chicken Nuggets:** Remove the chicken pieces from the buttermilk, allowing any excess to drip off. Dredge each chicken piece in the flour, shaking off any excess. Coat the floured chicken pieces in the panko mixture, pressing gently to adhere to the breadcrumbs. Set your gas griddle to medium-high heat (approximately 375-400°F). Allow it to preheat for about 5 minutes.
4. **Prepare the Griddle:** Once the griddle is hot, pour the vegetable oil onto the surface and spread it evenly with a spatula to ensure the entire cooking area is well-greased.
5. **Cook the Chicken Nuggets:** Place the breaded chicken nuggets on the hot griddle. Cook for about 3-4 minutes on the first side, until golden brown and crispy. Carefully flip the nuggets using a spatula, and cook for an additional 3-4 minutes on the other side until the chicken is cooked through and the coating is golden and crispy.
6. **Serve:** Remove the chicken nuggets from the griddle and place them on a serving platter. Serve immediately with your choice of dipping sauces.

Made in the USA
Coppell, TX
20 December 2024